KNOWLEDGE, INSTITUTIONS AND EVOLUTION IN ECONOMICS

As Adam Smith recognised, the division of labour is the division of knowledge. The division of labour is essential to the growth of knowledge, because knowledge grows by division.

In this volume, Brian J. Loasby explores how the limitations of human knowledge create opportunities as well as problems in the modern economy. Institutions emerge as a way of coping with the problems and helping to exploit the opportunities in an evolutionary process. However, this evolutionary process does not necessarily produce optimal results, making many of the optimisation techniques of modern economics less than useful.

The volume also explores how the biological foundation of human cognition helps us to understand both the role of institutions and the nature of capabilities or performance skills, both individual and organisational. Transaction and governance costs alone are not an adequate basis for understanding economic organisation: this is to be explained by capabilities as well as transactions.

Brian J. Loasby has held positions in Aberdeen, Birmingham, Bristol and Stirling, where he is currently Honorary Professor. The organisation of knowledge, within economics and the economy, is the theme of his three books – *Choice, Complexity and Ignorance*, *The Mind and Method of the Economist* and *Equilibrium and Evolution* – and many articles for journals and edited collections.

THE GRAZ SCHUMPETER LECTURES

KNOWLEDGE, INSTITUTIONS AND EVOLUTION IN ECONOMICS

Brian J. Loasby

London and New York

HB
133
.L6
1999

First published 1999
by Routledge
11 New Fetter Lane, London EC4P 4EE

Simultaneously published in the USA and Canada
by Routledge
29 West 35th Street, New York, NY 10001

© 1999 Brian J. Loasby

Typeset in Garamond by Routledge
Printed and bound in Great Britain by Biddles Ltd,
Guildford and King's Lynn

British Library Cataloguing in Publication Data
A catalogue record for this book is available from the British Library

Library of Congress Cataloging in Publication Data
Loasby, Brian J.
Knowledge, Institutions and Evolution in Economics / Brian J. Loasby.
p. cm. – (The Graz Schumpeter lectures; 2)
Includes bibliographical references and index.
1. Information theory in economics. 2. Economics – Methodology.
3. Knowledge, Theory of. 4. Institutional economics.
5. Evolutionary economics. I. Title. II. Series.
HB133.L6 1999 98-33940
330'.01–dc21 CIP

ISBN 0–415–20537–9

TO CHARLES SUCKLING FRS

CONTENTS

FOREWORD

The Graz Schumpeter Lectures

At the age of 28, in 1911, Joseph Alois Schumpeter (1883–1950) was appointed to the chair in political economy at the University of Graz, Styria (Austria). He remained a member of the Graz Faculty until 1922. Schumpeter used to call the third decade in the life of an intellectual 'the sacred age of fertility'. The final part of this age thus fell into his Graz period. His time in Graz was indeed fertile, seeing the publication of some of his major works.

In 1995 the *Graz Schumpeter Society* was founded. In the same year the *Graz Schumpeter Lectures* were inaugurated, thanks to generous financial support by the Government of Styria. The Lectures will take place on a yearly basis. A search committee will appoint well ahead of time the *Graz Schumpeter Lecturer* for a particular year. The Lecturer is chosen on the grounds of his or her originality and scholarship. The aim of the Lectures is to inform about the frontiers of knowledge in fields of socio-economic research characterised by rapid innovation and the potential applicability of the results arrived at in economic and political decision making. The Lectures are also meant to transcend a single disciplinary discourse and lead towards a more comprehensive view of socio-economic phenomena. While for obvious reasons the Lectures are named after Joseph Alois Schumpeter, the concern of the Lectures is not restricted to him and his work. It includes socio-economic study of individual decision making units in relation to their politico-economic environment (Governments, Corporations and Labour Organisations).

Heinz. D. Kurz
(Chairman of the *Graz Schumpeter Society*)

PREFACE

Heinz Kurz and his colleagues are to be commended for their enterprise in establishing the Graz Schumpeter Society; whether they should also be commended for inviting me to follow Stan Metcalfe in giving the second series of lectures in November 1996 may be more debatable, but I would certainly like to thank them for doing so, and for their hospitality during my visit to Graz.

My intention was to offer, both in the lectures and in the expanded version presented here, an exploration of issues that would be complementary to Stan's work, and a sequel to the lectures that I gave in Manchester at the invitation of Stan and Ian Steedman, the published version of which appeared as *Equilibrium and Evolution* (Manchester University Press, 1991). My original thought was to produce something like an expanded second edition of *Equilibrium and Evolution*, but I soon came to the conclusion that, although the basic theme remains an exploration of economics and the economy as ways of organising, using, and improving human knowledge, it would be better to develop the argument in a somewhat different way.

In the opening chapter, which corresponds to the first lecture, I attempt to identify the limitations of human knowledge, the opportunities as well as the problems that result from these limitations, the importance of institutions in coping with the problems and helping to exploit the opportunities, and the evolutionary process that results. It has sometimes been argued that evolutionary pressures within modern economic systems are strong enough to impose optimisation and that economists therefore have no need to concern themselves with evolutionary analysis; the second chapter investigates this claim and seeks to establish a basic conception of an evolutionary economy. In the third chapter (which, like the second, grew out of the second lecture in Graz) I seek to establish a minimal biological foundation for an understanding of human cognition, and suggest that institutions may be usefully considered as a major aid to cognition. The fourth chapter, which matches the third lecture in Graz, draws on the third to investigate the concept of capabilities, which escape the formal framework of modern economic analysis. The next two chapters, which are elaborations of the fourth and final lecture in Graz, examine the importance of both transactions and capabilities in explaining economic organisation and economic processes.

The remaining two lectures had no direct equivalent in Graz, but were part of the original design for the book. I had not been satisfied with the chapter on markets in *Equilibrium and Evolution* and had written papers for presentation at a Royal Economic Society conference, at the Judge Institute of Management Studies in Cambridge, and at the Turku School of Economics; reorganised and rewritten, the treatment of markets as institutions which embody knowledge and are both the product and the setting for evolutionary processes applies the theme of the preceding lectures. The original version of the final chapter, which is an overall view of the effects of economic organisation on the generation of knowledge rather than a summary, was written among my preparations for the Graz Lectures and delivered in the series of Jena Lectures at the invitation of Professors Manfred Streit and Ulrich Witt, Directors of the Max Planck Institute for the Study of Economic Systems; I would like to take this opportunity of thanking them for that invitation, and for subsequently welcoming me back to Jena.

Though the ideas and arguments of this book are hardly those of mainstream economics, they are part of the distributed knowledge of the community of economists; I have tried to cite the originators of these ideas and also those whose approaches are either similar or complementary and whose work is known to me, so that any interested reader can build up a personal set of connecting principles. There must be many others who deserve citation; to those I can only apologise and offer the excuse that I have no idea how to design an optimal search procedure. I am conscious of having derived benefit from contacts with a great many people; if I tried to list them I would greatly extend the length of this Preface, and would still leave some out; I hope that they will accept my thanks for providing ideas, comments and suggestions which I have been happy to treat as authoritative.

I have chosen to dedicate this book, not to any economist, but to the person who, directly and indirectly, has probably had the greatest influence on my thinking – and that includes some very strong competition. Charles Suckling is responsible for my move to Stirling, with all its consequences, notably my collaboration with Frank Bradbury, who had worked with him in ICI. His career has been devoted to managing uncertainty and generating knowledge, and to thinking keenly and imaginatively about the problems of doing so, on the basis of a first-class intellect and a capacity to seek and absorb ideas from a wide range of sources. Managers of innovation must cope with all the problems of knowledge outlined in this book, make selective and imaginative use of institutional supports, and, while conscious of the ever-present possibility of error, contribute intelligently to the generation and selection of variety in a continuing process of evolution. Not the least of my reasons for this dedication is Charles Suckling's confidence that the problems in which I have long been interested are of major practical importance, and that economists could actually provide some help to practitioners.

ACKNOWLEDGEMENTS

Some of the following chapters include passages (usually modified) from other publications. Part of Chapter 2 draws on 'Selection processes', in *The Evolutionary Principles of Economics*, edited by Kurt Dopfer (Dordrecht: Kluwer, forthcoming); part of Chapter 3 on 'Cognition and innovation', in *The Active Consumer*, edited by Marina Bianchi (London: Routledge, 1998); parts of Chapter 4 on 'The concept of capabilities', in *Economic Organization, Capabilities and Co-ordination: Essays in Honour of G. B. Richardson*, edited by Nicolai J. Foss and Brian J. Loasby (London: Routledge, 1998) and 'The organization of capabilities', *Journal of Economic Behavior and Organization*, 35, 139–60 (1998); and parts of Chapter 8 on 'The organisation of industry and the growth of knowledge', *Lectiones Jenenses* (Jena: Max-Planck-Institute for the Study of Economic Systems, 1996).

1

THE PROBLEM OF KNOWLEDGE

Robert Lucas, Nobel Laureate in Economics, once declared that 'in cases of uncertainty, economic reasoning will be of no value' (Lucas 1981: 224). It is true that in Lucas's model economies there is no way of handling uncertainty, in the sense of uncompletable lists of contingencies, causes, and even options; but it is no less true that only in cases of real-world uncertainty does economic analysis have any potential value. If uncertainty is absent, then every problem situation can be fully specified (if necessary with a probability distribution defined over a complete list of possible states of the world) and choice is reduced to a logical operation. This is indeed the world of rational choice models. But then the process of choosing, and the ways in which the process of choosing is organised, are empty topics, as has been observed by Knight (1921: 267–8) and Hutchison (1937). If all optima can be calculated (with due regard, of course, to future possible states of the world), well-motivated economic agents (and to economists like Lucas no other kind is conceivable) will have calculated them already; and economists will be the last to know. In such a world economists can demonstrate only that what has already happened in practice can also happen in theory. Thus not only are there no hundred-dollar bills lying on the street, there are no hundred-dollar bills on offer for economic advice. Economic analysis is of potential value only if people do not already know what to do: the foundation for useful economic theory must be incomplete knowledge, or partial ignorance. In these chapters I wish to suggest how useful economic theory can indeed be built on this foundation.

Obstacles to knowledge

The basic issue here is epistemological. What can we know? In this section we will briefly review six reasons why human knowledge is necessarily incomplete, before going on to consider institutions and evolution as ways of mitigating these problems, and of responding to the opportunities which are the obverse of the difficulties that they create. These six obstacles to complete knowledge may be summarised as the insufficiency of induction,

1

complexity, the limits of human cognition, exogenous change, the interdependence of individual initiatives, and conflicting ideas and purposes. Because the intention in this book is to focus on a particular set of economic consequences of uncertainty (a set which, it should at once be made clear, gives no emphasis to macroeconomic issues, where the neglect of uncertainty may lead to substantial error), the sources of uncertainty will be stated and not explored; but in order to understand the implications of uncertainty it is necessary to explain why '[e]rror is inseparable from all human knowledge' (Menger 1976 [1871]: 148).

The first and fundamental obstacle is David Hume's problem: the impossibility of certain, or justified, knowledge of universal laws, other than the knowledge of logical relationships. The instances that we observe, even when supplemented by the reported observations of others – which, of course, are not necessarily reliable – cannot be more than a tiny fraction of all possible instances, and they crucially and necessarily exclude all observations from the future; to treat the observations that are available as a representative sample we have to assume that they are drawn from a population which displays precisely those characteristics that we deduce from that sample. Hume reminds us that the existence of such a population can never be proved; all expectations, however carefully formulated, are conjectures which go beyond the evidence. Indeed, since knowledge of unique events is interpreted by the application of general laws, which no amount of attainable evidence can ever prove to be true, even 'the knowledge of the particular circumstances of time and place', to which Hayek (1945: 521) rightly attached such importance, can be disputed, as we observe often enough, and as Hayek (ibid.: 524) himself explicitly recognised.

There is a great diversity of views about the degree and even kinds of knowledge that are attainable, which I shall not discuss in this book. The view taken here is that all knowledge should be considered as conjectural, in Karl Popper's (1963) sense of hypotheses which, though apparently corroborated, always remain open to refutation, but that it is nevertheless possible in some circumstances to attain knowledge which is highly reliable, as John Ziman (1978) has argued with care, insight and lucidity. As Hayek became increasingly aware, the processes by which reliable knowledge may be obtained is a central issue in economic organisation; and Popper's transformation of Hume's problem of induction into a theory of scientific progress which liberated scientists' imagination (Medawar 1984) may be generalised into a theory of economic development, in which the economic system is not only an allocation mechanism but a prime source of novelty.

In both science and the economy, it is precisely because our present knowledge is incomplete, and some of it wrong, that we have the hope of improvement. Uncertainty is a source, not only of threats, but also of opportunities, even for economic theorists. The possibility of economic and social progress through the growth of knowledge inspired Marshall's work;

it pervades the *Principles*, though its presence may not be recognised by anyone obsessed with allocative efficiency. I believe – this, of course, is a conjecture – that, in the words of George Kelly (1963: 6), 'the universe is really existing and that man is gradually coming to understand it'; I also believe – this is a fundamental value judgement – that we should try to improve our understanding of this 'really existing' universe, and therefore that we should never be content with a record of apparently successful prediction from an instrumentalist theory. We may not, for the moment, be able to do any better; but we should always retain the objective of explaining why the predictions of a particular instrumental theory are successful. Only then do we have any chance of recognising when they may be expected to fail and how the theory might be improved.

Even when it is based on intendedly realist theories, human knowledge is always fallible, as Ziman explains, and knowledge within economic systems is liable to be especially so. Therefore the ability to cope with both incomplete and fallible knowledge, to take appropriate precautions against omissions and error, and to discover errors and generate novel conjectures – most of which will inevitably be false – is a crucial requirement in the organisation of an economy or a polity, as it is in every kind of scientific inquiry. This crucial requirement is inadequately represented in the great bulk of economic theory. In order to minimise confusion, the term 'learning', which is often used, especially by economists, in the sense of the acquisition of information from a prespecified set, or convergence on 'the correct model', will not be prominent in this book. Such a concept of learning may be entirely appropriate within specific limits of time and space, so defined as to allow one to identify a best-corroborated theory, a best available data set, or current best practice; but a good deal more is required for an understanding, let alone an evaluation, of economic systems. It is certainly insufficient for the generation of knowledge.

The inherent fallibility of human knowledge is compounded by the complexity of the universe, which is the second obstacle. The development of our understanding of this universe is hampered by the apparent fact that it 'functions as a single unit with all its imaginable parts having an exact relationship to each other' (Kelly 1963: 6). The failure of novel conjectures about products or processes is often attributable to false implicit assumptions about the structure of the physical, biological, economic and social systems into which they are to be introduced. This 'organised complexity' (Hayek 1978: 26–7) multiplies the difficulties of collecting relevant evidence, and, more fundamentally, of knowing what evidence is relevant. It is also the source of what is commonly called the Duhem–Quine problem: not only can we not prove any general proposition to be true; we cannot even prove it to be false, because we can test only complex conjectures, which embody many supplementary propositions that can never be proved true, and therefore we can never identify for certain precisely what element within that complex is responsible for a falsifying instance. Thus even the negative knowledge that is gained by falsification does not qualify as 'justified knowledge', and positive knowledge must be less secure.

As Hayek warned us, the complexities of human societies threaten the applicability of closed models of social science; but the complexities of the natural world also threaten the reliability of natural science, as Ziman (1978) is well aware. The foundations of knowledge are problematic. However tightly we control our experiments, our controls rest on principles of isolation which are necessarily fallible, and which are sometimes falsified; the well-established inertness of fluorine compounds, which had been put to beneficial uses – for instance as a safe refrigerant and anaesthetic – was eventually found to be inoperative in the ozone layer. As this example illustrates, important relationships may become apparent only after lengthy intervals; in Kelly's (1963: 6) words, 'time provides the ultimate bond in all relationships'.

Alfred Marshall's work as an economist was dominated by this problem of complexity, and by the interaction between complexity and time. He pointed out that 'a theoretically perfect long period...when carried to its logical consequences, will be found to involve the supposition of a stationary state of industry, in which the requirements of a future age can be antici-pated an indefinite time beforehand' (Marshall 1920: 379) and warned against misleading closure; it seems most unlikely that he would have regarded intertemporal general equilibrium as an adequate response to this problem. His biographer Peter Groenewegen (1995) has insisted that Marshall intended every theoretical proposition in what was originally published as Volume 1 of his *Principles* to be treated as provisional; the qualifications and revisions that were necessary for a full understanding of the economy and for the design of sensible policies were to be developed in Volume 2. But Marshall was so obsessed with the interconnectedness of everything, and with his Principle of Continuity which allowed for no clear distinction between the significant and the insignificant, that he could find no acceptable boundaries within which to develop his analysis. We may regret his caution, but after observing the damage that has been caused by later economists who scorned the clear warnings which Marshall had included in Volume 1, we can also respect it.

The third source of our imperfect knowledge, which interacts strongly with the second, is our limited mental capacity. This we can justifiably call Herbert Simon's problem, even though Simon's concept of bounded rationality is itself a boundedly rational definition of our cognitive limitations, implying that we choose by making logical deductions from a truncated information set, and diverting attention from those cognitive powers (for example, our ability to construct, recall, and apply complex patterns, to which Ziman (1978) gives particular attention) that do not seem to rely on what economists, in particular, regard as rational processes.

Conlisk's (1996) review of the evidence on human rationality and of economists' responses, though admirable within its declared scope, does not consider the full range of cognitive issues. There is much more to intelligent behaviour than procedures which are even limitedly rational, as we shall see; indeed 'the human mind...may often be better than rational' (Cosmides and Tooby 1994b: 329). But even when striving to be boundedly rational, in Simon's sense, we often find that, as well as being presented with more sensory input than we can handle, we have no means of access to information that would be necessary for an adequate understanding of our situation. Both deficiencies compel us to adopt simplified representations and simplified procedures. These cannot be optimally chosen, and often rely on linkages which cannot be classed as logical; they are conjectures, which go far beyond what we can possibly know. How these simplifying conjectures come to be adopted is a major theme of subsequent chapters.

Perhaps none of this would matter very much if we lived in an unchanging universe; for '[c]hange in some sense is a condition of the existence of any problem whatever in connection with life or conduct' (Knight 1921: 313). In such an unchanging universe, where the weather may be inconstant but the climate does not vary, 'things have time to hammer logic into men' (Schumpeter 1934: 80); routine behaviour is all that is required. In such an environment we, like other species, would not need to know why any routine works, or even to be conscious of the routines that we follow, although as human observers of such behaviour we might be more interested than Schumpeter was in the processes by which routines become established. (It is tempting to speculate whether such an environment would be hospitable to human consciousness, or even to the human species.) However, as Schumpeter also declared, the introduction of change is 'a distinct process which stands in need of special explanation'; it must therefore be included as the fourth source of our imperfect knowledge. The effects of change are not well represented by imposing shocks on a system within which knowledge is supposedly complete (except for the crucial knowledge that unpredictable shocks are to be expected), for, as Schumpeter pointed out, intelligent response to exogenous change requires something more than rational choice as that is currently interpreted. Frank Knight (1921: 313) identified the paradox of rational expectations long before the concept entered economic analysis: our ability to predict the future depends on its similarity to the past, but our need to predict the future results from our belief that it will be different from the past, in ways that are excluded from the definition of rational expectations.

As that experienced manager Chester Barnard (1938: 305) tells us, '[m]uch of the error of historians, economists, and of all of us in daily affairs arises from imputing logical reasoning to men who could not or cannot base their actions on reason'. Non-logical processes are essential to scientific discovery (ibid.: 306), and many decisions relate to unique events, in which causality is difficult to establish (ibid.: 307): in these circumstances the attempt to apply rigorous reasoning

> indicates a lack of balance of mental processes;...if there is no basis for calculation, it is more intelligent to guess than to manufacture data for false calculation....the correctness of such decisions must, therefore, depend upon the effectiveness of the mental processes of the type that can handle contingencies, uncertainties, and unknowables.
>
> (ibid.: 308, 311, 312)

As Barnard emphasises, the mental processes on which we must rely when economic analysis, according to Lucas, is of no value, are far more orderly, indeed intelligent, than 'guesswork' or 'hunches', for what is not rational may also be very far from being irrational; indeed, it may be much less irrational than a pretence of rationality which ignores significant elements of the situation, such as unpredictability. We shall see in Chapter 3 that human cognition seems to be remarkably effective in non-logical processes, though this may seem less remarkable when we reflect that without such abilities the conjectures that are embodied in our species would have been conclusively falsified by the processes of biological evolution.

Non-logical processes are even more important when, as in the telephone business in which Barnard worked, the purpose of many decisions is not to respond to events but to introduce change. It is a characteristic of modern societies that people wish the future to be in some ways different from the past: we therefore require knowledge not only to understand and adapt to what exists, and to the changes in what exists, but in order to create change which will be acceptable to others. This is not a problem in the development of the natural sciences, since it is universally assumed that fundamental particles, molecules, or genes are not purposeful; but it can be a problem for technologists who are trying to adapt scientific knowledge to particular ends. (That is one reason why the relationship between science and technology is not at all straightforward; another reason will receive some attention in Chapter 4.) This desire for purposeful change generates two kinds of systematic interdependencies, with their associated problems (the fifth and sixth) of knowledge.

If there is no disagreement about the kind of change that is desired, then the problem is that of co-ordinating activities: how can we know what other people are intending to do, and how can we bring the relevant pieces of individual knowledge into alignment? In orthodox theory, a fully-aligned system is represented by an equilibrium set of contracts, of which many variants are to be found in the journals; but the process of achieving this alignment appears as the problem of equilibration, which has now effectively been abandoned as insoluble, and is therefore routinely assumed to have been solved. We may give Hayek (1937) the primary credit for posing the issue in a manageable form, and George Richardson (1960, 1990) the primary credit for investigating possible solutions, and for demonstrating in the process that perfect competition is quite inappropriate as a way of even thinking about it. In modern macroeconomics, the effect of assuming that expectations are rational and that all markets clear is that the co-ordination problem cannot even be defined (Leijonhufvud 1998; Rühl and Laidler 1998).

The other kind of difficulty arises when there are conflicting purposes, which may range from straightforward rivalry between similar businesses, through the irruption of Schumpeterian entrepreneurship, to contradictory notions about the appropriate ways of arranging human affairs. Within standard economics, this sixth problem has plagued the analysis of oligopoly, which Simon (1982, vol. 2: 435) once called 'the permanent and ineradicable scandal of economic theory', and is currently manifest in the proliferation of solution concepts in game theory. This proliferation, and the variety of supplementary assumptions that have been introduced to generate solutions, has inspired some of the leading practitioners to widen their definitions of game-theoretic problems beyond the standard framework of highly rational and strictly self-interested agents to include elements such as bounded rationality, conventions, and even trust, in ways which may be consistent with some of the arguments of this book.

Organising knowledge

None of these problems of attaining true knowledge can be solved in any final sense; there is no general equilibrium of economic agents all equipped with the correct model of the universe, which would have to include the correct model of everyone else's correct model – a universal set of universal sets. As Alan Coddington (1975: 154) once commented, there can be at most one omniscient being. Our problems have to be managed: we have to try to make sensible use of what knowledge we think we have, to find ways of combining it effectively with the knowledge that we think other people have, and to protect ourselves against the consequences of our own and other people's ignorance. We also have to try to test and improve our knowledge; for, as George Shackle insisted, the hopeful consequence of our present deficiencies is the scope for imagination and the prospect of creating new ideas and developing new skills. These are problems for all those, including economists, who seek to improve the power of their particular discipline to aid understanding and to guide action, for all those who try to achieve success in their various enterprises, and even for those who simply wish to live contented lives. As Adam Smith (1980), Karl Popper (1959) and George Kelly (1963) all suggest, we should consider science as a somewhat special case of a very basic human activity, and, at least for some important purposes, consider people in their everyday lives as employing, often in a loose and sometimes in a distorted fashion, the principles of scientific enquiry, which are not well represented by rational choice theory.

'The economic analyst', Shackle (1972, Preface) observed, 'assumes that men pursue their interest by applying reason to their circumstances. And he does not ask *how they know* what those circumstances are.' I suggest that the fundamental question facing anyone who wishes to understand economic systems (and especially, but not only, their development) is this: how shall we organise our knowledge about the ways in which people organise their knowledge? The organisation of knowledge about an economy and the organisation of knowledge within an economy influence the kind of knowledge that is produced and the ways in which that knowledge is used. Any discussion of this question entails self-reference: this is a difficulty, but it can also be an opportunity because, as I have previously argued (Loasby 1991), we may learn something about the organisation of industry by examining the ways in which economists organise their work, and we may be able to improve the effectiveness of our work as economists by studying, from an appropriate perspective, the organisation of industry. I shall attempt to exploit this opportunity with the aid of Adam Smith, who was well aware of the problematic basis of human knowledge.

As is well known, Joseph Schumpeter was not unduly impressed with Adam Smith's contribution to economics; but what did impress him (Schumpeter 1954: 182) was Smith's (1980) set of *Essays on Philosophical Subjects*, and especially his 'History of Astronomy', in which he set forth and illustrated his psychological theory of the emergence of science as a consequence of the human desire for mental tranquillity. As long as objects or events are perceived as conforming to a familiar pattern, they

> fall in with the natural career of the imagination....There is no break, no stop, no gap, no interval. The ideas excited by so coherent a chain of things seem, as it were, to float through the mind of their own accord, without obliging it to exert itself or to make any effort in order to pass from one of them to another.
>
> (Smith 1980: 41)

But if objects or events fail to cohere in this way they generate 'confusions and distractions'; and so we turn to science to produce 'invisible chains which bind together all these disjointed objects', and thereby 'introduce order into this chaos of jarring and discordant appearances, to allay the tumult of the imagination, and to restore it...to that tone of tranquillity and composure, which is both most agreeable in itself, and most suitable to its nature' (Smith 1980: 45–6). As Smith's account of the succession of the four great cosmological systems (those based on concentric and eccentric spheres and those created by Copernicus and Newton) makes clear, the struggle to impose a new kind of order may be difficult and protracted. It is characteristic of Smith's view of human behaviour that this desire to avoid the need for thought should provoke the most intense and arduous thought; human minds may need to work very hard in order to be idle.

It is important to note that Smith made no claim that the connecting principles of science were true. Like Hume, he believed that no such claim could ever be justified. Even Newton's great achievement of linking together cosmological and terrestrial phenomena by the principle of gravitation was to be celebrated, not as 'the discovery of an immense chain of the most important and sublime truths' but as the invention of Newton's imagination. Smith (1980: 105) did, however, conclude his account by drawing attention to the rhetorical power of Newton's system, pointing out that, even in the process of representing it, like its predecessors, as a human invention, he had been 'insensibly drawn in, to make use of language expressing the connecting principles of this one, as if they were the real chains which Nature makes use of to bind together her several operations'. In stating that *the goal of science is a consensus of rational opinion* Ziman (1978: 3) recognises that 'much of the research literature of science is intended *rhetorically*' (p. 7). Both Smith and Ziman treat rhetoric as an essential link between the seeker after knowledge and the particular category of knowledge that is being sought, but both argue that rhetoric should be closely related to method and purpose.

It is entirely appropriate, therefore, that in his *Lectures on Rhetoric* Smith (1983: 146) should tell his class that, of the alternative means of didactical writing, 'the Newtonian method is undoubtedly the more philosophical, and in every science...is vastly more ingenious and engaging'. Because it offers the comfort of an encompassing framework, it is the most effective form of persuasion; and persuasion is not only the means of gaining agreement about what is to count for knowledge but also the means of gaining agreement about how to co-ordinate economic activities, since 'the propensity to truck and barter' arises, according to Smith (1978: 352), from the human desire to persuade. The institutions of science, of persuasive discourse, and of the economy are all responses to the imperfections of human knowledge.

More than two centuries after Smith had explained the emergence of scientific theories as the product of the human need for institutions that would make comforting knowledge possible, George Shackle (1967) reinvented Smith's theory – it was a genuine reinvention – in order to provide a framework to explain the development of economics between 1926 and 1939. Economists seek within their subject what we all seek in our lives: 'a satisfying conceptual structure, a model or a taxonomy' to protect us from 'the uneasy consciousness of mystery and a threatening unknown' (Shackle 1967: 288). This conception of science as an exemplification of the human need to impose the appearance of order on 'discordant appearances' was applied in reverse by the American psychologist George Kelly (1963), who sought to remind a profession which had been as committed as economists to the expulsion of mental activity from their theories that they prided themselves on their own mental activities, and might therefore reasonably treat people as scientists who are trying to find ways of constructing order.

Kelly's focus is on complexity, and the need to impose frameworks upon it, which are inevitably problematic. 'Experience', Kelly (1963: 73) writes, 'is made up of the successive construing of events. It is not constituted merely by the succession of events themselves.' It is essential to Kelly's argument that a succession of events may be construed in more than one way, so that different people may draw different conclusions from a particular sequence of phenomena (if indeed there is an objective way, accessible to humans, of describing such a sequence). This interpretative ambiguity is also essential to the understanding of economic evolution. Like Smith, Kelly recognises how attractive are interpretative frameworks of wide scope; but he is also aware of the fallibility of all frameworks, and of the potential obstacles to revising one element in a network that is closely connected – a combination of problems which, as we shall see, has its counterpart in the organisation of an economy. Though Kelly's objective was to improve the practice of clinical psychologists, his analytical system provides valuable cognitive premises for a study of economic behaviour. It also provides valuable guidance for the management of innovation; indeed, it was introduced to me by a distinguished research manager, Charles Suckling.

Representations, closure, institutions and evolution

It is therefore appropriate to set out in this chapter the connecting principles, or interpretative framework, of this inquiry into the operation of economic systems in which knowledge is seriously incomplete, fallible, and dispersed, but capable of improvement and co-ordination. The first principle is that all action is decided in the space of representations. These representations include, for example, neural networks formed in the brain by processes which are outside our conscious control, carefully constructed formal models, maps, organisation charts, corporate strategies, conventional wisdom and locally applied rules of thumb. None are direct copies of reality; all truncate complexity and suppress uncertainty. 'It is clear that to live intelligently in our world...we must use the principle that things similar in some respects will behave similarly in certain other respects even when they are very different in still other respects' (Knight 1921: 206). In other words, we need theories and policies (Loasby 1991: 15), which, as Smith (1980) so memorably explained, are fallible human inventions. To explain human actions, both successful and unsuccessful, we often need to understand the representations on which they are based.

10

Economic models in which information is treated as isomorphic to the real economy, and in which agents differ only in the fineness of their partitioning of the complete information set, are themselves representations which, like all others, replace the phenomena to which they purport to correspond. Representations of all kinds are often ordered differently from those phenomena, and sometimes they generate problems which are the product of the form of representation that is used. The conflict between increasing returns and perfect competition and the perception that the coherence of rational choice models requires agents to use the correct model of the economy are notable examples in economics; there are many others. This book is written in the space of representations, and it is unlikely that any reader will be in total agreement with the ways in which that space is used; although some of its topics appear in standard economics they are there usually located in quite different regions.

It is common to find apparently irrational behaviour attributed to 'framing effects', as if 'framing' were a remediable distortion. But any action must be taken within a framework, whether this is supplied by a neural network, a precisely specified model, a familiar procedure, a novel vision, or some other means. The second principle of this inquiry is that viable processes must operate within viable boundaries; in human affairs these boundaries limit our attention and our procedures to what is manageable without, we hope, being disastrously misleading – though no guarantees are available. Marshall failed to find any boundaries that he thought were viable for what he wished to accomplish in Volume 2 of his *Principles*, and so never came near to delivering it. In this section I am indicating the boundaries of the present inquiry. Economists often rely on separation theorems to legitimise independent frameworks for the analysis of production and consumption, of resource allocation and the choice of transaction mode, of labour and financial markets, or of the real and the monetary economy; accounting systems decompose production systems into cost centres; organisations assign responsibilities to heads of divisions and departments; managers classify difficulties as production problems, marketing problems, personnel problems, organisation problems; and so on. All knowledge requires a framework; and these frameworks must be imposed.

The third principle is that these frameworks are useless unless they persist, even when they do not fit very well, as will be explained in Chapter 3. Hahn's (1973, reprinted in Hahn 1984: 59) definition of equilibrium as a situation in which the messages received by agents do not cause them to change the theories that they hold or the policies that they pursue offers a useful framework for the analysis both of individual behaviour and of the co-ordination of economic activity across a variety of circumstances precisely because it is not to be expected that theories and policies will be readily changed just because some evidence does not appear readily compatible with them. But as Smith also clearly perceived, some kinds of change, of

11

knowledge and of economic activity, require a change of framework, or a new partition of the space of representations; and it is this balance between continuity and novelty that is fundamental to the growth of knowledge and to economic development, as I have argued elsewhere (Loasby 1991).

The fourth principle is that frameworks may be tightly or loosely defined, but that decisions require closure. Rational choice demands a complete set of premises, together with the assurance that they are indeed complete: systems must be both internally and externally closed, for example by defining a firm as a unitary decision maker and excluding cross-boundary effects; and all possible options and outcomes must be specified. But completeness can never be assured, because of the obstacles to knowledge which have already been noted; and so the achievement of sufficient closure to make logical deductions possible by human beings (or even by computer logic) requires all rationality to be bounded, either explicitly or by default. Behaviour which is strictly routine also requires closure: there must be a set of categories to which all phenomena can be assigned, and for each of which there is a predetermined response. Where complete closure is not provided, by familiar models or by complete systems of classification, some means of achieving closure must be invented if a decision is to be made. The gaps must be filled somehow, and different means of filling them have different consequences. These means and their consequences provide the underlying theme of this book. When no means which can be adapted or invented seems adequate, then decisions are hard to make, and it is perhaps because of the need to impose closure by non-logical processes that, as Barnard (1938: 308) notes, 'it is difficult to make correct decisions without responsibility'.

By a mixture of unconscious accretion and deliberate thought each of us develops an interpretative framework within which we construct our own experience through our perception of events, and develop responses to these constructions (Kelly 1963). Both experience and response are conjectures, which are fallible but may be resistant to falsification. These personal frameworks and procedures for achieving closure are substantially influenced by the assumptions, conventions, categories, practices, rules, routines and programmes by which we are surrounded from birth (Hodgson 1998: 172), and which develop through a cumulative mixture of deliberation and unintended consequences. The frameworks and procedures in common use within any group may be summarised as the institutions of that group. They help us to frame problems and offer guidance (sometimes imperative) on action, and thus provide us with the intellectual and social capital which allows us to function. Even an isolated individual requires cognitive frameworks within which to act, or even to think, and externally provided frameworks may be very helpful (Hodgson 1998: 171). The value of compatible frameworks in helping us to cope with interdependencies hardly needs emphasising – except perhaps to economic modellers. The link between cognition and institutions is explored in Chapter 3.

The fifth principle, therefore, is that the study of economic processes entails the study of institutions, for these processes are constrained, though rarely determined, by the institutions within which people think and act. As long as frameworks are susceptible to alternative closures, they permit individual choice; indeed, because they indicate how a situation should be represented, they organise the opportunities for choice. Thus the institutions of an economy frame the generation of variety. Moreover, institutions play an essential role in the co-ordination of economic activities. Co-ordination becomes a problem only when some of these activities change, but if the changes respect the institutional framework within which all those affected by them work, then the achievement of co-ordination is greatly simplified. Economies are stabilised by their institutions (Lesourne 1992), not by the perfect flexibility which is often illegitimately associated with a perfectly competitive economy; for if everything is perfectly flexible, nothing can be relied on. Some institutions may preserve stability by imposing rigidity; but others facilitate change while preventing the disintegration of order. We therefore need to understand the consequences of different institutions. Because different configurations in the space of representations will be appropriate for different purposes, we also need to understand the causes and effects of institutional variety within an economy, and the importance of sharing particular kinds of institutions within particular sectors and at particular levels of an economy. Much of this book is devoted to a selective exploration of economic institutions.

The economic processes which are framed by institutions may appropriately be categorised as evolutionary. That it is helpful so to categorise them is the sixth principle. The elements of evolutionary analysis will be considered in the following chapter; for the present it is sufficient to represent evolution as a process which relies not on correctly informed optimisation but on trial and error, which may include reasoned conjectures. At this introductory stage it is more important to emphasise the double relationship between institutions and evolution: the evolution of economic activities is channelled by human institutions, but these human institutions are themselves subject to evolution – within a broader framework and on a longer timescale. Institutions, whether crafted or emergent, are conjectures in the space of representations; the conjectures which are embodied in any institution may be amended or replaced, but since institutions are defined in relation to some group the amendment or replacement has to be accepted within that group and is therefore a much more complex change than a revision of one person's interpretative framework – though even that, as Kelly (1963) explains, may sometimes be extremely difficult to accomplish.

The seventh and final principle is that the study of evolutionary processes and of the institutions which frame them should therefore embrace a variety of levels and a variety of timescales. Marshall's four time-periods seem to fit more comfortably into an evolutionary analysis than into a model of general equilibrium, for each is used to analyse particular kinds of change within a particular institutional setting. We may choose to think more broadly of categories of institutions, which provide the context for categories of intelligent decisions, as framing distinctive but overlapping evolutionary processes. Thus we might seek to identify institutions which respectively guide individual thought and action, preserve (or are sometimes inadequate to preserve) social order at all levels from international relations to the family, and maintain the informal organisation on which all formal organisations depend. There is no attempt in this book to offer a comprehensive coverage of the kinds of institutions which help to frame behaviour, but in focusing primarily on economic behaviour we shall try not to forget – as Adam Smith did not forget – the effects on that behaviour of institutions which are not normally regarded as economic. What is part of the selection environment at one level of analysis and on one timescale may be a variant which is itself subject to selection at another level of analysis and on another timescale (Nooteboom 1992). But we cannot understand change except by assuming that some things – and usually many things – do not change.

Knowledge and methodology

As Smith, Shackle and Kelly (and many others) appreciate, all closures apply to representations; the phenomena themselves cannot be isolated. In attempting such isolation, we may even abstract away from rather than towards the essential features that we wish to study, both in axiomatic reasoning and in experimental design. Thus all closures are in some degree false. There can be no self-sufficient Cartesian scheme for deducing justified true knowledge from some original certainty. Logical structures carry forward truth values from premises to conclusions; but the truth values of the premises are always problematic. The premises of one chain of reasoning may themselves be deduced from higher-order premises, but, as Marshall was acutely aware, in any lengthy chain of argument it is almost inevitable that some necessary premises will be omitted because the problem is more complex than has been recognised, or that some premises which are included will be false. It was Descartes' theory of vortices that Adam Smith (1976a: 313) had explicitly in mind when he wrote 'A system of natural philosophy may appear very plausible, and be for a long time very generally received in the world, and yet have no foundation in nature, nor any sort of resemblance to the truth.' The axiomatisation of economics is not consistent with Smith's conception of human knowledge.

As Second Wrangler at a time when the theorems of Euclid held an important place in the Cambridge Mathematical Tripos, Marshall was quick to recognise that the internal coherence of non-Euclidean geometry undermined any general claim that empirical truths could be derived from axiomatic reasoning, and developed his own style of reasoning and presentation accordingly. Debreu (1991: 3) recognises that every rigorous axiomatic theory has a limited field of application, and claims that 'its explicit assumptions delimit its domain of applicability and make illegitimate overstepping of its boundary flagrant'; but when, two pages later, he justifiably celebrates Arrow's 'extension of the economic theory of certainty to an economic theory of uncertainty by a simple reinterpretation of the concept of a commodity', he notes its effect on the practice of financial markets without observing that the strict legitimacy of this application requires a complete set of contingent markets, and also assumes that a complete set of contingencies could be specified. The latter assumption is pervasive in economics, illustrating the continued relevance of Whitehead's (1951: 699) complaint about 'the absurd trust in the adequacy of our knowledge'. Overstepping of the boundaries is almost unavoidable if any theory is applied; what is avoidable is the pretence that nothing of the sort is happening. That is why Shackle's (1972) *Epistemics and Economics* was welcomed by a senior research manager and a head of corporate planning as a practical guide to running a complex business (Loasby 1994).

Logical arguments are not causal explanations, though they can be used as part of a causal explanation; for example, the identification of a stable equilibrium may be combined with an account of the reasons for a sequence of actions to explain why a system settles into a new configuration. Logical arguments are also very important as a consistency check on ideas which have been assembled by non-logical means, and as a means of deriving implications which may be more effectively examined than the premises from which they derive (Popper 1959). What logical systems can never directly produce — this is a simple logical proposition — is a genuinely new idea. It is impossible to deduce a Walrasian theory of innovation, as Schumpeter (1934) pointed out.

The categories, procedures, and criteria that we use, in all our activities, can only be representations of the reality that we believe exists. They simplify, approximate, and omit. The multiple levels of analysis, and the immense variation in the level of detail between the different levels (which of course is necessary to conform to the bounds of our rationality) are artificial decompositions imposed on a system which is integral, but which appears to behave as if it were decomposable within limited space and time. What these limits are is a question which we often get wrong — for example in ignoring the longer-run effects of burning fossil fuels, of tax changes, and of welfare provision, and in ignoring the implications of product or pricing decisions on other parts of the business or on responses by competitors. In suggesting, from time to time, reasons for particular kinds of failure, there is no intention to offer simple guides for public policy; that would require much more attention to the institutions of government and of policy-propagating organisations than can be afforded here — or than economists often bestow before offering policy recommendations.

Nevertheless, one general warning can be given: methodological choices can have real effects. The ways in which economists do economics, the ways in which a particular business is run, the ways in which we each try to manage our daily lives, have consequences, both good and ill, for what we can achieve. In each context there is a methodological prescription, partly explicit and partly implicit, of what questions are worth asking, what are the appropriate ways of trying to answer them, and what answers are acceptable; these are the parameters of a particular evolutionary process for generating and then reducing variety. On inspection, it is clear that every discipline has its own conception of what questions, what methods, and what answers are proper (Loasby 1995), though to an outsider it may be less easy to understand them, and sometimes quite difficult to appreciate the reasons for them, which may lie in the past evolution of that discipline.

The standard method of analysing economic policy in the middle third of this century assumed remarkable privileges for the economic analyst and policy-makers. Not only were they entirely exempt from the constraints and incentives which dominated the conduct of economic agents; these economic agents had no means of influencing analysts or policy-makers, or even of incorporating these strictly exogenous policies as premises of their own decisions. Macroeconomists now recognise the force of the 'Lucas critique', but the equivalent recognition has not yet spread to principal-agent analysis, even though the proposition that management control systems are endogenous to the behavioural patterns that they seek to control is not new (Loasby 1968). Perhaps the discovery by experimental economists that subjects may respond to the experimental design rather than the specific alternatives presented, for example in ultimatum and chicken games (Camerer 1997), may encourage a wider reappraisal. It is clear that evolutionary and institutional economists can have no such privileges; they are no less subject to evolutionary processes, and no less dependent on the institutions, both of their particular trades and of the various social groups to which they belong, than are the agents whom they study. Institutions and selection procedures, both within an economic system and among those trying to understand and analyse it, always foreclose and conceal options. The fundamental economic principle of scarcity ensures that there will be opportunity costs.

The institutions of economics, for example, influence the kinds of knowledge that economists can produce, and changes in these institutions have resulted in changes in knowledge. As Hahn and Solow observe:

> macroeconomics began as the study of large scale economic pathologies [such as involuntary unemployment]....Now, at last, macroeconomic theory has as its central conception a model in which such pathologies are, strictly speaking, unmentionable. There is no legal way to talk about them.
>
> (1995: 2)

As previously noted, Laidler and Leijonhufvud explain why. In this class of models, as we know, all observed states of the economy are to be understood as equilibria in which all economic agents are optimising, and so there can be no involuntary unemployment, or indeed any involuntary outcome. But though it may be rational to construct an economic model in which agents' expectations are consistent with the structure of the model, it cannot be rational for either agents or model-builders to commit themselves, without reserve, to the truth – or even to the predictive accuracy – of such a model. As we shall see in Chapter 5, what economists can say about the organisation of industry similarly depends on what kinds of analysis and what kinds of conclusions are acceptable.

In objecting to the unmentionability of involuntary unemployment, Hahn and Solow are warning us about the pathology of economic theory. Every discipline, like every economy, and every way of running a business, has its own pathologies, which result from the categories, processes and criteria on which it relies to make its problems manageable; sometimes, as with RCA's conception of what was an acceptable major innovation, where acceptable was defined in relation to members of the organisation and their interpretation of its history, the pathology can be fatal (Graham 1986). These pathologies may be regarded as an extreme case of opportunity costs, when the opportunities foreclosed turn out to be of major importance. If so regarded, they must not be forgotten in the following chapters; but neither do they constitute the main case. As Hayek warned us, before we can understand why things can go wrong (in an academic discipline or a firm, as well as in an economy), we need to understand how they could ever go right. To do that we must give proper attention to the non-logical elements in behaviour, adhering to the methodological principle that what does not conform to particular conceptions of rationality should not be dismissed as 'irrational'.

Knight (1933: xiv) declared himself 'puzzled by the insistence of many writers on treating the uncertainty of result in choice as if it were a gamble on a known mathematical chance', thereby rejecting 'the fundamental significance' of uncertainty. That insistence, which prevents any adequate discussion of many important phenomena, is a consequence of the evolved institutions of economics which, like other institutions, are paradoxically a response to uncertainty. The study of institutions and evolution requires a category of 'non-rationality' so that economic analysis may be extended beyond the limits set by Lucas, and thus acquire resistance to some of its own pathogens.

Before proceeding with our investigation, however, we should consider the argument that economists' concern with rigorous models of rationality, and the less than rigorous treatment of problems of knowledge that are necessary in order to define and manipulate these models, can be justified by the pressures on economic agents to achieve the outcomes that these models predict. What is especially pertinent to the theme of this book is that version of this argument that relies on evolutionary processes, but paradoxically claims that these processes are so effective that there is no need for economists to study them. Evolution is thus being invoked, not merely to explain the emergence of a particular set of institutions, but also (as is not uncommon in other contexts) to validate them. This proposition is examined in the following chapter.

2

SELECTION AND EVOLUTION

Selection and rationality

The modern interest in selection processes within economic systems originated with Alchian's (1950) intervention in the debate on the applicability of marginal analysis in economics. (The contributions to that debate to which I shall refer have been rigorously examined by Vromen 1995.) The critics, such as Harrod (1939) and Lester (1946), had argued that businessmen typically lacked the information that would be necessary to make the calculations on which profit-maximising actions could be based, and Machlup (1946) had responded by claiming that experienced business-men had developed the expertise which allowed them to maximise profits, just as experienced drivers developed the expertise which allowed them to overtake optimally. Machlup (ibid.: 521) then made the potentially fatal admission that 'all the relevant magnitudes involved...are subjective' and may differ from those observed by outside analysts, without recognising that even the explicit use of marginal analysis by businessmen may not then lead to the outcomes that the analysts would predict (Vromen 1995: 20–1).

Alchian began by apparently reinforcing the criticism of marginalism, in questioning the value of analysts' predictions as a standard by which managerial performance could appropriately be judged. He pointed out that only when we assume perfect information and perfect foresight can we specify unambiguously what is a profit-maximising choice: 'where foresight is uncertain, "profit maximisation" is *meaningless* as a guide to specifiable action' (Alchian 1950: 211). The maximisation of expected profits is optimal only for those who are risk-neutral, which we have no right to assume. (Alchian did not regard businessmen as the compliant agents of shareholders who managed risk by the diversification of their portfolios.) But even if it were deemed optimal, the maximisation of expected profits is consistent with any level of realised profit that is included within the probability distribution from which the profit expectation is derived; and so even if this probability distribution were objectively correct, the ability to predict choices would not be sufficient to predict outcomes. We may extend

Alchian's argument by remarking that if the envisaged possibilities are subjective, as Machlup insisted, then we have no secure anchorage for predicting either decisions or their consequences – as Hutchison (1937) had already emphasised.

As an advocate of formal modelling early in her career, Joan Robinson (1933: 6) declared that 'the assumption that the individual firm will always arrange its affairs in such a way as to make the largest profits that can be made…is [the] assumption that makes the analysis of value possible'. In her subsequent analysis she apparently conferred on firms the power of perfect, not merely probabilistic, foresight, including the ability to predict the outcome of interfirm rivalry (Robinson 1933: 21), but in practice finessed the difficulty in what has become the standard fashion by restricting her analysis to situations of equilibrium in which single-valued expectations had proved correct – a procedure that she later dismissed as 'a shameless fudge' (Robinson 1969: vi). Alchian agreed with the critics of marginalism, among whom Robinson was by then prominent, that marginalists had offered no justification for this procedure beyond its analytical convenience; but he then produced a distinctive justification of his own.

In this justification he took the radical step of discarding the 'assumption that makes the analysis of value possible' and indeed any attempt to explain choices. What matters, he insisted, are not choices but outcomes, both direct and indirect. The relevant direct outcomes are the profits which each firm actually realises and the relevant indirect outcomes are the survival of those firms which make positive profits and the disappearance of those that do not (Alchian 1950: 213). Thus, if our objective is to explain or predict aggregate behaviour in the economy, we do not need to bother with the ways in which particular firms decide what to do; 'the essential point is that individual motivation and foresight, while sufficient, are not necessary' (ibid.: 217). Alchian appears to be claiming that any sort of microeconomics is superfluous; our unit of analysis should be the population of firms in a particular industry, and our focus of interest the selection pressures which determine the characteristics of that population.

However, that is not the conclusion that he wishes to draw. Although he explicitly refuses to assume that selection pressures are generally so strong that only firms which somehow contrive to maximise profits will survive (ibid.: 217–18), he wishes to retain the profit-maximising model, on the grounds that the survivors will be those firms which have come closest to its predictions. Alchian believes that economists' ambitions should be modest, agreeing with Machlup that the proper objective of economic analysis is not the prediction and explanation of prices and quantities, but the prediction and explanation of the direction of changes in these prices and quantities in response to exogenous change. He also agrees with Machlup that marginal analysis is a convenient way of predicting that direction – but not for Machlup's reason. No appeal to skilful performance is necessary; all that we can legitimately say, in Alchian's view, is that the survivors will have achieved results which are closer to the maximisation of attainable profits than those of the firms which did not survive. But that is all that we need to say in order to predict the direction of change for an industry – though not, he points out, for any particular firm. As long as our concern is with the changes in the price and output of a commodity, we do not need to bother about individual firms, and certainly do not need to enquire how they make their decisions. Though Alchian is confident that comparative equilibrium models which assume profit maximisation will generally be sufficient for this purpose, he warns us that convergence over time to a profit-maximising equilibrium should not lightly be assumed, because environments are likely to change too rapidly for the selection of persistent optimisers (ibid.: 219); but only at this point does Alchian go beyond the very simplest kind of analysis of selection processes. He does not consider the adequacy of the profit maximisation assumption for the welfare appraisal of market economies.

Friedman's (1953) much-cited methodological paper, in which the choice of theoretical formulations is made to turn primarily on the success of the predictions which they yield, also includes a brief argument to explain why profit-maximising models may be expected to be good predictors. His argument, which was apparently developed independently of Alchian's, is much bolder – even perhaps reckless. For Friedman claims that the selection process is sufficiently powerful to ensure that the predictions of the profit-maximising model will be accurate not only at the industry level but for every firm, and that this will be true irrespective of 'the apparent immediate determinant of business behaviour' (Friedman 1953: 22). Now if only those firms which, for whatever reason, succeed in making profits survive, then indeed those whose behaviour depends on 'habitual reaction, random chance or whatnot' will survive if, and only if, that behaviour happens to deliver the profits which permit survival. But Friedman offers no reason why those firms which do well in the first period should continue to make maximum profits in succeeding periods, nor any reason why they should fail to survive even if they do not, since, by his argument, their rivals have already been eliminated. (This is not a difficulty for Alchian's carefully limited proposal, which is about movement, not equilibrium.) Friedman offers no theory of new entry, and thus fails to balance his account of variety reduction with an account of the generation of sufficient variety to make the effects of variety reduction significant.

Becker (1962) does not repeat Friedman's claim that selection is powerful enough to ensure that every firm which survives will be an ex-post profit-maximiser. His argument for the power of selection has an economic basis in the fundamental concept of scarcity, as manifested in the budget constraint which every firm has to face. Any firm which makes profits relaxes this constraint, and can therefore increase the scale of its operations; any firm which makes losses finds that its constraint is tighter, and is thus forced to contract. The result is a theory of differential reproduction which looks very similar to the biological model, and which has the happy effect of ensuring rational market response without any need for individual rationality. In Becker's formulation it is precisely because the market system does not require economic agents to be rational that we can confidently model them as expert optimisers.

However, Becker's theory is inadequate, because the biological model is inadequate for the economic context. Though consumer theory relies on individual budget constraints, they do not appear to be an essential component of the standard theory of the firm, as Becker (1962: 10) notes. In particular, they have no role in the standard neoclassical explanation of the size of the firm, which rests – though often implicitly – on the underlying assumption that capital markets can be relied on to supply whatever finance is justified by the firm's optimal plans, and none that is not so justified. But in denying the need for any rationality Becker has implicitly abolished efficient capital markets. Becker's argument also assumes that firms will generally operate on their opportunity frontier; for otherwise the shift of resources in favour of ex-post profit-maximisers will not ensure a steady increase in their share of the business. But just as the biological assumption that animal species will always take full advantage of opportunities for reproduction is clearly no longer universally applicable to human beings, so we may question the assumption that firms will take every opportunity of expanding – especially in the context of Becker's claim that rational economies do not require rational firms.

The insufficiency of selection arguments

Alchian, Friedman, and Becker develop a common theme: the realistic model of an economy is that of a continuing selection process, but there is, fortunately, no need to develop such a realistic model because the familiar models of well-informed optimising behaviour give adequate results for the issues which interest economists. To the question 'how adequate are these results?' somewhat different answers are given: Alchian believes that we should moderate our claims, Friedman is much more confident, and Becker is so convinced of the power of optimising models to mimic the results of selection that he later claimed that economists' rational choice theory was the only sound basis for analysis within the social sciences (Becker 1976). None of them even hints that economists might investigate the conditions in which selection processes will do what is required.

Economists, it appears, should continue to elucidate with precision the effects of different market structures on efficient allocation, by applying optimising models whose use is justified by the unanalysed effects of other poorly specified structures and behaviour on efficient selection. This remarkable methodological prescription signifies the abandonment of the centuries-old attempt to explain how economic systems work and, for policy-oriented economists, the acceptance of the dangerous principle that it is possible to control the economy without understanding it. (This principle has since been widely adopted in macroeconomics.) Selection processes are the most important operators in an economic system, but economists should nevertheless ignore them. We have here a striking example of selection processes at work within the economics profession; further examples are not difficult to find, indicating that a study of our own subject offers particular opportunities to develop skills in evolutionary economics.

The proposition that economists can safely substitute a false theory for one which they believe to be correct, and should be encouraged to do so, is open to a number of criticisms. First, a theoretical structure which depends, and has since increased its dependence, on hyper-rationality is being justified by the claim that any kind of rationality is unnecessary. Second, an intendedly rigorous theory which, especially in the versions put forward by Friedman and Becker, relies on the efficient operation of markets makes no attempt to model the operation of markets, but is content to represent the presumed market outcomes by equilibria of individual optimising agents. Third, because any selection process requires some variety on which to work, the selection argument which is invoked is incompatible with the assumptions of product and factor homogeneity and a common knowledge of production functions within most of the models which it is used to justify. In particular, ongoing selection is incompatible with perfect competition, which not only excludes variety but cannot exist outside equilibrium, and can therefore at best be a consequence of selection, but never a context for it. Selection processes cannot operate in perfectly competitive markets. This may be regarded as an alternative version of a familiar, but regularly ignored, argument that perfect competition can never be legitimately invoked to explain movement towards equilibrium. (Richardson 1960, 1990, offers a definitive treatment.) Fourth, and closely linked to the third, we have no explanation of how prices get changed; this was a major complaint raised by Kirzner (1962) against Becker's claim that rationality was superfluous.

Fifth, if we dispense with rationality, what grounds have we for supposing that what is selected is in any sense best? Becker's emphasis on the constraints of the opportunity set does not address that issue. If consumers have no intelligible ground for their choice of products, how do we know that those firms which make profits by supplying them are actually producing the goods which best conform to their preferences, and thus that their survival is evidence of their contribution to welfare? If banks and investors have no intelligible grounds for deciding whose activities to finance, Becker has no reason to claim that firms which fail to make profits will systematically lose control over resources. The argument that selection is an adequate substitute for rationality in economic systems appears to rest on an implicit theory of selection in consumer and financial markets which are populated by rational agents. Sixth, biological competition depends on excess entry, which is guaranteed by the urge to reproduce; this was Darwin's debt to Malthus, but the principle of excess reproduction is not obviously extendable to all economic activity. What drives excess entry into markets? Penrose (1952) put this question to Alchian; it carries a general warning that economic systems are not replicas of biological systems, but need rather more care than Friedman, Becker, and even Alchian were prepared to devote to them.

We thus arrive at the seventh and final criticism, also voiced by Penrose (1952: 808), which is that human beings do sometimes act purposefully, in a way which does not seem to be characteristic of flora and fauna; and some of these purposeful actions have significant consequences. There was, after all, a good reason for giving the notion of human choice – including rational choice but also the ways of choosing discussed by Barnard (1938) – a prominent place in economic theory. There was an especially good reason for doing so in an evolutionary theory, such as Alfred Marshall envisaged. In contrast to Alchian (1950: 219), who claimed to be following his lead, Marshall (1920: 5) clearly believed that individual motivation and foresight made an important difference to what he clearly regarded as an evolutionary process, and identified 'self-reliance, independence, deliberate choice and forethought', rather than competition, as the 'fundamental characteristics of modern industrial life'. Ex-ante selection, which should not be assimilated to ex-ante optimisation, as well as ex-post selection, is essential to evolutionary economics.

We therefore conclude that reliance on an ill-considered analogy to biological selection arguments is a logically inappropriate basis for justifying rational choice theory; it is a failure of rigour which, if detected within an economic model, would result in the summary rejection of any paper submitted for publication. If the validity of economic theorising is to be supported by selection arguments, these arguments should be set out with the care (though not necessarily the technique) which is normally deemed appropriate for economic reasoning. Such care requires considerably more than the replication of biological models with a change of nomenclature. Biological analogies should certainly be used where they are appropriate: for example, we need to think of both the variety and persistence of characteristics and the means by which characteristics are replicated. But we do not need to restrict ourselves to biological models; our analyses should reflect the distinctively human aspects of economic activity, not the least significant of which, as Mises (1949) insisted, is purposeful behaviour, both in response to events and in the origination of new products, new methods, and new forms of organisation. We have already argued that purposeful behaviour is entirely consistent with trial and error, as long as people have no way of knowing that their actions will achieve their purposes, and especially when people have different views about what kinds of behaviour will be effective and what kinds of conjectures will be corroborated. So instead of appealing to poorly specified natural selection arguments, from which conscious rationality is excluded, to justify the use of models which assume superhuman rationality and apparently divine omniscience, should we not try to develop a theory of economic evolution which incorporates reasoned choices?

The experimental economy

Evolution is here understood as a class of trial and error processes, which comprise three elements: the generation of variety, the reduction of variety, and some persistence both in the characteristics of the variants and in the environment within which they are selected. I have previously suggested (Loasby 1991) that the factors which were responsible for the persistence which is necessary for evolution might be analysed in terms of equilibrium, though not an equilibrium which is derived from the basic data of the economy; I still believe that this is a useful approach, but I shall not emphasise it in this book. It is very important to note that there may be many different evolutionary processes which depend on very different time-scales of persistence; biological evolution tends to work over much longer timescales than are likely to be of interest to social scientists. That is one reason why the processes of social evolution may not conform to biological analogies, though they must respect the present-day constraints on human behaviour which have resulted from biological evolution. In the first part of Chapter 3, the evolution of human cognitive capacity is treated as a problem of evolutionary psychology, but only in order to provide a credible basis for analysing the evolution of institutions in the context of unchanging human cognitive capacity (in effect, an equilibrium configuration) which these institutions have the potential to make more effective.

Popper's conception of science as a variety of conjectures, continually winnowed by refutation, was explicitly presented as an evolutionary process. It differs from biological processes in two respects. First, selection is in the hands of members of the relevant scientific community, and because of the Duhem–Quine problem the refutation of any conjecture is decided not by the evidence but by the interpretation that is placed upon it. Much of this evidence could hardly be called 'natural', since it is produced in circum-stances which are carefully contrived to exclude recognised complexity – though of course the experimental design is based on knowledge which is itself fallible; indeed, when experimental observations conflict with theory it is often the experimental design which is deemed to be falsified. Second, the conjectures which scientists offer for testing are often far from random; their ideas are influenced by their training, and some of them will be quietly suppressed without testing because they appear to conflict with currently accepted conventions (Kuhn 1962, 1970a). The institutions of each scientific community channel the processes by which that community develops its scientific knowledge (Whitley 1984). However, those who make these conjectures have no means of knowing whether their particular conjecture will be successful – and indeed the great majority are not. In this important sense, the generation of conjectures is 'blind'. As we shall have several occasions to note, the selection of conjectures is itself subject to error, and therefore some diversity in the basis of this selection is generally desirable.

Since evolution in economic systems depends on, if it is not constituted by, the evolution of knowledge, it is not surprising that it resembles Popperian science rather than biological models in both the generation and reduction of variety; for both the generation and the reduction of variety are substantially influenced by human intervention, and channelled by human institutions. Evolutionary analysis is in sharp conceptual opposition to the predilection of economists for designing optimal systems, once for whole economies, and more recently for monetary regimes and principal-agent relationships, for it denies the possibility of proving the optimality of any design. Nevertheless it can readily encompass processes in which rival designs for new products, new processes or new ways of organising a business are carefully worked out on the basis of the knowledge that is currently held in different organisations, and launched with very different degrees of success. But even if some of these designs are based on the assumption of secure and sufficient knowledge, they must be regarded as fallible – and often falsified – conjectures within an unintentionally evolutionary process (Nooteboom 1992: 286).

Design as conjecture is an important element in economic evolution, and some of these designs may be produced by the use of optimising models. Indeed, much of choice theory may be reconstrued as a theory of rational conjectures within a never-ending process rather than the basis of equilibrium. Mises' (1949) characterisation of human behaviour as a purposeful search for improvement – if not the whole of Mises' methodological prescription – seems particularly amenable to such an interpretation. But evolutionary analysis also opens up the possibility of system designs, still necessarily conjectural, which reject the possibility of ex-ante optimisation and seek to cope with the obstacles to knowledge that were outlined in the previous chapter, for example through a research programme which is intended to explore alternative possibilities, or an economic subsystem which encourages entrepreneurial initiative. As Hayek (1945: 520) observes, the question of how to organise economic activity 'is not a dispute about whether planning is to be done or not. It is a dispute about whether planning is to be done centrally...or is to be divided among many individuals.' Now a system of central planning has very different properties from those of a system in which rival plans are continually being launched into a competitive environment. In the present context the differences that are especially relevant lie in the capacity of each system to generate variety and its efficiency in selecting among the alternatives that are presented.

This is an issue that was completely ignored by those who invoked general equilibrium arguments to demonstrate not merely the feasibility but the likely superiority of planning; and, as Caldwell (1997) has pointed out, it is still ignored in the literature on incentive compatibility, which is sometimes presented as if it were a theory of management. However well designed the incentives for agents to do what they know their principals would want them to do, any formal organisation typically has only a very limited capacity to generate diverse options, and its ability to tolerate variety is often even less; that is why improvement so often seems to be associated either with multiple organisations or new entry to a field. General equilibrium theory is not an appropriate model of variety generation – though it may be useful as one of a variety of models with which to organise and improve our understanding of economic systems.

If we think of 'the economic problem' not as how to achieve an efficient allocation when all possibilities are known, or even of efficient allocation when this complete knowledge is initially distributed among many people, but as how to encourage an effective discovery process when there can be no demonstrably correct model either of what is available for discovery or how to go about it, then we may find a useful framework for our own enquiries in Eliasson's (1987) concept of an experimentally organised economy. If everyone knows the same things, not much will be known, and if everyone searches in the same direction, not much will be discovered.

In an economy as in a scientific discipline 'orthodoxy is the death of knowledge, since the growth of knowledge depends entirely on the existence of disagreement' (Popper 1996: 34). Because any particular conjecture is likely to be wrong, it is important that there should be many different conjectures; and that requires conjectures from many different people, with different backgrounds, relying on different institutions and experimenting with different forms of closure. It should be remembered that Kuhn, who is usually associated with the concept of paradigm-constrained normal science, not only recognised that agreement among scientists on the criteria which should guide choice was compatible with disagreement on specific theoretical choices, but argued that, since any such choice entails risks, 'variability of judgement may...even be regarded as essential to scientific advance' (Kuhn 1970b: 241, 264). Economic systems, like scientific or political systems, are likely to generate more knowledge and to use it more effectively if they are open societies.

This process of trial and error is inevitably wasteful in retrospect, and therefore does not appeal to the efficiency-minded. But it is the nature of discovery that it is not obvious; it requires, for example, a novel closure within a familiar framework, the removal of a traditionally accepted closure, or the application of a framework from a field hitherto believed to be irrelevant. All these are exercises of the imagination, and what might be imagined cannot be known. But, as Shackle (1979: 26) reminds us, an innovative idea is 'the imagined, deemed possible', and what each individual deems possible is heavily influenced by the impact of a particular set of institutions on personal ways of thinking. Innovative ideas sometimes need to be protected from those who would dismiss what is imagined as impossible; innovative organisations sometimes exempt their employees from their standard procedures for a portion of their time, and less innovative organisations may find that their imaginative employees leave in order to create their own protected environment. In modern macroeconomic theory, an economy of islands which are linked by an imperfect system of communications is a convenient device to inject trouble into a model of efficient co-ordination; but in a world of dispersed, incomplete, but augmentable knowledge, such an economy can facilitate innovation – which is, of course, a threat to co-ordination.

However, most conjectures are refuted. Much that is deemed possible by its creator turns out to be impossible; and an economy that encourages imaginative conjectures requires some means of sifting them, preferably before many resources have been committed. Harper's (1995) examination of entrepreneurship is notable for its insistence on the need to balance alertness and imagination in conceiving possibilities with rigour in planning the process of realising these possibilities and testing the assumptions which underlie that plan. It is also notable for its recognition that, contrary to the Schumpeterian image of the innovator who drives the original conception to success, most imaginative conceptions which succeed are substantially changed along the way. As in biological systems, selection is mainly rejection, but in economic systems it sometimes takes the form of adaptation and redesign, leading to another set of trials, which may result in further adaptation, or eventual rejection. Moreover, such responses may be evoked by both success and failure, though failure no doubt supplies the sharper incentive.

A major objective of the development process in commercial organisations is to anticipate the results of market testing, thus avoiding the costs of rejection in the market, and thereby improving the dynamic efficiency of the economic system. The producers thus act as agents for consumers, and for all those who, it is believed, may have some influence on the success of the product, including nowadays those who are concerned with its recovery or disposal after use; but the agency problems thus created are not primarily those of incentives but of the knowledge necessary to anticipate, and find adequate proxies for, the decisions which all these people are likely to make. The development process itself is therefore an important arena for selection through design. However, one should remember that the screens designed by research managers are fallible conjectures, which may differ between rival firms (see Loasby 1976: Chapter 3). It is well known that many products which come to market do not last long; it is less well known (for it is not something which there is any incentive to publicise) that firms sometimes abandon the development of products which, if persevered with, would have been successful. The selection processes themselves are subject to modification and sometimes to drastic revision; the tragedy of thalidomide changed the criteria by which animal species were selected for initial trials of new drugs. Studies of research and development therefore deserve a prominent place within evolutionary economics; and the name of Schumpeter has been of some service in bringing together economists with a primary interest in technology and those attracted by evolutionary concepts.

In economic evolution active selection by human agents occurs at all stages of the process. 'Market forces' respond to human choices. Economics therefore needs a theory of choice; but it is important to pay attention to the ways in which these agents set about making their selections, and the influences upon them; and that requires a much richer conception of decision processes, and of the learning processes which underlie them, than is found in conventional choice theory, even, as Caldwell (1997) demonstrates, including recent extensions of the theory of information. What characteristics are selected, by whom, using what criteria, within what framework and using what information? In what sequence are the selections made, and what do those choosing at each stage know about the factors which influence selection at other stages? The answers to these questions shape the outcome of particular selection processes. Since many of these decisions are taken within firms, the study of these processes requires particular attention to the capabilities of firms, which is the theme of Chapter 4, to the evolutionary processes by which these capabilities are developed, and to the organisational structures, both formal and informal, which frame the perceptions of productive opportunities and thus help to create the selection environment.

One characteristic feature of economic evolution is that, in contrast to biological systems, there is no universal difference in kind between the processes which generate variety and those which reduce it. Although the equivalent of mutation – unintended novelty – is certainly important, in a modern economy the generation of variety is a fundamental part of the economic process, and indeed a notable consequence of the division of labour. Adam Smith (1976b: 20–1) drew attention to the different kinds of inventions that would be produced by people whose attention was differently focused, and Marshall (1920: 355–6) emphasised the variation within each specialism which resulted from 'special opportunities and resources,...temperament and...associations'. This variety-generation process begins with an initial, and sometimes unconscious, selection of where and how to look for improvement, and continues with a drastic – and sometimes mistaken – winnowing of ideas even before the first attempt to try any of them out. The multiplicity of selection processes may be most clearly observed in the conduct of industrial research and development; the ideas which arise within any one organisation are a non-random subset of what might have been conceived, and the ideas that survive internal processing are a small fraction of these; moreover, the survivors typically emerge in a substantially different form from that originally envisaged. The variety reduction that occurs in markets is only a part, and often a small part, of the total; and it should not be forgotten that markets can also provide frameworks within which new ideas may emerge, from consumers as well as producers (Bianchi 1998).

Stability both in most features of the environment and in most elements of the various procedures for making choices is an essential condition of evolution. But each novelty produces some change in the environment and some change in the procedures used. In the course of discussing the effect of increasing returns in the chapters that were privately published as *The Pure Theory of Foreign Trade*, Marshall declared that '[i]n economics, every event causes permanent alterations in the conditions under which future events can occur' (Whitaker 1975, vol. 2: 163). Economists must therefore consider path dependency. This is a matter of degree, and sometimes the degree may not be significantly different from zero; the 'permanent alterations' may have no effect on the options which are relevant to the next move, or they may change the magnitude of costs and benefits without displacing the best. But some choices or events will lead others to act differently, and these differences may become cumulative. This is especially likely if existing conventions or procedures are affected, thus causing later decisions to be framed in a way which reflects history.

It is not difficult to identify 'technological trajectories', or indeed 'market trajectories', but it is not always clear to what extent the trajectory observed is a product, rather than a determinant, of particular sequences. The extreme case of path dependency is 'lock-in'; views differ about the practical importance of this possibility, and about the realistic chances of averting it by timely acts of public policy. In this book we shall be more concerned with the degree of path dependency which is manifest in changing constraints, both among outside opportunities and in internal frameworks of thought and action. It appears that both individuals and organisations are substantially conditioned by their history – this indeed is the source of much of the persistence on which selection processes can work – but that both individuals and organisations have a limited possibility of path independency. With some effort, often substantial, it is possible to switch between trajectories and to build, or adapt from elsewhere, new institutions; but no individual or organisation can do this very often. As Dr Johnson (1755) observed 'Change is not made without inconvenience, even from worse to better'; or, in modern terminology, switching costs are pervasive. However, the economic system is less constrained than any element within it, especially if that system has preserved diversity; and in the last resort, there is the biological expedient of birth and death. Constraints may therefore continue to evolve, as well as the activities which are bounded by those constraints; there is no foreseeable end to the process of economic evolution.

Human selection processes are subject to human limitations and are the product of biological, psychological, and sociological evolution; but humans have some degrees of freedom. Therefore, instead of assuming that people make logically impeccable deductions from preferences and opportunities, which are themselves not explained but are nevertheless treated as completely unproblematic, or alternatively that only those whose actions turn out to be consistent with optimisation survive, perhaps we should follow Simon's lead and look more closely at the process of decision making. Instead of beginning our analysis by assuming a set of options we should enquire what options come to be included in the choice set – for, as Alchian recognised, the optimum cannot be chosen unless it has been thought of. Shackle's insistence on the importance of imagination is a major contribution to evolutionary economics, but a contribution as yet scarcely recognised; its relationship to Schumpeter's conception of innovation has only recently been explored (Loasby 1996). The next stage of this inquiry is an investigation into the limitations and potential of human cognition.

3

COGNITION AND
INSTITUTIONS

Cognitive processes

In the opening chapter I drew attention to the importance of frameworks, conventions, and procedures as prerequisites of intelligent personal, and not only social, behaviour. In this chapter I shall first transgress the institutional limits of economics by exploring the limits of human cognition, before considering the emergence of these institutional constraints as a fallible solution to cognitive problems. Cognitive issues are ignored in conventional economics because, as Woo (1992: 167) points out, in rational choice theory the production function for decisions is not specified. Sir Dennis Robertson (1976) once asked 'What does the economist economise?' His answer was 'the scarce resource of love' – an answer that can be derived from Adam Smith, who believed that moral sentiments were essential but insufficient for the maintenance of a civil society. But Robertson might also have asked what, in their analysis of economic behaviour, do economists fail to economise? The answer is the scarce resource of cognition.

Contemporary North American economics, in particular, makes hardly any demands on love, or any moral sentiment, but prodigious demands on human cognitive powers. The energy cost of the supposedly rational procedures which are routinely imputed to economic agents is ignored, and the optima thus derived are therefore sub-optimal. This cost is not trivial: '[b]rain tissue is energetically among the most expensive tissues in the body' (Aiello 1996: 280), and the brain accounts for about one-fifth of human energy requirements. Since all life on earth depends on solar energy to compensate for its own relentless generation of entropy, human cognition deserves to be considered, at least from our own perspective, as one of the most significant externalities of the sun. One might add that even if there were no energy cost, decision making takes time, and therefore the making of any decision incurs the opportunity cost of the most valuable decision which might otherwise have been made in that time.

If '[an] economist thinks of himself as the guardian of rationality, the ascriber of rationality to others, and the prescriber of rationality to the social world' (Arrow 1974: 16), should he not heed Herbert Simon's repeated calls to apply the familiar analysis of rational allocation to the fundamental scarcity of human reasoning power? But economists seem deeply immersed in the bad habit, learned from Walras and reinforced by Arrow and Debreu, of assuming that all decisions are taken outside time, and so may be treated as free goods; few have yet begun to explore the ramifications of Coase's (1988: 14–15) claim that the costs of transacting – many of which, as specified by Coase (1937, reprinted in Coase 1988), are costs of cognition – should be included in any study of efficiency in exchange, and that because they are not so included 'current economic analysis is incapable of handling many of the problems to which it purports to give answers'. Very little serious attention has been given to the problem of the efficient allocation of resources, either of time or energy, to decisions, even though this is one of the central issues in organisational design and business management.

It is, of course, a central issue for each of us, and has surely been in the past a crucial factor in the survival of the human species. Indeed, we may regard the present organisation of the human brain as the product of evolution, at least in the sense that its architecture and procedures have survived the selection processes to which they have been subjected. There is no reason to believe that this organisation is optimal, since all that has been required is a level of performance that was adequate to cope with the environments that have so far been encountered, which included other living creatures with substantial cognitive limitations. Moreover, '[b]ecause moving mutations from low initial frequencies to fixation takes substantial time, and sequential fixations must usually have been necessary to construct complex adaptations, complex functional design in organisms owes its detailed organization to the structure of long-enduring regularities of each species' past' (Tooby and Cosmides 1996: 122); so we should not expect our cognitive apparatus to be appropriate to any distinctive features of modern environments. Though we have no reason to believe that biological evolutionary processes are not currently operative, it seems justifiable to assume an unchanging brain in examining the evolution of human activities.

In an early paper, written for a Cambridge discussion group a few years after the publication of Darwin's *Origin of Species*, Alfred Marshall (1994) produced a simple evolutionary model which still appears serviceable as an introductory parable to current ideas of human cognition. In this model, the evolution of the brain is governed by the basic needs for survival, which requires timely perception of threats and opportunities, closely coupled with swift and effective responses. Evolutionary fitness is therefore promoted by an architecture which can register many stimuli simultaneously, retrieve information which is widely distributed in the brain, match complex patterns of stimuli against patterns derived from stored information, and evoke rapid, complex and precisely ordered activities (see also Woo 1992: 86–9, 167–72). Marshall envisages a 'machine' within which these capabilities might evolve. The operating system of this machine is connected to a control mechanism (envisaged by Marshall as a very large number of wheels all linked by bands), which collects impressions from the environment, initiates actions, and collects further impressions of the environment as the action takes effect. A combination of positive and negative feedback then establishes increasingly strong links (represented by a tightening of selected bands) between particular clusters of impressions which represent particular artificial categories of phenomena and particular action sequences which have become associated with each representation. Here is an early model of self-organisation; it is not, however, a model of a general-purpose problem solver.

Marshall's conception of the evolution of the brain as a network of special-ised connections each oriented to a particular class of phenomena rather than as an instrument for rational thought corresponds well to that of modern evolutionary biology: 'natural selection is known to produce cognitive machinery of an intricate functionality as yet unmatched by the deliberate application of modern engineering' (Cosmides and Tooby 1994a: 42). The creation of such domain-specific connections has a clear evolutionary priority over the serial processing which is privileged in standard economic conceptions of rationality; a general-purpose 'logic of choice' cannot begin to match the speed, reliability, and efficiency of specialised mechanisms (Cosmides and Tooby 1994a: 59), and is thus most unlikely to have been favoured during the evolution of our species. Both the development and the use of this decision making procedure rely not on the consequential logic of choice but the retrospective logic of appropriateness: patterns that have been formed through a long series of past interactions are mapped onto present situations, with no reference to the future. 'Facts' are embedded in networks of relationships with other 'facts', and may not be recognised outside those relationships. 'We incorrectly locate the computationally manufactured simplicity that we experience as a natural property of the external world' (Cosmides and Tooby 1994a: 66); and this 'manufactured simplicity' evolved in a community of hunter–gatherers and is unlikely to be optimally adapted to modern societies.

Hayek's (1952) *Sensory Order*, which was developed, like Marshall's much briefer exposition, at the beginning of his academic career, provides a carefully worked out theory of the formation of such networks, which resemble the complex structures so characteristic of Austrian capital theory. They have similar implications too: they are resistant to meaningful aggregation, the uses to which they can be put depends on their orientation, and they are a strong force for conservatism, both when this is desirable and when it is not.

The problem that stimulated Hayek's interest was the disparity between the account of the external world which has been developed by the physical sciences and our sensory perception of that world: 'events which to our senses may appear to be of the same kind may have to be treated as different in the physical order, while events which physically may be of the same or at least a similar kind may appear as altogether different to our senses' (Hayek 1952: 4). This disparity is clearly at odds with the routine assumption within economics that information sets are isomorphic to the phenomena that they represent, differing only in the fineness of their partitioning, though it may provide a pattern for the use of economic models which are ordered differently from our perception of human behaviour. Hayek's explanation rests on the fundamental proposition that

> any apparatus of classification must possess a structure of a higher degree of complexity than is possessed by the objects that it classifies; and that, therefore, the capacity of any explaining agent must be limited to objects with a structure possessing a degree of complexity lower than its own.
>
> (ibid.: 185)

It is thus inconceivable that a single human brain can develop a complete explanation of a universe of which it forms an infinitesimal part.

Sensory perception, like the rest of our cognitive system, therefore relies on a classification system which interprets phenomena according to selected characteristics; and many different classifications may in principle be constructed by varying the basis of selection. Consciously or unconsciously, some basis must be chosen; when we think it inappropriate we may try to revise it; but we cannot escape the constraint that '*all* we know about the world is of the nature of theories and all "experience" can do is to change these theories' (ibid.: 143). Such theories are constructed over time as networks of relationships in the brain, developed as means of identifying categories of stimuli and connecting each category to an appropriate action, on the same principles as Marshall attributed to his machine; each system of classification 'will, as a result of its own operations, continuously change its structure and alter the range of operation of which it is capable' (Hayek 1952: 122). In Hahn's (1973, reprinted in Hahn 1984: 59) terms, some actions may generate messages from the environment which 'cause agents to change the theories which they hold and the policies which they pursue'. But as the record of interactions with the environment grows, so the influence of each subsequent interaction tends to diminish (Hayek 1952: 113). Messages which conflict with well-corroborated theories and policies may be ignored, as scientists often reject evidence which is inconsistent with a well-established body of scientific knowledge (Ziman 1978: 39–40). Path dependency is inherent in this process; as in Marshall's model it also constrains (though we should remember that it does not determine) the later development of conscious thought, which has to rely on the cognitive apparatus that evolved before consciousness. Hayek (1978: 41) later summarised this view of cognition by stating that 'what we call knowledge is primarily a system of rules of action assisted and modified by rules indicating equivalence or differences or various combinations of stimuli'.

Within a stable environment (in which stability is to be interpreted in terms appropriate to the climate rather than the weather) evolutionary success depends on the formation of connections which are appropriate to that environment; and so successful adaptation gives the appearance of rationality, even though no rational calculations whatever occur. Within this environment a retrospective logic of appropriateness has become isomorphic with the anticipatory logic of consequences. Such an evolved isomorphism is the basis for the claim that selection validates the predictions of optimising models, which was examined in the preceding chapter. As Schumpeter (1934: 80) observed, though rational choice is always a fiction, it can be a good predictor of behaviour if time has hammered logic into men – or, we should add, into other animals; and some biologists have duly adopted this fiction in order to explain patterns of animal behaviour in terms of optimisation. But if this behaviour, in either biological or economic systems, is a selected adaptation and not a specific application of a general logic of choice, then the introduction of substantial novelty – a change not of weather but of climate – is liable to be severely disruptive, as Schumpeter also insisted. In biological systems it can lead to the extinction of species, sometimes on a very large scale.

However, as Marshall recognised, the human species has acquired some capacity to escape from this backward-looking behaviour: in his evolutionary model the control system of his machine later begins to develop a second compartment which deals, not with impressions and actions, but with ideas of impressions and actions, and can project these ideas into the future. It is this faculty of imagination which allows people to conceive of future possibilities in possible future states, and thus to contemplate a future which is more than a mapping from the past, and which might be influenced by reasoned choice. It seems perverse to argue, as Becker and Friedman did, that such a development makes no significant difference to the performance of economic systems. But it is only when people are capable of quick responses in critical situations that they have the time and mental energy to contemplate such consequential reasoning; that is why, as Marshall clearly indicated by the evolutionary sequence of his model, the faculty of reasoning and the power of imagination, though so important in human development, must emerge later than the skills, both mental and physical, that are needed for effective action. The reasoning capacity to which economists assign logical priority cannot achieve priority in an evolutionary sequence; and it remains a scarce resource.

In this early work, before Marshall's mind had turned to economics, his argument rests, not on scarcity, but on plausible evolutionary pathways; but the consequent restrictions that he places on the development of human reasoning, which seem to be confirmed by modern biology, are rather similar. Because reasoning is expensive in time and energy, it should supplement the procedures developed earlier, and cannot replace them. Whitehead (1948 [1911]: 41–2) castigates the 'profoundly erroneous truism...that we should cultivate the habit of thinking of what we are doing. The precise opposite is the case. Civilisation advances by extending the number of important operations which we can perform without thinking about them.' The significance of this proposition is enhanced by its appearance in Whitehead's *Introduction to Mathematics*, which we might naturally be inclined to regard as the supreme embodiment of formal reasoning; but Whitehead reminds us that expert mathematicians are those who have become so familiar with the recurring patterns in mathematics, and with the operations that are appropriate to each, that they can rely on the logic of appropriateness to cope with everything but the crucial novelties on which the scarce resource of reasoning can be focused. Marshall anticipated Whitehead's argument; only by ceasing to think about old problems can we find the time and energy to tackle the new. Once the imaginative powers of the brain have produced a satisfactory linkage between ideas of impressions and ideas of action, the corresponding linkage between impressions and action is installed in the control system, where it works by imposing patterns rather than by anticipating consequences. Thereafter new possibilities may be imagined in other contexts, and new choices may result; but the proportion of human activities which is governed by routines increases. 'Operations of thought are like cavalry charges in a battle – they are strictly limited in number, they require fresh horses, and must only be made at decisive moments' (Whitehead 1948 [1911]: 42).

In Marshall's model, not only does the practical management of daily life remain the province of routine behaviour; the stimulus to imagination arises from failures of routine. It is when a standard response no longer seems to work, and the sequence 'impression of situation – action – impression of satisfactory outcome' cannot be completed, that a signal is sent to the part of the brain that is capable of imagining alternative ways of classifying situations and of assembling action sequences in response. Conscious thought is a response to a perceived problem; and what is perceived as a problem within an individual brain is a mismatch between the operating routines of that brain and the perceptions of the situation with which it is trying to cope. This may be retrospectively regarded as a precursor of the 'aspiration-achievement gap' in behavioural theory. It is also an application of Smith's (1980) psychological theory of scientific progress; for Smith anticipated Kuhn (1962, 1970a) by two centuries in arguing that the perception of new anomalies was a necessary stimulus to the generation of new knowledge. It is apparent from many passages in Marshall's *Principles* that he believed such stimuli to be important for human progress; the capabilities of each person's imaginative faculty are developed by exercise, and so satisfaction with all current routines is hardly compatible with 'self-reliance, independence, deliberate choice and forethought' (Marshall 1920: 5). But we should not forget the dual importance of these routines, both in economically preserving successful products of the imagination and also in providing the impetus to thought which may lead to further innovation.

In allocating responsive and anticipatory cognition to distinct parts of his 'machine', Marshall implicitly extends Smith's principle of the division of labour to intellectual operations, and he later developed this application in his analysis of the organisation of industry. However, we must be careful not to assimilate this division of labour to the distinction between logical and non-logical processes; for in Marshall's model, as in Schumpeter's (1934) account, reasoned choice among possible futures is a process which is clearly distinguished from formal rationality. The human capacity for imaginative reasoning is adapted from a mental apparatus which is especially adept at pattern making and pattern matching; the formation of logical sequences is therefore less natural, and takes more time and energy, than non-logical processing. The attempt to construct more effective patterns does not employ a set of logical operations within a problem situation which is assumed to be already unambiguously defined, but begins with a search for an appropriate way of defining that situation and a search for possible alternatives, not necessarily in that order. March's garbage can model of decision making in organisations (Cohen *et al.* 1972) may be an application of what is a basic means of making individual decisions.

Because rational choice theory ignores the costs of choosing, it has no need to pay attention to the magnitude of the benefits; any gain, however small, is worth having and immediately available; therefore all opportunities for improvement should be instantly perceived and implemented. In effect, everyone is continuously in equilibrium, because there is nothing to prevent them getting there. As Coase (1988: 15) has observed, this is what makes the assumption of costless choosing so attractive to theorists, and many of their conclusions so irrelevant. But primitive humans, like all other species, had to conform to some strict priorities if they were not to become extinct; and these priorities entailed not only a clear focus on identifying certain kinds of decisions, but also reliance on particular ways of making them. Modern humans, who are still genetically programmed for past environments, must attempt to reason with brains which are adapted to earlier priorities. For a striking example, compare the difficulty of programming the identification of a face, from any angle, with the identification of a name; yet most of us find the former much the easier: the reason, no doubt, is that rapid and reliable identification of faces, as of other complex patterns, was crucial to survival long before the emergence of a capacity for language (on which see Aiello 1996).

The implications of cognition for behaviour

The present comparative advantage of the human brain over the brains of other species may lie in its capacity for ratiocination; but considered simply as an instrument of cognition its absolute advantage is not in the formation of rational sequences but in making and using combinations. However, this is not such a disadvantage as a well-trained orthodox economist might suspect. If economic reasoning, construed as rational choice theory, is of no value in cases of uncertainty, then, since uncertainty is so pervasive, some other kind of reasoning is essential, as Barnard (1938) pointed out; and proficiency in constructing and using combinations is invaluable in non-logical intelligent operations. Thus the human predilection for imposing patterns on all kinds of phenomena, though sometimes misguided, is hardly less valuable now than it was to our ancestors. Indeed, 'pattern recognition is every bit as reliable as a source of consensual knowledge and as a means of arriving at a scientific consensus, as discourse in the logico-mathematical mode' (Ziman 1978: 94): in Ziman's view the non-logical process of pattern recognition is indispensable to scientific progress. It may be no less indispensable to innovation. The architecture of the brain, certainly in humans, has the potential for the formation of a very large number of alternative networks; but they are alternatives – the establishment of one set of connections precludes the establishment of many others within the same brain. Thus for each person at any time many possible phenomena, some of which may be important in other locations or other conjunctures, have no means of representation. But within a human population there is the potential for many different combinations, and so the cognitive range of a population is potentially far greater than that of any individual – provided that connections are formed differently in different individuals. We shall need to consider in what circumstances this is likely to happen.

In appraising the efficiency of human cognition, we need to be careful in our definition of effective, let alone optimal, action. The costs of error are often highly biased: consider, to take the extreme example, the relative costs of mistaking a shadow for a dangerous predator and of mistaking a dangerous predator for a shadow. This warning may be applied, in less apocalyptic forms, to many present-day decisions, and to many contemporary models. In a theoretical and empirical analysis of production decisions which is mainly conducted within neoclassical assumptions, Aiginger (1987) presents strong evidence to suggest that, even if we convert uncertainty into risk and assume no risk-aversion, it is probably the exception rather than the rule that an optimising firm should treat the expected value of a probability distribution of sales as the value on which production plans should be based. The gearing effects of commitments on profits, and the costs, sometimes very different, of dealing with unsold stocks and unsatisfied demand typically generate asymmetric costs of error.

Adjusting prices to clear the market, Aiginger reports, is not a common policy; firms are much more likely to plan to underproduce, in relation to their mean expectation, while maintaining some reserves of productive capacity to supply those customers who are prepared to wait a little rather than accept the uncertainty of dealing with an unfamiliar supplier. Indeed, many firms – and not only those engaged in producing idiosyncratic items of capital equipment – produce wholly or mainly to order; as Aiginger (1987: 128–32) points out, the size of order books in the US, Germany, and Austria is much bigger than the size of inventory. Aiginger recognises that these policies, and the circumstances which make them possible, imply substantial departures from perfect competition; it is beyond his remit to consider how continuing relationships between supplier and customer can mitigate the effects of uncertainty on the customer also.

Because of the highly biased costs of error in the early stages of human development, we should not be surprised to find that present-day humans exhibit patterns of behaviour which lead to systematic error in decision making, even when present-day costs of error are properly allowed for. Changes in the cost of error do not lead easily to the replacement of routines which have long proved effective, for evolutionary biological processes are not driven by rational expectations, but by lengthy exposure to stable environments. The persistence of systematic errors is even more understandable when we allow for the advantages of the automatic 'framing' of problems in ways which increase the speed and reduce the opportunity cost of decisions; simplifications and the collection of somewhat heterogeneous instances into categories which are treated as homogeneous may prove of benefit on average or – what may be more relevant – in crucial instances. Even when the persistence of systematic errors imposes net costs, these costs may appear less than the costs of avoiding them, when that requires the creation of a new framework. For each of us, the costs of creating a new framework (which, as Kelly (1963: 9) observed, must be compatible with other frameworks which still appear to be serviceable), its range of usefulness and the magnitude of its benefits cannot be known in advance; and such frameworks cannot be created solely by conscious thought and memorisation. Once established, whether by lengthy evolutionary sequences or within an individual lifetime, such patterns of decision making are not easy to change; that is one of the more obvious features of human nature, and has to be recognised in any account of human behaviour.

We may therefore expect to find substantial differences between people in the frameworks that they use, resulting from differences in the phenomena previously encountered and the interpretations which have been placed upon them, and also substantial differences in their readiness to consider a revision of any framework in response to anomalous messages; situations which some take in their stride will stimulate others to extensive cogitation. That those with more detailed knowledge of particular phenomena will perceive problems that will be passed over by those less expert was noted by Smith (1980: 45) as part of his explanation of scientific discovery, and later applied to the division of labour within an economy (Smith 1976b: 20). Such cumulative processes may trace out divergent paths of learning, as may be observed by comparing industries or academic disciplines; the effects of such differentiated learning are pervasive in modern societies and modern economies. There may even be substantially different repertoires of action for what might appear to be similar circumstances, because these circumstances will not appear similar to people whose knowledge has come to be organised in different ways. This produces the 'tendency to variation' within each industry, and within each discipline, that Marshall (1920: 355) and Popper respectively thought so important as a source of progress. When people work together within distinct administrative frameworks, they generate the differential growth paths that characterise Penrose's (1959, 1995) *Theory of the Growth of the Firm*. Thus an economy or an academic discipline may be able to escape from path dependencies by which organisations and individuals within that economy or discipline are constrained.

By focusing on evolutionary cognition we may hope to explain, and even, in favourable circumstances, to predict, how particular people react to particular kinds of shocks, among them particular kinds of innovations, and even what kinds of innovation they may themselves produce. We may be more confident in predicting what kinds of innovation they will not produce, as a knowledge of a large firm's technology base allows one to predict with some confidence what that firm will not produce. To do this we need to examine the history of events and actions, and the mental maps into which this history has been incorporated, the strategies employed for search and the evaluation of alternatives, the balance between memory and imagination, and the partition between binding constraints and possible options. If there is situational rationality, it depends on the way in which the agent defines the situation. Knowledge is dispersed and subjectively held, as Austrian economists insist – though it is also subject to intersubjective criticism (Ziman 1978); it is also organised in a variety of ways, and indeed what appears as knowledge to an individual is partly dependent on the way in which it is organised. Thus, for example, some economists claim to have knowledge of involuntary unemployment, while others, as Hahn and Solow (see Chapter 1) have noted, find the concept meaningless; some economists see market failure where others see institutions which make market co-ordination possible. So too may a manager in one firm see a novel business opportunity in a situation which elicits a routine response from other firms, and a consumer may see how to put a product or service to a use which its supplier had not envisaged.

We choose by making connections. Logical connections between premises and conclusions (or sometimes, because we all make mistakes, illogical connections) are an important category but, contrary to mainstream doctrine, they are not sufficient either for prediction or prescription. Many choices, even deliberate choices, result from connections between clusters of stimuli and clusters of responses, both of which are the product of our own experience, supplemented, as we shall shortly explain, by vicarious experience embodied in practices that we have adapted. The assignment of a new situation to a particular cluster is typically unconscious; even so, the response may sometimes appear as an innovation to an observer who has a different way of ordering stimuli and responses. The recognition of a new possibility may require an extension of our value system; rather than determining choice, preferences may be a product of the process of choosing, for when cognition absorbs time and energy, it cannot be sensible to formulate a complete preference system let alone a complete set of contingent plans. But sometimes no existing category is acceptable; then we need to create, or adapt, a new way of ordering some phenomena; and this may lead to novel choices, not only in the immediate situation but through the application of new schemes of ordering to familiar activities.

Pareto improvements within an economy are very rare; and the equivalent of a Pareto improvement is sometimes difficult to find for an individual. Our knowledge of facts and values is distributed within our mind in quasi-autonomous groupings; the amount of processing required to reduce this diversity to a single ordering is far too great to be contemplated; and so the kinds of difficulty which inhibit the construction of a social welfare function may impede our own decision making. The application of Lancaster's (1966) theory of characteristics takes for granted consumers' ability to weight alternative bundles of characteristics – an assumption which seems to derive from a consumer theory, now officially discarded, in which all forms of consumption contribute to a single pool of utility. But it may be more appropriate, if less simple, to think of each individual as a coalition of multiple selves, as Amartya Sen has suggested, and of each self as a composite of multiple roles, as is often assumed in the formation of marketing policy. Many significant consumer purchases invoke the values associated with more than one role, and often with more than one self; and the alternatives which are most highly valued for one role, or for one self, may evoke strong negative reactions for other roles, or other selves. Many products have failed to gain acceptance from particular groups of customers, despite the undeniable advantages which they offered, because they were not compatible with one of the sets of values by which those customers appraised them (Rogers 1983).

Such unresolved conflicts may, however, present an opportunity for innovation, by producers or even by consumers. Indeed, the psychological discomfort caused by a conflict between perceptions and accustomed patterns provides the stimulus to search for new patterns in Smith's (1980) theory of the development of science and for the modification of an individual's interpretative framework in Kelly's (1963) theory of personality. Since both the content and the arrangement of knowledge are in some degree unique to each individual, we can never be sure when anyone will experience a conflict which may stimulate a significant modification of existing patterns, or the content of any such modification. The number of potential novel connections is extremely large, and it continues to grow with the creation of new fragments of knowledge (Weitzman 1996: 211); the creation of new connections depends on the variety of human imagination. The consequences of such new combinations are not predictable; human cognition may have chaotic properties. What we can reasonably conclude is that the differences between people, partly endogenous, and partly the result of their particular cognitive development, in the patterns of connections by which they make choices, or recognise a need for a reconstruction of their strategies for making choices, are primary contributors to the generation of variety and thus the evolution of economic systems.

The formation of institutions

The need to act in a world of uncertainty has influenced the evolution of human cognition as a system of classifications and procedures, which are often tacit, and necessarily fallible. Choi (1993) has used the human imperative of coping with uncertainty as the foundation for his explanation of our reliance on conventions – which he frequently refers to as paradigms. It is usual to think of conventions and paradigms as group phenomena, but Choi's insistence on starting with the assumption of pervasive uncertainty ensures that the basic concept of a convention appears, and is explained, at the level of the individual. Thus his explanation of institutions is firmly based on the moderate variant of methodological individualism, according to which all human action is to be explained in terms of individual actions, though not necessarily by avoiding any concepts which cannot be defined in relation to single individuals. As we shall see, it also deepens our under-standing of institutions and their effectiveness in co-ordinating human activities.

The need for rules and patterns, though accentuated by interactions with other people, does not originate in such interactions; it arises, as I have just argued, from the inescapable limitations of individual human knowledge. Choi's (1993: 37) Proposition 1 states that 'People decide and act in a given situation based on a paradigm identified as appropriate for that situation. Without a paradigm there will be no decision and no action.' Unlike Barnard (1938), Choi (1993: 31) accepts the universal applicability of the logic of choice, but insists that this logic must be framed by some artificial but credible pattern. Logical choice requires closure, and that closure cannot itself be logical. When people must act, he argues, uncertainty is not acceptable; and it can be resolved – it would be more accurate to say suppressed – only by the imposition of a paradigm (ibid.: 45). Neoclassical economics is just such a paradigm for the suppression of uncertainty, and a particular interpretation of that paradigm has made possible new classical macroeconomics.

Choi's paradigms are human conjectures, fallible but indispensable. Paradigms have to work for each individual; they must therefore be tolerably compatible with the experience of that individual – though among academic economists what matters is likely to be experience of economic theory rather than of economic systems. Because the applicability of any particular set of procedures and assumptions for corralling uncertainty is context-specific, different people may be expected to use different paradigms; their actions must therefore be regarded as indeterminate by outside observers. Since they cannot, except by occasional accident, be accurate representations of reality their use entails selective vision, coupled with a failure to recognise how selective it is, limited flexibility and the possibility of systematic error (Choi 1993: 38–43). Opportunity costs take many forms.

Choi chooses not to explore such pathologies; instead, he explains that individual paradigms, like Kuhn's (1962, 1970a) scientific paradigms, will sometimes fail to generate any satisfactory result, and that the failures of particular paradigms will tend to accumulate to the point where the user will no longer be willing to use them as a basis for decision making. But since, in Choi's scheme, no action is possible without a paradigm, rejection leads directly to his Proposition 2: 'When faced with uncertainty, an individual will search for a suitable paradigm; the search will continue until one is identified and uncertainty is resolved' (Choi 1993: 47). As in Popper's theory of the growth of knowledge, we learn as a consequence of recognising our mistakes, for this recognition stimulates a search for something better. Choi, however, does not suggest that people are likely to make the bold conjectures advocated by Popper; instead he argues (Choi 1993: 48–51) that people will follow a process of sequential search, which suggests something closer to Kuhn's 'normal science' than scientific revolution, though since what seems most promising to one person may never occur to another, the outcome of such searches may be very surprising to outside observers – and sometimes even to the searcher.

Kelly (1963) likewise points to the need for interpretative frameworks to be compatible with individual circumstances if people are to cope adequately with their particular situations, and to the interpersonal differences which result; but as a clinical psychologist he is particularly interested in what Choi would call paradigm failure; and economists too might take more interest than most of them do in the pathology of interpretative systems, which can frequently be observed in individual managers, business units, large organisations and sometimes in large sections of an economy. By Kuhn's analysis, as with the evolutionary view of human cognition presented earlier, people as scientists should not be expected to change paradigms easily, and therefore, as Schumpeter argued, the creation of major new combinations is typically destructive of pre-existing order. What economists should be interested in is pervasive failure (which is by no means only a macroeconomic phenomenon), and to explain this we need to examine why paradigms or interpretative frameworks should be widely shared.

The basic reason is that the search for new paradigms may be a stressful and even dangerous business, for it is not always possible to put off major decisions until we have tested our proposed new way of dealing with them. The difficulty of finding an adequate paradigm for ourselves encourages us to observe the paradigms that other people seem to be using because, as Keynes (1937: 214) observed, when we are unable to resolve our own uncertainty we look for someone who appears to know better than us and whom we can therefore copy. This immediately allows us to supplement our own experience by drawing on the results of the far greater volume of testing which we may observe within a supposedly relevant reference group (Choi 1993: 54). The vicarious tests on which one person relies need not be carried out by people who would recognise that person as a member of their group; indeed, the identification of a novel reference group seems to be an important way in which people invent new ways of defining problems, and of associating them with ready-made solutions. Cognitive development thus becomes a social process which exploits the variety of people's interactions with their environments.

Choi (1993: 63–6) is no less impressed than Keynes with the importance of confidence about the means by which we resolve uncertainty into action, and observes that our confidence in the way that we do things is enhanced by the approval of others, and even by our belief that our behaviour is such as to merit the approval of others. Choi (ibid.) bases this part of his argument on Smith's *Theory of Moral Sentiments*, where we find not only the emphasis on the imagined 'impartial spectator' as a guide to action but also the observation that the judgements of others, expressed or imagined, are 'more or less important to us, exactly in proportion as we ourselves are more or less uncertain about the propriety of our own sentiments, about the accuracy of our own judgements' (Smith 1976a: 122–3).

The more dependent we become, the more important it is that the judgements of others are accurately represented, but we can draw on another passage in Smith's writings, this time in the 'Early Draft' of part of the *Wealth of Nations*, to find reasons why they may often be: for if any person reflects on the source of his knowledge outside the sphere of his own particular occupation,

> a very small part of it only, he will find, has been the produce of his own observations and reflections. All the rest has been purchased...from those whose business it is to make up and prepare for the market that particular species of goods.
>
> (Smith 1978: 574)

Of course this knowledge, like all knowledge, is subject to error, but as Simon (1982, vol. 2: 399) has observed, 'it may be more important, in some circumstances, to have *agreement* on the facts than to be certain that what is agreed upon is really fact'. If people of many occupations derive their non-specialised knowledge from a common source, then they are likely to resolve many of their uncertainties in a similar way – including their uncertainties about what to expect in their dealings with other people. Shared conventions within a specialised group thus may result from distinctive shared knowledge; shared conventions between disparate groups may result from a shared absence of direct knowledge, and consequent recourse to a common pool of those who may be presumed to know.

Institutions are a response to uncertainty. They are patterns acquired from others which guide individual actions, even when these actions are quite unconnected with any other person. They economise on the scarce resource of cognition, by providing us with ready-made anchors of sense, ways of partitioning the space of representations, premises for decisions, and bounds within which we can be rational – or imaginative. They constitute a capital stock of other people's reusable knowledge, although, like all knowledge, this is fallible. In fact, just as Marshall recognised the importance for firms of supplementing their own internal organisation with an external organisation, so each of us finds life much more manageable if we supplement our own internally organised cognition with the externally organised social capital which is the accretion of many other people's cognition. We are therefore not restricted to our own apparatus of classification in trying to make sense of our surroundings.

A major consequence of our attempts to cope with uncertainty by adopting the practices of others is that when we come to deal with other people the basis for successful interaction is often already substantially prepared. This analytical sequence helps to explain how the institutions which facilitate co-ordination come to be adopted, and suggests a method of explaining which institutions come to be adopted in particular circumstances. The institutions which we have already found indispensable for our own private purposes now suggest interdependent solutions to the problems of interdependence; our reliance on conventions and procedures, many of them adapted from other people, as a consequence of our cognitive limitations helps to resolve the co-ordination problems which result from those limitations. We find ourselves using similar assumptions, similar taxonomies, and similar methods of argument; and these substantial pragmatic advantages are reinforced by the rhetorical effect of shared conventions on our moral sentiments. Shared conventions make it easier to predict the behaviour of others, even when we cannot predict their circumstances (Heiner 1983); indeed, Choi (1993: 89) argues, they help to predict the values which will influence behaviour, for 'perceptions of justice are conditioned by conventions'. Conventions thus remove a good deal of perceived uncertainty from human interaction – not least, as we shall see in a later chapter, in markets.

However, they cannot abolish the uncertainty which is inherent in the human situation, and so we should expect to find that they carry an opportunity cost. Because they give comfort and make action possible, they tend to persist even when they become rather ineffective comforters and lead to action which produces rather unsatisfactory outcomes. As Kelly (1963: 9) points out, a part of an individual's interpretative framework which is working very badly may be retained because it is firmly embedded in a complex structure of human capital to which that individual is committed; and even if that individual has found a replacement which seems satisfactory, it may prove incompatible with the frameworks and procedures used by others that form an indispensable part of the social capital on which that individual depends. The extreme result in these two cases is personal breakdown, which was Kelly's professional concern, and the collapse of a hitherto effective social group, which should be a professional concern of more economists than those who call themselves post-Keynesians.

However, as circumstances become less and less amenable to representation within existing paradigms, the potential rewards from creating a new paradigm increase; and though most people conform to conventions, there are always deviants (Choi 1993: 92). So, although 'x-inefficiency is a predictable, not aberrational, consequence of conventions and...firms, like other groups, rarely operate with maximum efficiency' (ibid.: 104), the consequences are not, in Choi's view, as bad as Olson (1982) has suggested. Choi prefers Kirzner's proposition that the greater the range of unexploited opportunities, the greater the chance that someone will discover them, and the greater the incentive to search for a new paradigm (or what, since connections matter, we might in this context prefer to call a 'new combination') to apply to them. Choi thus produces a theory of entrepreneurship which combines Kirznerian alertness and a smaller-scale version of Schumpeterian discontinuity, without requiring Schumpeterian heroes. In all these theories, entrepreneurship is indispensable for successful economic performance.

To adapt someone else's procedure for making a particular class of decisions, or the assumptions on which to base such decisions, is to acknowledge that person as an authority on those decisions. Barnard (1938: 163) insisted that authority was no simple product of hierarchy: 'the decision as to whether an order has authority or not lies with the persons to whom it is addressed, and does not reside in "persons of authority" or those who issue these orders'. Acceptance may sometimes be achieved by the incentive structure, but there are many ways of evading unwelcome instructions, and so hierarchy is not a sufficient condition for authority. But neither is it necessary. Accepting someone else's authority is usually interpreted as allowing that person to decide what one should do; but it is helpful to extend the concept to allowing someone else to supply some or all of the information and procedures to be used in reaching a decision. Such authority will constrain, and may even precisely determine the decision; but it is often acceptable, and even welcome. We cannot possibly make all the decisions that we have to make without repeatedly 'taking someone else's word for it', whether 'it' is an item of information or a method of reaching a decision.

We may find our sources of authority anywhere; but for many important activities there are clear advantages in organising the sources of authority: then the institutions, in the sense of conventions, routines, and procedures, on which we rely, are structured by the institutions, in the sense of organisations, to which we belong. If, therefore, evolution is structured by our institutional arrangements, the influence of formal organisations on those institutions must be a crucial issue. We must therefore include the theme of authority as a co-ordinating device in our examination of the role of those formal organisations that we call firms. But the next step is to use our analysis of cognition as a basis for understanding capabilities.

4

CAPABILITIES

The concept and context of capabilities

The term 'capabilities' was introduced to economics by Richardson (1972). As he makes clear, his analysis is developed from Penrose's (1959, 1995: 24–5) conception of a firm as a collection of physical and human resources which may be deployed in a variety of ways to provide a variety of productive services. Penrose explicitly avoids the term 'factors of production' because it fails to distinguish between resources and the services that they yield and thus obscures the range of orientations that may be implicit in any collection of resources, which is essential to her explanation of the growth and distinctiveness of firms. Richardson insists on a similar distinction.

> It is convenient to think of industry as carrying out an indefinitely large number of *activities*, activities related to the discovery and es-timation of future wants, to research, development, and design, to the execution and co-ordination of processes of physical transfor-mation, the marketing of goods, and so on. And we have to recog-nise that these activities have to be carried out by organizations with appropriate *capabilities*, or, in other words, with appropriate knowledge, experience, and skills.
>
> (Richardson 1972: 888; 1990: 231)

Richardson's focus was on the distribution of economic activities between firms and the ways in which these activities were co-ordinated, and Penrose's on the sources and directions of growth for individual firms; both rely on the differences between firms in the capabilities that they possess and in the uses to which they put these capabilities, and in the differential development of these capabilities and uses over time. Together they provide the economic basis for what has come to be called the capabilities (or competence) theory of the firm. We shall consider this theory in Chapter 6; the purpose of this chapter is to clarify the concept of capabilities by relating it to the limitations and potential of human cognition, and especially to the

49

connections between intelligence and action. Our discussion will not be limited to firms, for capabilities, being related to cognition, have a much wider significance for human knowledge and human behaviour.

The first requirement is to make a clear distinction between capabilities and production functions. In standard economic analysis, production functions, representing complete sets of feasible input combinations, are part of the apparatus which is designed to show how the input combination that is chosen reflects relative prices; and economists assume that decision makers have complete (and costless) knowledge of the relevant functions. That is sometimes a conscious assumption; but economists rarely seem to be aware that they are also assuming that knowledge of the input combinations is sufficient for production to take place, ignoring the skills, and the observance of productive sequences (Leijonhufvud 1986: 203), which are necessary in order to transform inputs into outputs. The impossibility of complete justified knowledge is the foundation of this book; the principal theme of this chapter is the structured combination of skills which underlies effective performance. The use of the word 'capabilities', as Richardson (1972) makes clear, signifies that the universe of discourse is not that of rational choice and equilibrium allocations which is the natural habitat of production functions, but one in which skill, and therefore the quality of performance, is both important and problematic. We should therefore begin by identifying the universe of discourse in which the concept of capabilities can flourish.

The relevant economic context for the concept of capabilities, as Richardson (1975) has pointed out, is the increase of wealth through the division of labour, which is the fundamental principle of Adam Smith's (1976b) economic theory. It is especially relevant to note that the central importance of the division of labour in Smith's scheme derives not from its power to make the best use of differences in natural aptitudes, which had long been recognised, but from its power to create increased, and also novel, specialist competences (Smith 1976b: 28–30), which make new activities and new products possible. The evolution of capabilities is therefore a necessary element in any comprehensive theory of economic change. Capabilities are endogenous, for their development is endogenous; and they are idiosyncratic, for this development is influenced by its context, and the way in which this context is interpreted by individuals, guided by the institutional framework that is provided by formal and informal organisations.

Hayek (1937: 49) criticised economic theories of equilibrium for neglecting the problems caused by the division of knowledge, but he did not recognise that the principal cause of the division of knowledge was the division of labour; for knowledge grows by division. Specialisation allows each person to focus on a particular group of activities, and to create new personal knowledge about them; and it is a simple inference from Smith's (1976b: 20–1) account of the different sources of invention that each kind of specialist knowledge develops in a way which is likely to be in some degree peculiar to the institutions of that specialism and produces results which are conditioned by the distinctive features of its development. The growth of knowledge proceeds through the differentiation and dispersion of knowledge, and the organisation of economic activity should respect the diversity of knowledge-generating systems. There is no calculable destination for this process of increasing productive knowledge, either for those engaged in that process or for those who seek to analyse it.

Categories of knowledge

It may be helpful to distinguish four kinds of knowledge, which may be arranged in a simple two-dimensional matrix. The principal dimension is defined by Gilbert Ryle's (1949: 28) distinction between 'knowing that' and 'knowing how'. 'Knowing that' is knowledge of facts, relationships and theories, the primary subject-matter of formal education and the news, and may be subdivided into 'knowing what' and 'knowing why' (Lundvall and Johnson 1994); 'knowing how', by contrast, is the ability to perform the appropriate actions in order to achieve a desired result, and includes skill both in performance and in recognising when and where this skilful performance is appropriate. The other dimension is provided by the distinction between direct and indirect knowledge. We may possess the relevant knowledge ourselves or know where we can find it; we may know how to do something or know how to get it done. Capabilities are know-how, both direct and indirect; they represent the kind of knowledge which plays little or no formal part in mainstream economics, but which is crucial to the performance of a person, a firm, an industry, an economy – and, as we shall see, an economist.

Ryle's analysis is particularly, though unintentionally, appropriate because he was criticising the philosophical conception of the mind as the arena for intellectual operations and the location for 'knowledge that', which was regarded as separate from and superior to the practical management of the machinery of the body. He claimed that 'In ordinary life...we are much more concerned with people's competences than with their cognitive repertoires, with the operations than the truths that they learn' (Ryle 1949: 28), and observed that it is generally not the case that effective operations depend on the understanding of truth, nor that the understanding of truth leads directly to effective operations. Barnard (1938: 312) records a friend's judgement on someone 'of extensive knowledge and experience in his business that "he knew more about it and could do less with it than anyone else he had met" '. 'Knowledge how' is not deducible from 'knowledge that' but requires separate attention.

What is true of ordinary life is also true of economic activity, but not of orthodox theorising about economic activity. The exaltation of rational choice is also the exaltation of intellectual operations (even though economists are extremely uncomfortable when agents in their models are actually free to choose). These intellectual operations are firmly based on 'knowledge that', and economists are happy to extend them to the analysis of information, when that is treated as assured and manipulable data; they are prepared to make heroic, even incredible, assumptions about the accessibility and authenticity of such knowledge, and may be encouraged to do so by the Nobel Prize Committee. Few economists, however, seem to be aware that they are also making heroic and incredible assumptions about agents' ability to perform the operations that they are supposed to have rationally chosen. For example, Arrow and Hahn (1971: 53) define a firm's production set as 'a description of the state of the firm's knowledge about the possibilities of transforming commodities' without recognising that a firm may be fully aware of these possibilities without being capable of realising them: the knowledge that it is possible to convert crude oil into a specific range of plastics is quite compatible with total ignorance of how any of these conversions could be accomplished. Indeed, the formulation of standard models assumes that the only obstacles to successful performance arise from inadequate incentives: knowing how is never a problem. This is precisely the sort of model of the mind that Ryle was criticising. Far from providing, as Becker (1976) claimed, the only satisfactory basis for theory in the social sciences, it is a formidable obstacle to our understanding of the organisation of industry and of economic progress.

Knowing how to achieve a desired result may be quite independent of any understanding of the reasons why the procedure appears to work; all of us make use of procedures that we do not understand. We have seen in the previous chapter that there are good evolutionary reasons why we should have developed such a pronounced ability to be instrumentally knowledge-able while remaining substantively ignorant, even when we do not know how to set about removing that ignorance. The inability to remove our substantive ignorance does not prevent us from improving our performance, and this improvement displays intelligence. 'It is of the essence of merely habitual practices that one performance is a replica of its predecessors. It is of the essence of intelligent practices that one performance is modified by its predecessors. The agent is still learning' (Ryle 1949: 42). What is being learnt is not a precisely defined drill, but a capability which can be applied to a range of situations; it is not, however, a general-purpose procedure, as we have seen in the previous chapter. Like all learning, this is a process of trial and error; unconscious learning, as we saw in the preceding chapter, depends on cognitive ability, and conscious intelligence allows us to make appropriate trials and to interpret the results sensibly – in particular, to decide which parts of the procedure to think about *next*.

We learn *how* by practice, schooled indeed by criticism and example, but often quite unaided by any lessons in the theory...Even when efficient practice is the deliberate application of considered prescriptions, the intelligence involved in putting the prescriptions into practice is not identical to that involved in intellectually grasping the prescriptions.

(Ryle 1949: 41, 49)

Though it is not appropriate in this chapter to pay systematic attention to 'knowledge that', it is relevant to note that its production and its effective use depend on particular kinds of 'knowledge how'. Archaeological knowledge, for example, rests on the skills with which archaeologists conduct a dig, and on their ability to interpret their discoveries by making connections to a pattern of relationships, or occasionally by the invention of novel patterns. Ziman (1978) has argued that the reliability of scientific knowledge depends primarily on the processes by which it is generated and tested, and on the appropriateness of these processes to the subject matter; there may be fundamental principles which are common to all branches of science, but these branches do not share a common body of know-how, and it would not be helpful if they did. A satisfactory universal model is hardly compatible with human cognition, and Ziman, who is a physicist, clearly explains why physics cannot provide one.

The development of appropriate capabilities is what academic scientific education is principally designed to achieve (though course designers do not always appear fully to appreciate this). If one looks back, as student or as teacher, one may reflect that the substantive content of a complete undergraduate programme could be set forth in a single semester; but the development of sufficient skills to put the acquired knowledge to use, even within the confines of classroom exercises, takes much longer, and the development of the skills that are needed to produce new 'knowledge that' takes longer still.

Learning *how* or improving in ability is not like learning *that* or acquiring information. Truths can be imparted, procedures can only be inculcated, and while inculcation is a gradual process, imparting is relatively sudden....'Part-trained' is a significant phrase, 'part-informed' is not. Training is the art of setting tasks which the pupils have not yet accomplished but are not any longer quite incapable of accomplishing.

(Ryle 1949: 58)

Within a discipline what is inculcated is the institutional framework of that discipline, which provides substantial, but highly selective, reinforcement of the students' cognitive processes. Good research scientists know how to develop testable implications from hypotheses, how to devise experiments that will test them, and how to interpret the results in a way that will foster the continuing process of discovery – all within the evolving conventions of their own science. Kuhn (1962, 1970a) introduces his concept of paradigm as an exemplar of 'knowledge how' to develop a specific field. Moreover, the content, as well as the reliability, of knowledge within each discipline depends on the procedures that are followed. In science as in business and in everyday life, we can learn only by restricting our attention to particular skills or particular topics; and we cannot know – though we may guess – what we might have learned had we attended instead to other skills or other topics.

The knowledge that is presented in economics textbooks is conditioned by the ways in which economists have sought to develop it, and economics students learn by practice how to deal with problems in ways which are approved within the profession, thereby avoiding issues, and potential 'knowledge that', which are not amenable to their 'knowledge how'. That can be seen most clearly by observing what is left out of standard economics, for example, in the explanation of firms solely in terms of market failure and incentive problems, the lack of interest in interfirm differences in productivity, which are often substantial and persistent, and the exclusion of involuntary unemployment from the knowledge that can be produced within new classical macroeconomics. The institutions of orthodox economics require models to be fully specified: the information currently available to a particular agent may be incomplete, but the information sets employed by the analyst cannot be. It can therefore never be rational to operate inside the possibility frontier, as that can presently be specified, in order to be able to respond quickly to threats or opportunities which cannot be clearly identified – because what cannot be identified cannot be included in the economist's problem definition; and strategy as a set of decision premises for future choices, which to non-economists is an obviously sensible and useful definition, must be replaced by a game-theoretic strategy of commitment to conditional actions. Though these examples are specific to economics, the principles which they exemplify are not. Institutions are focusing devices, and the pathology of focus includes bias and oversight. Some examples of this pathology in the course of technological innovation are examined by Garud et al. (1997). Institutions may have substantial consequences, for good or ill, that were no part of anyone's intention.

We should also note that the centrality of rational choice in modern economics has not perceptibly improved the ability of trained economists to make rational choices, either as managers or as policy-makers; but why should it? The ability to make good decisions is not closely related to an understanding of the logical principles of choice, but depends more on skill in defining the problem, selecting the important factors and seeking out crucial information. As Barnard (1938) pointed out, many decisions must be taken by non-logical means; and even rational choices require a pre-rational closure in the space of representations. Choice theory in economics was not developed as a means of making decisions, but as an instrument – indeed, as an institution – for developing propositions about the economy. The skills of economists are not in making choices, but in using particular concepts of choice in creating knowledge – or perhaps, remembering Popper's warning that all scientific knowledge is conjectural, we should say in creating knowledge claims. Whatever we think of these knowledge claims, we should recognise the highly developed capabilities which are often employed in producing them.

Here too, economists exemplify a general tendency: those proficient in developing and expounding the theoretical structure of a discipline often seem to be remarkably ineffective in its practical application. These are different skills, appropriate to different activities. This contrast in skills is particularly important in understanding the relationship between science and technology. The declarative content of science is 'knowledge that' (remembering that what is treated as knowledge is a set of hypotheses which have been not yet been refuted), and technology is 'knowledge how'; so we should not be surprised that science is rarely an adequate guide to the development of the technology which it might seem to suggest, or even that the technological implications of a scientific theory may not be recognised until long after the theory has become textbook material. What good academic scientists know how to do is to develop, test and criticise scientific theories; there is no general reason why they should know how to develop new technology, unless they have had specific training and experience: these are different capabilities. As Rosenberg (1994: 140–1) points out, the magnitude of development costs, even when the development is related to old science, provides an impressive indicator of this mismatch. A less public indicator is the number of scientific problems that are first identified during the development process: in a time of rapid technological change, technology may lead science as often as the other way round (ibid.: 141) – not least in suggesting the value of interdisciplinary research (ibid.: 147–9). The capabilities of the academically trained scientist are directed towards a different purpose from the knowledge of how to achieve technological goals; indeed, in many fields science and its related technology have effectively become what Smith called distinct trades, and examples of the division of labour which has led to a remarkable development of specialised skills.

This division of labour and skills is often conveniently organised by a clear separation between university and industrial science, which minimises the operational conflict between very different concepts of what constitutes good practice. But, like any organisational solution, and indeed any choice worth considering, this has its opportunity costs. As a simple example, developed by Rosenberg (ibid.: 144–6), scientists become extremely skilful at achieving results in the conditions and on the scale of a laboratory, but rarely give attention to the skills that are required to achieve equivalent results in very different circumstances. The well-known relationship between the volume and surface area of a reaction vessel, for instance, means that exothermic reactions which pose no problem in a laboratory may present formidable challenges to the design and operation of a commercial plant; but there is no reason why most university research chemists should develop any special skill in handling such challenges. Similarly, because the accumulated expertise of economists in developing theories of rational choice has been directed towards modelling various kinds of equilibrium, in which no further choices are required, we should not be surprised – though we may be embarrassed – to observe how limited is the help that rational choice theory can give in making decisions, even to rational choice theorists. The gap between the knowledge of how to do research into chemistry and the knowledge of how to develop new chemical technology has been filled by the emergence of a whole new discipline of chemical engineering; the gap between the knowledge of how to develop economic models of choice and the knowledge of how to make good managerial decisions has been filled by that amorphous collection of disciplines known as management studies, although (as we should expect) many of its practitioners are more successful in developing skills in building theories for classroom exposition than skills in practical decision making. Each science develops its own 'knowledge how', which guides the evolution of that science; and the division of intellectual labour leads to substantial differences between sciences, and also between each science and its related technology.

Knowing how to do things ourselves is not enough. Anyone who is not self-sufficient needs to know how to get many things done; indeed if we consider the standard co-ordination problem in economics from the point of view of the individual, as Smith (1976b: 26–7) did, it appears precisely to be the problem of how to get many things done on which that individual depends for comfort or even survival, but which, because of the differentiation of skills as a consequence of the division of labour, must be entrusted to others. Smith's perspective has been obscured by the modern practice of seeking to define an efficient allocation, and then using this to appraise the efficiency of various market structures, sets of contracts, or game forms, within each of which everyone makes the rational choices that are determined by the structure of the model. Modern economic analysis works best when the individual is of measure zero (Hahn 1984: 64). As usual, the focus is on incentives and not knowledge, and everyone responds in exactly the same way to particular incentives in particular situations.

Smith did not neglect incentives, but he took a much broader view of human motives, including a sense of propriety and the desire to be worthy of the approval of others, on which, as we have seen, Choi (1993) drew in explaining people's readiness to adopt other people's practices; and his theory of economic progress was founded on the generation of differentiated knowledge through the ever-increasing division of labour, as a consequence of which our wants are provided by 'the assistance and co-operation of many thousands' (Smith 1976b: 23), whose knowledge we cannot share. Economists have constructed a theoretical world of perfect markets in which no one has the slightest difficulty in getting done anything that they are willing and able to pay for; but Coase (1937) and Hayek (1937) both argued, in different but complementary ways, that this model ignored the question of how people were actually to accomplish what perfect markets theoretically made possible: a good deal of knowledge is required in order to use markets effectively, and much of this, though neither Coase nor Hayek make the point explicitly, is 'knowledge how'. Using markets to obtain what one wants, like using inputs to create the outputs that one wants, requires the appropriate capabilities.

Instead of relying on markets to gain access to other people's capabilities, either in the form of labour services or embodied in products, we may seek to get some things done by establishing a continuing relationship with people who will agree to do them as required. This kind of relationship, which when embodied in a formal organisation we may call a firm, avoids the need for either a futures market or precise forecasts of future needs; but it does require a general agreement on the kinds of things which are to be done, and on who is competent to do them. Reaching such agreements with appropriate people, and managing the resultant relationship, require indirect capabilities which are not identical to those by which consumers manage market relationships. If however, as is usual, this firm is intended to be a source of income, its success will also depend on the indirect capabilities needed to manage relationships with both suppliers and customers, including 'knowledge how' to develop the kind of 'knowledge that' on which to base analyses of consumer preferences, alternative materials and sources of supply, and relevant developments in technology. As Richardson (1972) points out, the operation of a modern economy depends on very many activities, each requiring its particular direct capability, and the co-ordination of these activities requires its own set of indirect capabilities. Economic performance cannot be satisfactorily explained solely by building models of inputs, production functions and market demands. Unless proper attention is paid to both direct and indirect capabilities, economists will continue 'to neglect the main activity of a firm, running a business' (Coase 1991c: 65).

Cognitive foundations

Hayek (1937: 45) declared that 'hypotheses or assumptions that people do learn from experience, and about how they acquire knowledge...constitute the empirical content of our propositions about what happens in the real world'. Recognition of the importance of 'knowledge how' reinforces the argument for an approach to the analysis of learning which does not rely on an extension of rational choice theorising, but on ideas about human cognition such as those examined in the preceding chapter; and it is fitting that Hayek's *The Sensory Order* (1952) contains four references to Ryle's *Concept of Mind*, which is also cited by Richardson (1972: 895). We may prefer to say, with Kelly (1963: 73), that each person's experience is constructed, not by events, or what economists call 'information', but by the interpretation which that person places upon those events or that information, although, as Kelly observes, the particular kinds of events and the sequence in which they occur will typically have some effect on the construction systems which an individual develops. In Kelly's account there are many possible construction systems, and in Hayek's there are many possible networks of relationships; but in both accounts the establishment of one particular pattern of interpretation or response inhibits the development of many alternatives (as happens when an infant learns to speak a particular language).

The development of knowledge is a path-dependent process, in which the acquisition of certain kinds of 'knowledge how' facilitates the acquisition of further knowledge of the same kind, and impedes the acquisition of knowledge of incompatible kinds; and this principle applies both to the performance of productive operations and to the procedures by which we seek to develop new 'knowledge that'. Each person's cognitive repertoire develops within an institutional context, and becomes to a greater or lesser extent dependent on that context both for its structure and its applicability. Penrose (1959, 1995: 53–4) suggests that individuals are likely to develop capabilities with very different breadths of application, some for example being useful only within a particular firm, some within a group of firms, some within manufacturing industry, and some in any productive activity.

Henry Boettinger, who was Head of Corporate Planning at AT&T in the 1970s, sought to raise awareness of the effects of the institutional structure of professions, skills and disciplines on ways of thinking by identifying seven styles of mental architecture. The mind of the engineer he compared to a steel and glass skyscraper, ruled by function; the research scientist operates within 'a haunted gothic castle, fog shrouded and built on the ruins of unnumbered previous foundations'; the lawyer's mind resembles a Moorish palace, harmonious from a distance, but full of peculiar detail; the economist's world of ideas suggests a large circus tent, subject to unpredictable short-term disturbances by mischievous boys hacking at the ropes; the manager lives in a capacious Victorian house, much adapted over the years; the humanist's mental home is in a sidestreet off a great city plaza; and the politician operates in a children's playground, where he must follow the children from activity to activity (Boettinger 1974). The variety of cognitive frameworks is no less desirable than the variety of architectural styles: the division of labour leads to different kinds of 'knowledge how', substantial parts of which could not otherwise be developed, and even within a specialism people will acquire skills that differ somewhat in context and scope, as well as quality, thus generating the variety which Marshall expected within each of the forms of organisation that aid knowledge. This variety must somehow be accommodated within any society, by a mixture of segregation and integration.

In Marshall's, Hayek's and modern artificial intelligence models, we have systems by which phenomena are represented, and linkages constructed between perceptions, actions and outcomes; but in none of these models are there any processes available which could ensure that these representations are correct, and that the linkages in the human brain correspond to the linkages which actually operate in the environment. As Smith (1980) knew, patterns are invented and imposed; and if cognition is an evolutionary process, we should remember that evolutionary success requires no more than a performance which is satisfactory in relation to rival cognitive systems in the circumstances that have hitherto been experienced. All four kinds of knowledge that we have distinguished are acquired by trial and error, which may be carefully designed, especially for the acquisition of scientific knowledge, fairly casual, or often controlled by the unconscious processes of our brain. Not one of the four kinds can ever be more than provisional, or, in Popper's terms, conjectural. The next time that we try to use any piece of knowledge, it may be falsified. Our theorem may fail, a hitherto reliable source of information may lead us astray, a well-proven routine may fail to produce the expected result, a colleague or regular supplier may be unable to deliver what we expect. As we shall see, there are ways of protecting ourselves against the consequences of falsification, but these in turn are fallible.

Using capabilities

The capabilities of an individual or a firm can rarely be precisely defined. As Ryle (1949: 33) pointed out, 'a skill is not an act', and should not be identified with any particular performance, or even set of performances, which it has made possible. 'Knowing *how*, then, is a disposition, but not a single-track disposition like a reflex or a habit. Its exercises are observances of rules or canons or the application of criteria' (ibid.: 46). Moreover, capabilities may be, and clusters of capabilities always are, clusters of dispositions, which may be realised in many ways; and, through the exercise of intelligence, they may be developed in ways which are not foreseeable. The limitations on their development cannot be foreseen either, for, as Nelson and Winter (1982: 84) remind us, 'performance takes place in a context set by the values of a large number of variables; the effectiveness of the performance depends on those variables being in appropriate ranges';

and we cannot possibly know what all the ranges – or indeed all the relevant variables – are. As with scientific hypotheses, what matters is always the next trial, and the result of that can never be guaranteed; a change of circumstances or the emergence of a new or improved rival system may invalidate years of experience. Nelson and Winter's emphasis on the ambiguity of scope inherent in any skill should be matched by an emphasis on the variability of its quality. 'We never speak of a person having partial knowledge of a fact or truth…On the other hand, it is proper and normal to speak of a person knowing in part how to do something' (Ryle 1949: 57–8). Thus many firms may know how to make cars, market new products, or manage a supply chain, but not all know how to do so equally well; and what level of performance is 'good enough' at any time depends on those – such as one's customers – who make the judgement, and on the alternatives that they perceive to be available to them. The effectiveness of any capability, even in a familiar situation, is never definitively established.

Unless we restrict ourselves to explaining the past, our interest in capabilities, whether direct or indirect, and whether embedded within individuals, firms, or economies, is in their future uses and their future development, and neither are fit subjects for rational expectations. In Menger's (1976 [1871]) terms, capabilities provide a reserve when the list of future contingencies cannot be closed: they are a structure of complementary skills which is oriented towards a particular range of possible futures. (We should have learnt from Austrian economists to think of capital in terms of both its structure and its orientation.) Ansoff (1965) included flexibility among the objectives of corporate strategy, and flexibility may be increased by investing in the development of those capabilities which are judged to be both desirable and attainable, given the present set of capabilities and the cognitive and institutional constraints that are associated with them. Education develops capabilities for future contingencies, and should also develop the ability to develop those capabilities further – though how many educational programmes develop the capability for understanding very different styles of mental architecture is an open question. Capabilities have an option value, but that value must be conjectured.

The scope and level of capabilities sought, and also the rate of improvement, must depend on a view of future possibilities, for no-one can afford to prepare for every prospect that can be imagined, let alone those that cannot. So any plan to develop capabilities involves a double conjecture, about the kinds of future that it is reasonable to prepare for, and about the appropriateness of particular capabilities to those kinds of future. Both judgements must be right if a firm is to be able to undertake the activities which match the requirements of the situation. Charles Stine's fundamental research programme for Du Pont was carefully judged as a means of enhancing the company's capabilities for a future which could not be predicted, and succeeded brilliantly (Hounshell and Smith 1988: 223–7, 233); on the other hand, despite a long record of imperfect success it is apparently still very common for firms to misjudge their capacity to manage successfully businesses that they propose to take over (Norburn and Schoenberg 1994: 32). Even intelligent procedures do not preclude unintended consequences, welcome or unwelcome.

Capabilities of the kind so far discussed are not sufficient to explain what activities an individual or a firm undertakes, though they can explain what activities they are unlikely to be successful in undertaking. A cluster of capabilities resembles a production set in one important respect: it indicates (with some ambiguity and a significant potential for error) a range of possibilities; we need something else to explain what is chosen. For that it is helpful to adopt Penrose's (1959, 1995: 31) concept of a firm's 'productive opportunity', which combines capabilities with the perception of a profitable use to which they can be put; and as can frequently be observed, either perception or capability may be missing. Productive opportunities, too, are conjectures. Penrose is well aware of this, though because her purpose is to explain how firms can grow by developing and deploying their capabilities, she explicitly recognises only errors of omission. However, although knowledge, whether true or false, of an attractive market should be regarded as 'knowledge that' rather than 'knowledge how', nevertheless the ability to seek out relevant information or to draw inferences from newspaper reports, conversations, political or social changes, or even price movements, is certainly 'know-how'. 'To know something is to be able to understand and otherwise make sense of it' (Minkler 1993: 520). 'Knowledge that' may be a public good, but the capability of making sense of it, in any one of the ways that are conceivable, is not:

> [people] differ in their capacity by perception and inference to *form correct judgements* as to the future course of events in the environment. This capacity, furthermore, is not homogeneous, some persons excelling in one kind of problem situations, others in other kinds, in almost endless variety.
>
> (Knight 1921: 241)

However, this capability, like others, is generally susceptible to analysis in terms of experience and the patterns that have consciously or unconsciously been imposed upon that experience, and Penrose treats it accordingly. The alertness which characterises each of Kirzner's (1973) entrepreneurs is a differentiated capability, relying on a distinctive interpretative system; that is why appropriately oriented capabilities may be sufficiently scarce in each local economic environment for alertness to be a source of profit. Casson's (1982) entrepreneur is especially skilled at interpreting the conjunction of different kinds of knowledge. Sony is a good example of such capabilities, most spectacularly in their perception of the productive opportunity in portable radios that was offered by Bell Lab's development of the transistor. But because both the knowledge of potential applications and the knowledge of how to realise that potential are fallible, so too may be the conjectured connections, as has been illustrated more than once by Clive Sinclair; and Sony was apparently so impressed by the doubtful complementarities between its television business and Hollywood film-making that it underrated the rather obvious contrasts in 'knowledge how'.

Choice, routines and codification

We will conclude this chapter by noting three implications of our discussion of cognitive-based capabilities. The first is that Nelson and Winter (1982: 82–5) are fully justified in challenging the orthodox distinction between choices and productive operations, the latter being chosen but requiring no choices in their performance. Schumpeter observed that

> the necessity of taking decisions occurs in any work. No cobbler's apprentice can repair a shoe without making some resolutions and without deciding independently some questions, however small. The 'what' and the 'how' are taught him; but this does not relieve him of the necessity of a certain independence.
>
> (1934: 20)

After noting tasks which entail greater discretion, Schumpeter continues:

> Now the director or independent owner of a business has certainly most to decide and most resolutions to make. But the how and the why are also taught him....He acts, not on the basis of the prevailing condition of things, but much more according to certain symptoms of which he has learned to take heed.
>
> (ibid.: 21)

Nelson and Winter were particularly anxious to elide the standard distinction between technologies as data and the choices of what technology to use, by drawing attention both to the technologies of choice and to the scope for choices within technologies, which generate improvements in the manner of Smith and Marshall. There is always at least a potential element of choice in skilful performance; and the quality of the choices that are made depends on the capabilities of the chooser.

Decisions about what to produce, what methods to use, what marketing strategy to follow, what capital structure and organisational design to create, along with household decisions about labour supply and consumption, may legitimately be distinguished from decisions made in the process of production or of consumption; but all depend on 'knowledge how' which is associated with a particular category of decisions. The capabilities required of a proficient marketing director are different from those of a proficient electrician; but the marketing capabilities of the former may be no more helpful in managing a research department than the electrician's in chemical engineering. People learn how to make choices in a particular range of circumstances – which may include discovering, or creating, their own preferences (Woo 1992); they also learn, as is often overlooked, how to identify the occasions for choice: what needs to be decided and when. Like all capabilities, these may be of varying quality and applicability. For craftsman, manager, or consumer, problems or opportunities are identified by matching perception against some reference model (Loasby 1976), which may be a cognitive map of which the individual is not conscious, a carefully worked out individual conception, or an institutional model of what is appropriate within the group to which that individual looks for guidance. If this reference model is tightly specified, then the identification of the need for decision immediately generates the response, as with Kirzner's (1973) alert entrepreneur or an expert games player; if it is not, then there must be some procedure for closing the option set and applying some decision rule, such as those invoked by economists. There may be an intermediate stage during which the problem is opened out to incorporate additional factors and additional options, and this may be crucial to the quality of the decision; like the procedure for applying closure, that process relies on 'knowledge how'.

In all situations where action is required, people have recourse, consciously or unconsciously, to what Simon (1957) has called 'decision premises', which provide partial closure by specifying assumptions about the possibilities and the criteria by which to choose between them. For the cobbler's apprentice, the closure is almost, though not quite, complete; for the director it is a good deal less, though the how and the why are closely specified. Schumpeter's entrepreneur, of course, is a breaker of constraints, but, by Schumpeter's own account, not a breaker of all constraints. His new combination is based on novel premises – but not on any premises that he might fancy: it is the imagined, deemed possible (Loasby 1996), and so an obvious question to ask of the Schumpeterian entrepreneur is why certain things are deemed possible, and why others are not. Like Penrose, Schumpeter is interested in developing a theory of successful enterprise; but it would be a reasonable extension of both theories to investigate the cognitive and institutional factors in success, and in failure. Perhaps most instructive of all is the not uncommon sequence of success followed by failure, where we may find that success created the cognitive and institutional conditions for failure in a different environment. The computer industry provides some striking illustrations of this sequence (Langlois 1997).

All decisions, like all knowledge, depend on frameworks: the preselection of phenomena and of the methods by which to handle them. No one can cope with an unlimited decision space; partial closure is essential, and routines may provide such closure. The second implication of our discussion is the perspective that it offers on the concept of routines. Nelson and Winter (1982) discuss capabilities as routines, with due emphasis on the linkages between them. Routines reduce cognition costs and save time by imposing closure; they provide the stable patterns on which selection processes can work, and also the stable patterns of individual and sub-unit behaviour which permit the development of the indirect capabilities which impose coherence on the activities of an organisation. But 'routine' is an ambiguous label, as is demonstrated in the discussion by Cohen *et al.* (1996). The definition which the discussants eventually and hesitantly offer is as follows: 'A routine is an executable *capability* for repeated performance in some *context* that [has] been *learned* by an organization in response to *selective pressures*' (Cohen *et al.* 1996: 683).

What is defined, it will be observed, is not a category of behaviour but a category of 'know how' which is realised in performance, and we have noted that both the quality of performance and the range of context in which it can be applied are problematic. Any individual may perform inconsistently, some people may perform better than others, and an apparently minor variation in the task or the environment may cause unsuspected trouble. That routines economise on cognition, often governing 'classes of perform-ance in which intelligence is displayed, but the rules or criteria of which are unformulated' (Ryle 1949: 30), makes prediction of such variations difficult. Routines are representations within the brain, and definitions of routines, even in the form of standard operating procedures, are public representations which are constrained by language and the concepts available, as the discussion between Cohen and his co-authors abundantly demonstrates; such public representations are therefore doubly removed from the performances which are to be explained. We should also observe that organisations as such do not learn; what is true, and very important, is that many routines, and not only those which involve interactions with others, are learnt within an organisational context and may be relevant only in that context.

It seems best to recognise the variety of performances within which we may usefully recognise elements of routine, the contribution of which varies between categories. The most rigid interpretation is a single sequence of actions – the ideal, or perhaps caricature, of Taylorist efficiency. This interpretation can be readily extended to a complete set of condition-action rules which elicits a standard response in each situation, like single-exit models in economics. The first type of routine requires no co-ordination between individuals, even if they are closely interdependent, once the set of activities has been correctly assembled and the routine established; the second requires the ability to identify each situation in order to predict the outcome, and in cases of asymmetric information may therefore give rise to the agency problems which constitute the standard economic analyses of organisation. Neither, by definition, can directly generate any improvements in productivity, though they may well embody such improvements (as in Marshall's 'machine'); but they provide stable units which may be inserted into new combinations. Such routine elements may constrain non-routine behaviour; they may also make such behaviour possible by making the cognitive task manageable. We should also recognise that what appears to be routine behaviour may actually be a manifestation in a stable situation of a capability which can cope very effectively with a range of situations, perhaps without conscious thought. This is the nature of skilful performance, and should only be called routine if that term is to be extended to cover all tacit 'knowledge how'.

Routine seems to denote the absence of change; but all change requires substantial elements of stability; whatever may be the physical constraints, the limitations of our cognitive capacity make it impossible for any of us to revise our knowledge, either 'that' or 'how', or our behaviour, unless much the greater part remains unchanged. In explaining the course of improvement in engineering design, Vincenti (1990: 223) emphasises that '[v]ery little change would occur if new operational principles had always to be devised at all levels'. But even the change process itself relies on established capabilities, and so many elements of routine may be embodied in the processes by which change occurs. Nelson and Winter (1982) provide a lead by distinguishing between operating, investment, and search routines: even if the procedure for deciding on investment is tightly programmed, the investment itself is certain to make some difference to some aspect of operations, and any search which is more than Bayesian is expected to generate some kind of novelty. Search routines are focusing devices; they remove closure, but do so only in parts of the current system of knowledge. Which parts these are may be crucial in explaining the outcomes of search.

Rules may be thought of as routines, and may similarly be divided into the prescriptive and the procedural: the latter, as Hayek pointed out, may be abstract (such as many constitutional provisions) and intended to require interpretation in any specific case. All have the function of imposing constraints on the choice set – otherwise they are irrelevant – thereby saving time and reducing cognition costs, and perhaps bringing a decision within the bounds of rationality by supplying sufficient premises for logical processing. A particular virtue in an interdependent society is that rules which are widely shared help each of us to predict the behaviour of other people and thus interact effectively and avoid conflict. (This was Smith's (1976a) *theory* of moral sentiments.) Of course, problems may be inappropriately defined and wrongly closed; and closures which are effective for one purpose are likely to be ineffective for others, and so attempts to tackle unfamiliar classes of problems by proven methods often produce disappointing results. Far from being surprising, that is a natural corollary of the advantages of specialisation; the opportunity cost of capabilities in one kind of activity is incapabilities in many other kinds. There can be no universally valid framework, and no universally applicable skill. It was Hayek's view that the best general rules were those which had survived the testing of many generations, and had been incorporated into the cognitive systems of vast numbers of people.

Rules and routines, most of which are not clearly defined, or even explicitly stated, provide an institutional setting for each individual's use of knowledge; might not formalisation and clear specification make that use more effective? This is the third, and final, issue to be discussed in this section. By converting tacit knowledge into knowledge that is public, unambiguous and readily transferrable, codification may be an investment which would produce substantial and continuing benefits. Like other institutions, it economises on individual cognition and increases the compatibility of thought and action between those who use the same categories and procedures. It is difficult to deny that the amount of codified knowledge has been increasing, but whether the proportion of knowledge that is codified has also increased is less certain – partly because codification and the epistemic status of knowledge claims are both matters of degree. Codification is best developed in the sciences, and it may appear obvious that it should be more vigorously applied to technology and to many practical and managerial skills. However, we must remember the distinction between 'knowing that' and 'knowing how'; the latter is harder to codify and is likely to require a different coding system. As Hayek (1952) realised, the attempt to develop a systematic account of what our senses appear to be telling us has led to the development of 'knowledge that' which employs a coding system that does not map onto the 'knowledge how' of our sensory order; and this disparity can be repeatedly matched in other comparisons of 'knowledge that' and 'knowledge how'. We should also recognise the differences, noted earlier, between the substantive content of each science and the knowledge of how to develop and use that knowledge: the persistence of methodological disagreements indicates the difficulty of codifying scientists' 'knowledge how'.

Since any complete codification should encompass all the possible situations encountered by code users, no universal code can go beyond generalities; as with other kinds of institutions, the more specific the guidance, the narrower is likely to be the range of application. Because cognitive processes occur in the space of representations, every person's knowledge is partly codified; every brain develops its own codes, many of which are not at all susceptible to conscious control – for good evolutionary reasons noted in the previous chapter. Different areas of knowledge, having evolved in the process of dealing with a particular range of situations, may be expected to use local codes which resist incorporation into a single system which humans are capable of handling. Arrow (1974: 55–6) presents a similar argument in terms of information processing, but does not explicitly recognise that the differentiated framing of problems is the key to differentiated knowledge.

Much 'knowledge how' is very poorly articulated, being controlled in parts of the brain which developed prior to consciousness; that this tacit knowledge includes some of the most effective skills indicates the quality that can be attained by unconscious coding systems. Nevertheless, the process of explicitly codifying routines may be helpful in clarifying both the routine and its domain, thus both defining and limiting closure, and raising the performance of those whose tacit knowledge within the relevant field is well below the standard of the experts. Within one specialism, formal codification can be very helpful: Whitehead's advice to economise on thought is used to extol the value of mathematical symbols. But it can never be complete, for however elaborate they may be, the codes must always be interpreted by the use of uncodified knowledge; it is a familiar experience that messages in a shared language – even the language of mathematics – are subject to diverse interpretations. There is no attainable base of justified knowledge. 'There is not a sentence which adequately states its own meaning. There is always a background of presupposition which defies analysis by reason of its infinitude' (Whitehead 1951: 699). However incompleteness, of an appropriate kind, is a virtue; for ambiguity and even conflict between perceptions and established patterns are the conditions of creativity.

Conclusion

A proper understanding of capabilities is crucial to an understanding of economic organisation and economic development. Although we rightly celebrate the power of human reasoning and the human imagination, we should give full recognition to the pattern matching and performance skills which create time for this reasoning and imagination to be applied. The division of labour between these two kinds of activities is essential to progress. So too is the division of labour between capabilities. The human brain has the potential for developing an enormous variety of alternative networks to constitute an enormous variety of alternative kinds of 'knowledge how'; but for any individual most of these are necessarily alternatives – the establishment of each set of connections precludes the development of many others. The enhancement of each person's 'knowledge how', and indeed of each person's 'knowledge that', requires specialisation. But if different people specialise in different areas of knowledge, then the total knowledge available within the group becomes far greater than what is attainable by any single person. The division of labour generates the growth and the division of knowledge as joint products.

5

TRANSACTIONS AND GOVERNANCE

In November 1970, Ronald Coase (1972, reprinted in Coase 1988: 58) told a meeting at the US National Bureau of Economic Research that '[v]ery little work is done on the subject of industrial organization at the present time,...since what is commonly dealt with under this heading tells us almost nothing about the organization of industry'. He added, 'We all know what is meant by the organization of industry. It describes the way in which the activities undertaken within the economic system are divided up among firms;' but industrial economics had become applied price theory and therefore had nothing to say about this division (Coase 1972, reprinted in Coase 1988: 60). That price theory also (and for similar reasons) tells us nothing about the growth of firms had been discovered by Penrose (1959, 1995: 11–14), whose alternative approach was not mentioned by Coase, although it had already been in print for eleven years. In the last quarter-century, Coase's complaint has been met – though not quite to his complete satisfaction – by the development of transaction cost economics. Following our exploration of capabilities in the previous chapter, it is now time to consider the explanations of industrial organisation which are based on transaction costs; but rather than examining these explanations in detail I wish to set them in a wider context, both historically and methodologically. In the first chapter, I suggested that studies of the organisation both of economic systems and of economic analysis could help us to understand how evolution is shaped by institutions; in this chapter we shall see how historical sequences may constrain perspectives or provoke reactions to perspectives, and how methodology may define what is a proper question and what is a proper answer.

Coase's problem

In this investigation, Coase is a central figure, and his paper of 1937 on 'The nature of the firm' a central document. Fortunately, in the last ten years he has told us quite a lot about the circumstances of its composition, and of his present attitude towards it. So let us begin by asking what problem Coase was trying to solve in his 1937 paper, and why this problem seemed important to him. We may then be able to explain why neither the problem nor the solution that Coase offered to it seemed important to other economists. At the London School of Economics he took a Bachelor of Commerce degree, which included no formal instruction in economic theory; but it did include a course in business administration, in which he had learnt how the economic system responds to consumer demand through the profit-seeking activities of firms. The system therefore 'worked itself', without any central direction. Coase found this account entirely satisfactory as far as it went; but it was not complete.

Because he had taken no course in formal economics he was not bothered, as were his better-trained contemporaries, by the twin demonstrations that allocative efficiency required competition to be perfect and that perfect competition was incompatible with increasing returns; what was lacking was a reason why each individual productive operation should not also 'work itself', without central direction – why, in other words, there should be any firms at all, and therefore any such topic as business administration, which he had been studying (Coase 1991a: 38). He looked for an answer which would preserve both the theory of a self-regulating system and the topic of business administration; and he had worked out the substance of his proposal by the summer of 1932, on the basis of a year spent visiting firms in America, during which he 'tried to find the reason for the existence of the firm in factories and offices rather than in the writings of economists' (Coase 1991b: 52) – as Alfred Marshall had visited firms to resolve his difficulties with Cournot's microeconomic theory. Such practices are not encouraged nowadays.

Coase's problem was one of theoretical coherence; but it was coherence within a different style of theorising than that which brought perfect competition into conflict with increasing returns. He wanted to reconcile the existence of firms with his understanding of the working of competition, which was what Nelson and Winter (1982) have called an 'appreciative theory'. How might this be done? Clearly firms had to be given a justification that was compatible with this appreciative theory: therefore both owners and employees must choose an employment relationship rather than a market relationship, and that choice must be based either on preferences or costs. In his article, Coase (1937, reprinted in Coase 1988: 38) noted but dismissed as a general theory the possibility that many people may prefer to be employed, and reinforced this dismissal towards the end of the article by arguing that Knight's (1921) emphasis on uncertainty as a reason for the division of labour between uncertainty-bearing entrepreneurs and uncertainty-avoiders who seek guaranteed income from such entrepreneurs does not explain why 'the price mechanism should be superseded' (Coase 1937, reprinted in Coase 1988: 48–51).

70

Having rejected the idea that replacing market activities by a firm could generate any kind of systematic benefits on which a theory might be built, Coase was left with the only acceptable alternative: there must be some general way in which the organisation of a firm may save costs. Coase at that time shared the standard assumption that these cannot be production costs, since such costs are treated as 'engineering data' and are therefore not subject to choice but technologically determined – an assumption which, as we have seen in the preceding chapter, excludes some of the most important features of economic activity; they must, therefore, be the costs of arranging what is to be done. But since, as Coase well knew from his degree course and his observations in America, running a business organisation generates substantial costs, it could be rationally preferred only if the alternative to organisation – using markets – entails even greater costs.

So Coase (1937, reprinted in Coase 1988: 38) simply invoked 'a cost of using the price mechanism'. This was not just armchair empiricism; Coase had not dreamed up such costs but observed them during his American tour. Since he did not further define these costs, we may specify them as costs of search and information, bargaining and decision, and policy and enforcement (Dahlman 1979: 148). However, it was empiricism which was aimed at preserving the appreciative theory of a competitive economy, by reconciling a conflict between an apparent implication of that theory, that all economic activity can be effectively co-ordinated in markets, and abundant evidence that much co-ordination is managed within firms, which appeared to contradict that implication. His studies of business administration had left him comfortable with the assumption that costs of internal organisation increase with the range of activities undertaken, and the juxtaposition of such rising costs with the costs of using markets allowed him to explain the boundaries of every firm as a particular instance of 'substitution at the margin' (Coase 1937, reprinted in Coase 1988: 34).

In attributing this concept to Marshall, Coase failed, like other economists who had been much more thoroughly trained in theory, to distinguish between the marginal equalities which characterise an equilibrium allocation and active but incremental experimentation at the margins of knowledge. Marshall's (1920) own presentation of his Principle of Substitution does nothing to clarify such a distinction (Loasby 1990). Hence Coase's (1937 (reprinted in Coase 1988: 47)) claim that '[t]he whole of the "structure of competitive industry" becomes tractable by the ordinary technique of economic analysis' is open to interpretation either as a proposition about the efficiency with which economic activities are divided up among firms or as a theory of economic processes. These two interpretations lead to two different theories of the firm – and, as we shall see, one of these has two variants which might reasonably be regarded as distinctive theories.

The implications of Coase's solution

In his original article Coase suggested how economists might account for the presence of firms within a generally self-regulating market economy, but he did not present a formal explanation. Thirty-five years later he observed that the 'ordinary technique of economic analysis' had not yet been applied to the allocation of economic activities; his article had been 'much cited and little used' (Coase 1972, reprinted in Coase 1988: 62). What made this neglect initially surprising to Coase was the abundance of books that were available in 1937 on the organisation of particular industries, as well as others – notably Marshall's (1919) *Industry and Trade* – which attempted a comprehensive survey of organisational patterns. In studying for his Commerce degree Coase had become more familiar with such work than with formal economic theory, and he believed that he was connecting it with marginal analysis. But Lionel Robbins, the head of the economics department at the LSE, and whose precepts Coase thought he was following, took no interest in his article (Coase 1991b: 51).

Only much later did Coase realise that the books with which he had become familiar exemplified for Robbins 'the incredible banalities of much of the so-called theory of production', which failed to explain how internal organisation is governed by 'the relationship of prices and cost....In the modern treatment, discussion of "production" is an integral part of the Theory of Equilibrium' (Coase 1991b: 53, citing Robbins 1932: 65, 70). What mattered to Robbins was the determination of factor combinations by the price mechanism, not which particular institution actually did the combining. Marshall's interest in firms as means of organising production, and thus as means of reducing the costs of production, which was derived from Babbage and Mill, and probably also from Rao and Roscher (Streissler 1990), had no place in modern economic analysis; nor, as we shall consider in detail in Chapter 7, did the organisation of markets. Economists had failed to understand why Marshall (1920: 139) had suggested that 'it seems best sometimes to reckon Organization as a distinct agent of production'.

Robbins' attitude was consistent with the drive to formalism which characterised what Shackle (1967) called 'the years of high theory', and in particular with the central and pervasive importance of scarcity, which has since led to an exaltation of the logic of rational choice. Economic theory was to be based on three kinds of individual decisions: the work–leisure choice, which determined labour supply and income; production decisions, which determined the supply curves for every commodity and the demand curve for labour, and consumption decisions, which determined the demand curves for products. Consumers were reduced to preference functions and firms to production functions, which were assumed to be public knowledge; and production was just one category of exchange. The task of economists, according to Robbins, was to demonstrate how the allocation of resources was determined by the fundamental data of preferences, resources and technology. That these data should be treated as both fundamental and clearly specified was so clearly essential for sound economic theory as to be undiscussable, even though, as Hutchison (1937) pointed out, the practice has no epistemic basis. Whatever the institutional setting, decision makers were constrained to make precisely the choices that were dictated by these economic fundamentals; therefore the relocation of some decisions from markets to firms, like the use of money to replace barter, could have no real effect on outcomes but were veils which concealed the truth from the uninitiated, and might lead them into analytical error. Robbins' view is still implicitly, and sometimes explicitly, prevalent among economic theorists. The consequent divorce between theory and subject matter, which is endemic in rational choice theory, has, in Coase's (1988: 3) view, had 'serious adverse effects on economics'.

Whereas Robbins, and those who thought like him, were seeking to restrict economic theory to the principles which ensured that an economic system, properly guided by prices, would work itself efficiently, and were content to treat the firm as a unitary agent responding to market signals, other economists were critically examining the proposition that the system did indeed work itself efficiently. If Coase had received a thorough training in economic theory, he could hardly have failed to notice that this was an issue of some interest; and even if he had not been drawn into thinking about that topic, it seems very unlikely that he would have formulated his problem in the way that he did. The simple implication of the emerging theory of imperfect competition was that firms existed for their monopoly advantages. In this theory, firms were not a solution to a problem of economic organisation but themselves a major source of problems. What mattered was not organisation but market structure.

Thus, as O'Brien (1984: 39) has pointed out, in what came to be called the theory of the firm the very concept of a firm as an organisation was banished. In Meade's (1936) intendedly practical guide to economic policy, the manager of a firm has simply to calculate optima; Meade was therefore confident that the weakening of incentives, which would accompany the conversion of managers, as he proposed, from independent profit-maximisers to operators of planning rules in which they had no direct interest, would be more than compensated by the simplification of their task from setting output, in a world of monopolies, at the level which equated marginal cost with marginal revenue to setting output at the level which equated marginal cost with price. Instead of having to calculate two marginal values from the data, they would need to calculate only one, and that the easier of the two (Meade 1936: 195).

Why firms existed was therefore not a relevant question for economic theorists in the 1930s, whether or not they believed that markets generally worked well. Lionel Robbins and Joan Robinson disagreed about the appropriate model of the firm in price theory, but they were equally opposed to accepting the concept of the firm as an organisation, because that would divert attention from the (disputed) model of the fundamental determinants of economic phenomena. So, although economists might be comforted by the notion that the allocation of activities between firms and markets could be explained by standard optimising principles, and might therefore be happy to cite Coase's article, this was not knowledge that they wished to apply, and so they had no reason to use it. What concerned industrial economists was the relative allocative efficiency of different market structures – what came to be called the structure-conduct-performance model. Firms which were too large to form part of a perfectly competitive industry were necessarily a source of welfare losses. That their size might reflect economies of scale was occasionally admitted – though this was not logically compatible with the implicit, but essential, assumption of zero transaction costs (Loasby 1976: 69); that it might reflect lower costs of internal governance was not even contemplated. Even if it did, such lower costs could do nothing to counter the logically irrefutable proposition, most imperiously stated by Samuelson (1972 [1967]: 39) that increasing returns were a threat to economic welfare.

However, if we now consider the implications of Coase's article, which Coase himself did not until much later, we can see that Robbins should have taken more notice of it; for it threatened, almost in passing, to undermine the theory of equilibrium which he valued so highly. If 'there is a cost of using the price mechanism', should one not at least consider whether that theory, in which none of these costs are allowed for, needs revision? The assumption, which is almost as unconscious as it is orthodox, that production uses resources but exchange does not, protects the choice-theoretic autonomy of price theory from the potentially troublesome question whether the cost of transacting might have some important effects on the formal models of perfect and imperfect competition, and the policy conclusions that have been drawn from them.

Coase (1988: 15) eventually came to think that such effects were important and pervasive. He argued that externalities could not be a threat to efficiency within the setting of rational choice and zero transaction costs in which they were currently analysed (Coase 1960); and he later extended this criticism into a broader judgement – which is orthogonal to what is misleadingly known as the Coase Theorem – that, because it ignores transaction costs, 'current economic analysis is incapable of handling many of the problems to which it purports to give answers' (Coase 1988: 15). We may at least agree on the need to consider the appropriateness of perfect competition as either a predictive model or a standard of comparison when transactions entail costs. Exchange at the margin cannot then be an exchange of equal values, because the parties have also to bear the costs of the exchange process. Furthermore, it is impossible fully to restore the

74

initial situation by reversing the exchange, because the costs of both transactions must be deducted from the initial endowments. Every transaction causes an increase in entropy. On the other hand, transaction costs might provide some welcome frictions to stabilise an economy which otherwise is liable to generate a wholesale rearrangement of activities in response to even a modest change in the data. The conflict between perfect competition and increasing returns, we may also observe, appears from this perspective to be an artefact of a questionable formulation – as George Richardson (1975) also concluded from the perspective of Adam Smith's theory of economic development.

If the use of markets entails costs, then it is hardly compatible with the basic assumptions of optimisation to assume that the set of markets is complete; moreover, where are the resources that are needed to undertake transactions to come from if they have all been deployed in the equilibrium allocation? Chamberlin's (1933) *Theory of Monopolistic Competition* may readily be interpreted as assuming that some of them come from the producer, for selling costs are clearly transaction costs in Coase's terminology – indeed, Coase (1937, reprinted in Coase 1988: 42) attributes the emergence of the firm 'primarily to the existence of marketing costs'. They cannot therefore be dismissed as welfare reducing. Chamberlin did not so dismiss them; in contrast to Robinson, he was very wary of drawing welfare conclusions from his analysis. Marshall thought it superfluous to note that transactions are costly, and was content to observe that

> [p]roduction and marketing are parts of the single process of adjustment of supply to demand. The division between them is on lines which are seldom sharply defined: the lines vary from one class of business to another, and each is liable to modification by any large change in the resources of production, transport, or the communication of intelligence.
>
> (Marshall 1919: 181)

Coase (1937, reprinted in Coase 1988: 51–3) pointed out that a rising cost curve for a particular product cannot determine the size of a firm, since firms can always turn to another product. The firm of price theory, being an analytical fiction, may be restricted to a single product for analytical convenience; but then applied price theory becomes a questionable basis for the study of economic organisation, as Coase (1972) observed. The scope of Coase's intendedly real-world firms is not measured solely by the degree of vertical integration. 'Which activities tend to be associated and which do not?' (Coase 1972, reprinted in Coase 1988: 74) is a much broader question. Coase suggests that the answer depends on 'the marketing costs (that is, the costs of using the price mechanism) and the costs of organising of different entrepreneurs' (1937, reprinted in Coase 1988: 53), for the cost of managing a particular transaction within a particular firm must be compared not only with the cost of using the market but also with the cost of managing it within any other firm. He did not seek to explain these costs by assuming an exogenously determined production function for transactions.

That Coase's explanation of firms should fail to enthuse economists who wished either to formalise or to undermine theories of price-mediated efficient allocation is therefore not surprising. But what to an outside observer might seem more surprising, though it has been little remarked, is the failure to recognise a fundamental complementarity with another approach to economics. Coase's article was published in the November edition of *Economica*; in the preceding February, the same journal had published Hayek's 'Economics and Knowledge'; and Hayek was a colleague of Coase. In that article Hayek (1937: 39) argued that 'the assertion of the existence of a tendency towards equilibrium is clearly an empirical proposition', which requires some account of how people can acquire the knowledge that will lead them to take those actions which are compatible with equilibrium, and noted (ibid.: 48) the analytical neglect of the press and advertising as communicators of knowledge. (Hayek did not mention Chamberlin.) Now the transaction costs which Coase discussed are explicitly costs of acquiring the knowledge which is necessary to make transactions or the costs of making arrangements to counteract the irremediable lack of knowledge about the future. Firms replace the missing markets in which future contracts might, on counterfactual assumptions, have been made.

Hayek and Coase were both asking how an economic system can function in a world where the information which is regularly postulated by theorists at the beginning of their analyses is only partially available to any of those who actually have to decide what to do; and they both recognised, though imperfectly, that the problem required to be handled by a theory of processes, in which institutions are important. Unfortunately, Coase had his mind on firms, and did not think to examine more closely the appreciative theory of markets which he had too readily accepted, whereas Hayek was beginning to realise that the conventional equilibrium models of markets failed to explain the processes by which the actions of individuals, each based on their own particular but incomplete knowledge, could result in well-co-ordinated behaviour, and not unnaturally focused exclusively on improving our understanding of markets. Neither recognised the need to consider both as means of organising knowledge.

By 1945, Hayek (1945: 523) had come to emphasise that 'economic problems arise always and only in consequence of change'. Transaction costs, whether in markets or in firms, are incurred only when some new arrangement is required, and firms, as Coase had realised, are likely to be created in anticipation of the future need for new arrangements. Microeconomic equilibrium is a condition in which there is no change, in Hayek's (1937:

35) sense of divergence from what was expected; in such a model of equilibrium there is indeed no place for transaction costs, for all transactions have already been arranged. In microeconomic equilibrium there is no role for either firms or markets – nor indeed any role for central planning; there is simply routine behaviour. Coase's problem disappears, but so do all other economic problems; as we noted at the beginning of Chapter 1, everything of interest has already happened. If nothing changes, no kind of economic reasoning is of any value. But as soon as we allow change, Coase's problems reappear, and so do Hayek's objections to central planning, and the well-known difficulties of adapting the analysis of equilibrium to the explanation of what happens out of equilibrium.

One economist who was impressed with Hayek's (1937) call for a better theory of economic behaviour outside equilibrium attempted to provide one by focusing on decision making in firms. George Richardson's (1960) *Information and Investment* did not refer to Coase's analysis, but may be interpreted as an extension of it. Coase explains the firm as a means of replacing a series of transactions for various future dates with a single transaction which will provide a basis for decisions to be taken later, and that requires some means of forming expectations about future circumstances. Richardson asks how anyone running a business can construct a set of expectations on which to base a reasoned response to a change in the data, when that requires expectations about the responses of other firms.

Richardson's negative answer is that perfect competition cannot generate the requisite expectations, because although it excludes interdependencies between individual firms, it cannot exclude interdependencies between each firm and the consequences of the aggregate actions of all other firms, and it cannot provide decision makers with timely information about those actions. His extensive discussion of the possible ways in which adequate expectations may be generated includes differences between firms in their capacity to respond to particular kinds of opportunity, various kinds of understandings between rival firms, and established relationships between each firm and its suppliers and customers. Differences in capacity we shall return to shortly; established relationships are entirely consistent with Coase's original article. Richardson is thus on the way to developing a theory of markets to match Coase's theory of the firm. In a subsequent article, which we will consider later, he was to give content to Coase's theory.

Transaction costs and comparative institutions

Transaction cost theory in its present form is predominantly the work of one man. Oliver Williamson was trained as an engineer, discovered economics at Stanford, and was encouraged to move to Carnegie Tech, which was then experiencing its greatest days, with Simon, Cyert and March developing new ways of analysing business organisations. Like Coase, he was therefore something of an outsider; but, as we shall see, his greater immersion in economic theory has resulted in a moderated analytical scheme. Williamson's (1964) dissertation at Carnegie on managerial objectives in the theory of the firm incorporated the behavioural concept of 'organisational slack' into a model of managerial optimisation, which he later noted 'was only partly in the behavioral theory tradition' (Williamson 1996: 24); he followed this with a paper analysing the limits to the size of a firm which were imposed by control losses (Williamson 1967). Such losses, in the form of mistakes – not adverse draws from a probability distribution nor the consequences of opportunism – had been identified by Coase (1937, reprinted in Coase 1988: 45–6) as a major factor in restricting the size of firms; but Coase's specific reference to 'the dissimilarity of transactions', which might lead to such mistakes, was not taken up by Williamson, either then or later. Williamson gradually came to the conclusion that the performance of firms as organisations could not be properly appraised without specifying an alternative; the analysis of relative transaction costs at the margin which Coase had proposed should therefore be developed into a comparison of institutions.

This comparison is based squarely on the presumptive advantages of markets in providing 'high-powered incentives' to efficiency, which lie at the heart of standard economics. As Williamson (1975: 20) puts it, 'in the beginning there were markets'. This is explicitly a methodological assertion rather than a claim of historical succession; as we have seen, Coase had adopted the same starting point, but without apparently recognising that any methodological issue was involved. But their shared assumption that the existence of costly markets requires no explicit attention, while the existence of costly governance structures does, is not innocuous; in the evolution of economic theory, as in the evolution of the economy, history matters. Incentives are important, but they are not the only consideration in organisational design.

Williamson's alternative institutional form is a hierarchy – an amplification of Coase's conception of the firm as an employment relation, in which subordinates respond to directions rather than price signals. This alternative is viable only when market incentives generate inefficient outcomes; markets fail if incentives fail to move people towards efficient allocations. In standard theory this, of course, is precisely the problem with monopoly and with externalities; profit maximisation, which delivers Pareto-efficient outcomes in a perfectly competitive economy, guarantees inefficiency if competition is imperfect or the set of markets incomplete. Thus neoclassical economists have no difficulty in accepting Williamson's operating principle. Furthermore, in Williamson's analysis monopoly, in the form of either a single source or a single customer for a product or service which is dependent on a highly specific asset, is a basic requirement. In contrast to standard price theory, however, for Williamson monopoly alone is not sufficient.

We may note in passing – though it really deserves much more than a paragraph – that the neoclassical identification of monopoly as a sufficient cause of market failure is open to question; since the failure consists essentially of the inability of some consumers to obtain goods for which they would be prepared to pay a price greater than the producer's marginal cost, one should ask why the potential gains from trade which are the obverse of this failure should remain unexploited. In standard microeconomics, setting up transactions is implicitly costless; so if they are not set up whenever gains from trade are available someone apparently is not optimising. Here is another example of Coase's (1988: 15) proposition that microeconomic theory which implicitly assumes that transaction costs are zero is incompetent to analyse, or even to identify, market failures. What is actually demonstrated by the standard textbook demonstration of market failure is a failure of analytical rigour. Williamson clearly agrees with Coase in this specific instance: in the absence of transaction costs neither monopoly nor monopsony of productive assets is an obstacle to efficient market contracts. He has, however, shown no enthusiasm for investigating the wider implications of Coase's proposition.

Williamson (1985, 1986, 1996) insists that a combination of three conditions is required to frustrate efficiency. The first is a high degree of uncertainty – though in Williamson's analysis uncertainty is to be thought of as a very large number of contingencies rather than an open-ended list, as Knight, Shackle, and also Coase thought of it. This increases the complexity of contracting, but does not, in itself, impair its efficiency. But if we now add bounded rationality – a limited ability to process information – we may make it impossible to draw up a complete contract (Williamson 1996: 37). One may conceive of an incompletely specified contract being drawn up in good faith, so that in any contingency for which no provision has been made the party which happens to have acquired an ex-post bargaining advantage will not press it; and efficiency may thereby be preserved. If, however, either party is unwilling to trust the other, which is rational behaviour on the assumption of self-interest seeking with guile, then 'the convenient concept of contract as promise (unsupported by credible commitments) is vitiated by opportunism' (ibid.: 6), markets fail, and the way is open for an administrative solution. Whether this solution is adopted depends on its relative effectiveness in mitigating the failure; hence Williamson's insistence on the comparative institutional method, and the feasibility test for all proposed solutions.

Just as Coase in 1937 may be seen as bringing comfort to the high theorists of the time by suggesting that the apparent anomaly of firms in a market economy could be incorporated in marginal analysis, and thereafter ignored, so Williamson may be seen as bringing comfort to practitioners of a more highly developed neoclassical theory by incorporating bounded rationality into a rational choice framework. Williamson has proclaimed transaction cost theory as part of the 'efficiency branch' of economics: the allocation of economic activities to organisational forms is explicable by a variant of rational choice theory, supporting a variant of the Arrow–Debreu contractual system. Williamson (1981: 1545) believes that 'the theory of comprehensive contracting has been fully worked out' in that system; transaction cost economics provides the corresponding theory of 'incomplete contracting in its entirety' (Williamson 1996: 9); and 'the study of governance is concerned with the *identification, explication, and mitigation of all forms of contractual hazards*' (ibid.: 5).

Williamson (1995: 188) accepts the standard conception of an equilibrium of optimising agents, and assimilates the threat of bounded rationality by arguing that Simon's underlying argument that mind is a scarce resource (Simon 1978: 9) clearly requires a logic of maximisation. 'Economising on transaction costs essentially reduces to economising on bounded rationality' (Williamson 1985: 32). Scarcity necessarily implies optimisation, even when it is the capability of optimising that is scarce. Simon's concept of satisficing is dismissed with the arguments that 'it is more closely associated with psychology' and 'is now generally agreed' to have 'not been broadly applicable' (Williamson 1996: 36–7). Williamson thereby evades the problems of knowledge and cognition which Shackle insisted were a threat to ex-ante optimisation, and the problems of analysing the process of adaptation and the possibility of discovery.

The trick is to assume that boundedly rational agents can accurately predict the consequences of their own and other people's bounded rationality: although they do not know, they do know the effects of not knowing. Thus, though *'all complex contracts are unavoidably incomplete'* (ibid.: 37), 'limited but intended rationality is translated into incomplete but farsighted contracting' (ibid.: 9); 'transaction cost economics examines incomplete contracts in their *entirety* – hence the absence of surprise, victims and the like' (ibid.: 46). Williamson thus extends the scope of the familiar microeconomic principle that allocative efficiency rests on an optimal set of contracts. He also extends a familiar principle of theory construction: the process of anticipating future consequences in the design of organisational forms, like the process of completing the set of pure market contracts in a Walrasian model, apparently takes place outside the working economy, and implicitly before economic activity begins. No processes are modelled, and the operation of governance systems does not generate any further change in the arrangements.

Williamson is still following, in a more elaborate but less formal way, the research strategy of his dissertation, that of imposing an equilibrium model of optimising agents on a structure which is built on the denial of optimisation. The 'absence of surprise' is a clear indicator that the underlying concept is of rational choice equilibrium, in which the identity of individuals has no significance, the only learning is Bayesian, and optimisation is accomplished by design; it is not an evolutionary process in which all designs are conjectural, may differ between individuals, and are liable to have unintended consequences. 'Adaptation is taken to be the central problem of economic organization, of which two types are distinguished: autonomous or Hayekian adaptation (in which markets enjoy the advantage) and cooperative or Barnardian adaptation (in which the advantage accrues to hierarchy)' (Williamson 1996: 26). But what is offered is a model of a structure which is already adapted, corresponding to the familiar models of economic systems that are already in equilibrium, not one which is designed to adapt to future events and to fresh knowledge.

The sources of change are exogenous, and economic agents are 'farsighted' but not creative; and although Williamson (1996: 31–2) appears to endorse Barnard's (1938: 5) observation that 'successful cooperation in or by formal organizations is the abnormal, not the normal condition', and claims only that observed arrangements are relatively efficient (Williamson 1996: 56), he has no general explanation for varying degrees of efficiency, either between firms or between economies. He does not seem to have yet decided whether his fundamental belief is in the power of rational choice or of efficient market selection; like other economists, such as those considered in Chapter 2, who have invoked selection mechanisms to mimic rational choice, he has not considered at all carefully whether such mechanisms exist. His analytical system avoids any direct confrontation with knowledge or process, and is entirely free of evolutionary concepts.

Opportunism and optimality

It is a notable feature of Williamson's analysis, which he has emphasised himself, that the absence of trust is the general case; and so his is presented as a general theory. Market incentives are high-powered because they appeal to self-interest, and self-interest leads people to take whatever advantages are on offer, by the most effective means available. Thus perceived opportunities are always exploited, even if the exploitation involves 'making self-disbelieved promises' or any other form of 'self-interest seeking with guile'. This insistence on opportunism accords well with contemporary North American economics. In particular, it provides a natural link to principal-agent and property-rights theories of the firm, which are the principal alternatives to transaction cost explanations, though in these theories it is asymmetric information, rather than uncertainty and bounded rationality, that offers scope for opportunism (Conlisk 1996: 690–1).

Coase (1991b: 58) does not accept the analytical significance of opportunism for transaction cost theory. He tells us that he considered including it (in the form of fraud) as a reason for firms, but could find no basis for a general presumption that it could be more readily avoided in firms than through interfirm relationships. As we have already noted, he was not thinking in terms of perfect markets, but allowed for continuing interactions, in which the evolution of relationships was more important than the specificity of contracts. Though General Motors acquired Fisher Body, it had no difficulty in working closely with its supplier of car frames, A. O. Smith (Coase 1991c: 71–2). What underlies this difference with Williamson is a difference in focus: Williamson's is on incentives, but Coase's is on incomplete and dispersed knowledge – the need to discover prices and potential trading partners and the need to make provision for future decisions without knowing what those decisions will be. For Williamson, the incompleteness of contracts brings the threat of opportunism; for Coase it creates the opportunity for flexibility.

In an important sense, Coase's analysis of 1937 is still little used. What is used instead is what might be called Williamson's neoclassical synthesis, which in one crucial respect resembles the neoclassical synthesis which enveloped Keynes' *General Theory* (1936). Just as the impossibility of adequate knowledge of the future that motivated the search for liquidity and excluded the possibility of rational long-term expectations in Keynes' theory had to be replaced by a system of rational choices which were frustrated by rigidities, so the problems of future knowledge on which Coase (1937, reprinted in Coase 1988: 39–40) relied have been replaced by the rational choices of incentive-compatible structures which result from inadequate knowledge and apparently neutralise its inadequacies. This synthesis has been extremely successful; indeed it is a model of innovation, and demonstrates the fundamental principle that novelty must be carried by continuity.

Williamson challenges one of the strongest policy implications of price-theoretic industrial organisation by offering a novel – and undeniably valuable – explanation for vertical integration: instead of a monopolistic move, leading to market failure and inviting government intervention, it is often an efficient response to market failure, produced by the economic system itself. Not only is Williamson's work, as he insists, within the 'efficiency branch'; it carries the implication that governance structures will always be adjusted to support the requirements of productive efficiency – notably that when the most efficient technique requires dedicated assets, whatever organisational arrangements are necessary to ensure that those dedicated assets are made available will be forthcoming. Consequently economists who wish to confine themselves to the modelling of production in standard ways can feel confident in the applicability of their results.

However, as in the macroeconomic neoclassical synthesis, there is a snag, which is immediately visible by comparison with agency and property rights theories.

The current working hypothesis is that the privately owned firm arises to solve the shirking-information problem of joint production, and that a firm is simply a set of contracts among the individuals who participate in a business: owners of firm-specific assets, managers, employees, creditors, and others.

(De Alessi 1996: 345)

As much as possible is specified in these contracts, and the rights to make decisions in contingencies which have not been specified are allocated to the owners of those assets, the deployment of which is most important to the profitability of the business. The choice between rules and discretion is thus resolved by confining discretion to those whose discretion has the most impact and providing them with the incentives, through their right to a share in the surplus, to use their discretion to maximise that surplus, leaving everyone else to observe contractually-specified rules. No-one has any power to give orders, for no orders are necessary: the contract plus the designated right to make whatever profit-maximising decisions become necessary are sufficient to close the system (Hart 1995: 160–4) – provided, as Hart (ibid.: 166) notes, that those who own the assets personally manage them, which might be thought a significant proviso in modern economies.

The advantage of this formulation, from a neoclassical perspective, is that firms are thereby assimilated to what purport to be markets: all economic relationships are contractual relationships. This Williamson (1996: 149) has consistently and explicitly refused to accept: a hierarchy is not a contractual relationship, even though it may be created by contract, but a mechanism of post-contractual governance, to handle issues that can neither be adequately defined in complex contracts which are necessarily incomplete, nor resolved by allocating the right to make crucial decisions to the owners of critical assets. He agrees with Coase (1937, reprinted in Coase 1988: 36) that 'the distinguishing mark of the firm is the supersession of the price mechanism', and he consequently takes administrative arrangements far more seriously than do agency and property rights theorists. Thus he rejects the famous claim by Alchian and Demsetz (1972: 777), about which Demsetz himself is no longer confident, that the firm 'has no power of fiat, no authority, no disciplinary action any different in the slightest degree from ordinary market contracting between any two people'; inside firms principals have the power, within the limits discussed by Barnard (1938), to decide, without negotiation, what agents should do. This is the aspect of Williamson's work which is clearly not neoclassical, and allows us to distinguish his variant of transaction cost theory from that which relies on contracts and the ownership of critical assets. His emphasis on the post-contractual management of relationships brings him into contact with the institutions of procedural rationality, and even with Barnard's institutions of non-logical decision making; but he is unwilling to admit such institutions into his analysis of precontractual choice. Coase's (1988: 6) recognition of the ubiquity of transaction costs implies that they should be admitted.

For Coase as for Marshall – though Coase does not make the connection – a firm is a way of organising knowledge. This is what makes the lack of mutual recognition between Coase and Hayek so surprising. Williamson is essentially a theorist of economic agency, distinguished by his willingness to consider direct control of agents. All orthodox microeconomics is essentially a theory of economic agency, since all producers are agents of the consumer, and the central problem of economic theory is to design efficient incentives for people who are ruthlessly self-interested. Coase (1991a: 38) recalls his teacher Arnold Plant speaking of the consumer as the 'ultimate employer'; but he was not inspired to think in terms of agency models, which require knowledge to be asymmetric but always in principle sufficient for costless optimisation through the exchange of property rights. Coase knew that arranging market transactions can be costly even if good faith is never in question.

Transactions and activities

Williamson's theory may also be distinguished from Coase's by his treatment of production. Coase (1937) introduced his original article by referring to the firm's role in co-ordinating production, and in 1970 was asking for more attention to the scope of firms' activities, with no special emphasis on vertical integration (Coase 1972), while Williamson takes vertical integration as the focus of his analysis in presenting the firm as a device to prevent opportunism, or the fear of opportunism, leading to inefficient allocations. Williamson reminds us from time to time that a comparison of institutions must include both transaction and production costs, and justifies his own neglect of the latter with the argument that they have been thoroughly analysed. In practice he assumes that the two parts of the comparison can be kept separate; the same conditions of production, summarised by a production function, obtain within markets as in hierarchies. As in microeconomic theory, production functions are independent of their institutional setting; the discussion of production remains, as Robbins wished, an integral part of the theory of equilibrium. But we now have a dichotomy as remarkable as that embodied in the assumption that production is costly but exchange is not, which Coase objected to; for in the analytical systems of Williamson and the agency and property rights theorists '[a]lthough information is treated as being costly for transaction or management control purposes, it is implicitly presumed to be free for production purposes. What one firm can produce, another can produce equally well' (Demsetz 1988: 150).

We have argued in the previous chapter that production consists of a series of activities, which are not adequately represented by production functions, and which have to be linked together in an appropriate way. Coase, Williamson, Hart and others argue that the market linkages which have long characterised microeconomic theory are not always adequate and that some other means may sometimes be preferable, though, as we have noted, they do not agree whether these means should include non-contractual linkages. What we should now note is that transacting, operating a hierarchy, agreeing property rights, and exercising discretion are all themselves activities. (A glance at the number of businesses whose main activity is transacting should provide evidence enough.) Now activities require capabilities, and capabilities are problematic. Though he does not give adequate weight to 'knowledge how', Demsetz (1988: 158) is right to insist that '[e]conomic organization, including the firm, must reflect the fact that knowledge is costly to produce, maintain, and use. In all these respects there are economies to be gained through specialization.' The benefits of the division of labour apply to transacting and governance skills, which are indirect 'knowledge how', as well as to productive skills: the cost of transacting, or of operating a business, depends on who is doing the job. Demsetz (ibid.: 151) exposes a weakness in transaction cost theories by pointing out that 'the same organizing activities often characterize exchange *and* management', but (as he would presumably agree) that does not imply that any specific individual will be equally skilful at both. Williamson has occasionally hinted that management is an activity: before he focused so sharply on incentives he wrote of adaptations being 'accomplished by administrative processes in a sequential fashion' (Williamson 1975: 9), and his more recent formulation of the principle of aligning 'transactions, which differ in their attributes, with governance structures, which differ in their costs and competences' (Williamson 1996: 311) hints at the relevance of capabilities; specialised assets, by contrast, appear to be precisely the kind of factor that one would find in a production function.

In the Arrow–Debreu system there are good analytical reasons why markets open once only; but it is not at all obvious why transaction cost analysis should also close with the initial choice of organisational form, since the expectation is clearly of a series of decisions about future activities. As that analysis is crucially dependent on incomplete knowledge, it seems peculiarly inappropriate not to consider the possible implications of changing knowledge, especially when the relationship must generate knowledge about the participants. The argument in the preceding chapter that capabilities require a process analysis strengthens the case. As we begin to think about the process of managing transactions, we may be led to consider whether the individual transaction should be replaced as the unit of analysis by the transaction capability which is relevant to a class of transactions. This capability, which should be distinguished from the transactions that it makes possible, can be developed by deliberate investment, as well as the incidental investment which is called experience.

From this perspective, transaction costs do not offer an alternative theory of industrial organisation to that based on capabilities but provide an extension of it in which particular attention is given to the indirect capabilities that were discussed in the preceding chapter. There is no need to choose between a production basis and a transaction basis; the cognitive potential and the cognitive limitations of human beings imply that economic development results from the division of labour, which requires both productive and transaction capabilities, and contributes directly to the development of both.

We may therefore agree with Williamson (1996: 50) that 'the boundary of the firm ought to be set with reference to the capacity of the firm (compared with the market) to provide useful organizational functions', but not with his conclusion that this requires an organisational theory to set alongside a technological theory. Nor should we accept his conception of what these organisational functions should be: his assertion, in a criticism of Demsetz, that 'the study of contract and organization is economically uninteresting in a world of zero opportunism (where engineers would suffice)' (Williamson 1997: 130) seems to reveal a fundamental lack of understanding of what firms (and markets, for that matter) do and of the fundamental problems of human living. The costs which Coase identified are those of finding, interpreting, and using knowledge, and in particular knowledge of future possibilities and capabilities, with which we have been concerned throughout this book. The institutions of firms and markets which provide a setting for evolutionary processes, as well as being themselves subject to evolution, do contribute to the management of opportunism, but that is not their primary function. Coase was much nearer the mark in calling his Nobel Prize address 'The institutional structure of production' (Coase 1991d); and that is what we shall consider in the next chapter.

6

ECONOMIC ORGANISATION

The purposes of organisation

It is arguable that Coase (1937) actually posed his original question the wrong way round: rather than explaining firms as organisations which economise on market transactions, it may be more enlightening to use firms to explain markets. But the most enlightening approach of all may be to continue the line of argument of the first four chapters. Knowledge is irretrievably incomplete, but new knowledge can be created; it is also irretrievably dispersed, and the principal means of increasing it is through the division of labour, which increases the dispersion. People must therefore develop capabilities which will help them to cope with what cannot be predicted, and which will help them to make use of other people's knowledge. If it were not for the effectiveness of specialisation in generating capabilities, thereby exploiting the potential of the human brain while circumventing its limitations, we could all be substantially self-sufficient; then we would undertake few transactions, and would therefore incur few transaction or governance costs. But there is no way that knowledge, especially the 'knowledge how' that is required to deliver a well-balanced set of activities, can all be collected in one centre, or understood by any one cohesive group of people. The indirect capabilities that are required to co-ordinate activities are themselves dispersed. This is 'the really central problem of economics as a social science' (Hayek 1937: 49).

However, as Hayek came to realise, this specification does not match the normal definition of the co-ordination problem in economics. Not only is the application of knowledge a continuous process which must be managed by many individuals in situations which are never completely understood; a major purpose of co-ordination is to enhance, or at least maintain, the performance of the economy as a knowledge generator; and that requires the creation and testing of novel conjectures – and also, since all knowledge is provisional, the continued testing of currently accepted conjectures. Both of these tasks require the co-ordination of capabilities as well as activities: the former to create and maintain the potential to cope with a range of possibilities, the latter to improve the scope and quality of the combinations of productive services that are deployed. As Marshall (1920: 241) saw, both the pattern of specialisation and the relationships between specialists have decisive influences on the performance of an economic system; greater differentiation must be balanced by greater integration, but without destroying the generation of variety on which the selection processes in the economy can work.

In orthodox economics, variety, and especially novelty, appear as the enemy of efficient co-ordination; variety which is not predictable even appears as the enemy of rationality. In evolving economies, however, variety and novelty are essential, and co-ordination therefore requires an appropriate set of transaction and governance capabilities and an appropriate mix of institutions to constrain the decision space. This appropriate mix includes both differentiated local classification systems and procedures to provide different groups with distinctive ways of closing their cognitive models, and a broader set of general rules and procedures which will maintain compatibility between these differently evolving paths of knowledge. Marshall's (1920: 139) identification of three forms of industrial organisation which aid knowledge – 'that of a single business, that of various businesses in the same trade, that of various trades relatively to one another' – distinguishes three institutional settings which contribute to this evolutionary process of creating stable environments and stable relationships to facilitate change. Beyond these are the institutions which guide the practices of a community and which facilitate transactions between members of that community. There are many such communities, often overlapping, and correspondingly many clusters of institutions. All these institutional constraints develop over time, and all help those who observe them to develop their own transaction and governance capabilities and thus reduce transaction and governance costs.

However, it is necessary to take seriously the formal proposition that what matters is the sum of production and transaction or governance costs, because the reduction in production costs which can be achieved by abandoning self-sufficiency necessarily entails the acceptance of otherwise avoidable costs of co-ordination. We may expect that entrepreneurs will seek to minimise the costs of developing and using their chosen modes of transaction and governance; but their choice of mode is intended, not to minimise the costs of these activities but to maximise net benefits, like all reasoned choices. As Neil Kay (1997: 37) points out, transaction cost economics neglects value considerations. The creation of productive capabilities, through the dynamic processes of increased specialisation and learning by doing which mediate Marshall's increasing return, often justifies additional costs in co-ordinating these specialised activities and in extending markets in order to relax the constraints on the division of labour. Chandler (1977, 1990) has provided abundant evidence of this process in action. His central theme is that it has been the triple investment in production, marketing, and management which has given large firms their advantages in many industries, an investment which does not seem explicable by any theory of transaction cost minimisation, and especially not by one which assumes that the only reason for increasing the scope of a firm is to prevent the frustration by opportunism, or the threat of opportunism, of the productive efficiencies which are technically accessible in any transaction mode. That seems to explain why Chandler (1992) has become less enthusiastic about transaction cost theory; the choice of organisational arrangements is indeed crucial, but for its effects on production as well as transaction costs.

Because of the effects of organisation, both internal and external, on the development of production capabilities, reductions in the cost of particular transaction and governance activities need not mean a reduction in the total amount of transaction and governance costs within an economy. Transaction and governance capabilities, like other capabilities, may be developed by specialisation, and the greater these capabilities, the finer the division of labour that can be afforded. If the division of labour is limited by the extent of the market, the extent of each market is limited by the transaction capabilities of those who use that market, and especially of those who develop the institutions of that market, as we shall see in the following chapter. If the costs of individual transactions in a market can be reduced, then the volume of transactions may respond sufficiently to increase the total quantity of resources that is devoted to transactions; and if further division of productive labour leads to increased productive capabilities, and so to lower prices, it is perfectly possible that the total share of economic activities accounted for by transactions and governance may increase. Indeed, this is what seems to have happened. Though there have been great improvements over the last two centuries in transactional efficiency as people have developed new transaction capabilities, the share of national income which is accounted for by transactional and governance activity, in a broad sense which includes the supply of information on past and possible future transactions, has clearly increased. Instead of considering transaction costs and capabilities as alternative explanations of the organisation of economic activities, we may do better by combining them in an institutional and evolutionary economics of incomplete but augmentable knowledge.

The capabilities of the firm

In 1931, or even in 1937, Coase could not be expected to be familiar with the concept of efficient intertemporal allocation, as Hayek was; but he did recognise the obvious problem of making provision for an unpredictable future. Carl Menger (1976 [1871]: 82–3) had already identified a general response to this problem in the creation of reserves, and offered fire extinguishers and medicine chests as examples; but Menger's particular concern was to explain the emergence of money – purchasing power which could be deployed at will, and which therefore provided, as Shackle (1972: 160) was to put it a century later, 'the means by which choice can be deferred until a later and better informed time'. Now anyone who makes a long-term contract which includes the right 'to specify what the other contracting party is expected to do' (Coase 1937 (reprinted in Coase 1988: 40)) is also creating a means by which choice can be deferred to a later and better informed time. This means of deferring choice Coase calls a firm. Thus firms and money are alternative means of preparing for an uncertain future (Loasby 1976: 65; Laidler 1990: 22).

This is not the occasion for an extensive comparison between money and firms as economic institutions; but it is relevant to note that money is used in markets, because of its transaction advantages over barter, and that it offers a wider range of options than a firm. This suggests that a comparison of transaction modes should include their particular benefits as well as their costs. Menger's discussion of reserves provides the clue. It is not, in general, a good idea to wait for a medical emergency or an outbreak of fire before deciding what to buy in order to deal with it; and a firm provides the means of reacting quickly to a particular (if often ill-defined) set of problems or opportunities. This is exactly the argument that Coase (1937 (reprinted in Coase 1988: 39–40)) makes: when the future services required can be expressed in general terms, but the choice between alternative realisations cannot yet be sensibly made, then an imperfectly specified contract giving control over the relevant capabilities may be the lowest cost option. What Coase does not say, but is a natural deduction from his emphasis on the problems of knowledge, is that the continuing direction of these capabilities is likely to improve both the productive and managerial skills available to the firm. Creating a firm may thus be the high value option.

Coase was therefore mistaken in explaining the choice between market and firm solely in terms of costs; this mistake was remedied by Penrose, whose conception of the firm as 'a pool of resources the utilisation of which is organised in an administrative framework' (Penrose 1959, 1995: 149), though unquestionably Penrose's own inspiration, seems in retrospect to be a natural development of Coase's idea. The focus of this definition is on capabilities, both direct and indirect; indeed the modern conception of the firm as a set of capabilities is no less Penrose's creation than transaction cost theory is Coase's. The firm is 'an autonomous administrative planning unit, the activities of which are interrelated' (Penrose 1959, 1995: 15), and its boundaries are defined by its 'area of "authoritative communication"', a phrase which Penrose (1959, 1995: 20) adopted from Barnard (1938) precisely because it incorporated informal as well as formal communications.

Penrose's work, like Coase's, was for many years little used, and not often cited. The increasing recognition of its importance seems to have resulted partly from a growing interest in the role of the firm in technical change, exemplified by Nelson and Winter (1982), but perhaps even more from the desire of writers on business strategy to find some recipe for exceptional profits which does not depend on welfare-reducing monopoly advantages. Yet the fundamental role of Penrose in this theoretical development creates a puzzle in the filiation of ideas; for Penrose's definition fits very well Marshall's (1920: 138–9) conception of the firm as one of the forms of organisation which aid knowledge; and Marshall's theory of economic development through the growth of knowledge was explicitly derived from Adam Smith. But Penrose, having learnt Marshall's equilibrium model of the firm – which does not exist – produced her own theory quite independently.

All knowledge requires a framework; in order to develop factual, theoretical or practical knowledge, we must limit our ambitions. As Adam Smith saw, specialisation is a condition of progress; but if it is to deliver progress, the specialised activities must be integrated, and any close integration requires compatibility between the frameworks that are being used. A viable firm provides a particular set of compatible frameworks within which people can pursue their specialism without the need for continual clarification and negotiation, thus reducing the costs of individual transactions. As Benedicte Reynaud (1996b: 14) has said, 'it is the distributed knowledge among workers, and not their shared knowledge', that provides the basis for organisational effectiveness. The combination of direct and indirect capabilities that enables the members of a firm to produce their particular range of outputs is not directly accessible to any single person (Winter 1991: 185), because of the fundamental cognitive limitations discussed in Chapter 3. 'Knowledge how' is 'embedded in the social practices of a community' (Boehm 1994: 162), and firms draw on such practices to create environments which facilitate the embedding of complementary structures of capabilities.

Penrose (1995: xiii) insists that 'growth is an evolutionary process and based on the cumulative growth of collective knowledge, in the context of a purposive firm'; and any theory of this process requires a definition of a firm with 'insides' (ibid.: xi) – which cannot be found among transaction cost, agency, or property rights theories. 'It is the heterogeneity...of the productive services available or potentially available from its resources that give each firm its unique character' (Penrose 1959, 1995: 75). Firms are clusters of differentiated knowledge, and the incompletely specified contracts by which each firm is constituted allows some choice of closure. The different realisations of these dispositions, to use Ryle's (1949) term, and the effects of these realisations on the capabilities that are available within each firm, trace out the growth paths of these firms. Penrose emphasises the 'receding managerial limit', which recedes because governance skills improve; her explicit discussion of the need to invest in new areas of governance is an unintentional echo of Marshall, which has not been heard by many of those who espouse equilibrium models of transactions and governance. Productive skills receive less explicit attention, but the rate and direction of growth of each firm clearly depend on what can be produced as well as on what can be managed.

The conventional but problematic concept of knowledge as a public good makes important issues undiscussable, as does the central conception of macroeconomics according to Hahn and Solow, Laidler and Leijonhufvud. Coase explains how a firm can provide privileged access to knowledge, and Penrose how it can provide the framework for a local discovery procedure, based on manageable units of knowledge, that develops capabilities which can be most effectively used within the context of discovery. Because the growth of knowledge, especially of 'knowledge how', is stimulated by the interpretation of experience, the productive activities of the members of a firm, including their interactions, constitute an interlocking set of experiments: running a business helps to develop the knowledge with which to run that business better. This was a view shared by Marshall and Penrose; Marshall's (1920) 'Principle of Substitution' was a principle of experimentation, and part of the normal task of management (see Loasby 1990), and in Penrose's (1959, 1995) theory the use of a firm's resources was the means to augment those resources. Opportunism plays no part in this basic explanation, though it needs to be considered in any comprehensive theory.

This changing stock of capabilities may be interpreted in Austrian fashion, as a firm-specific structure of complementary capitals, created through repeated interactions, distributed through the organisation, and oriented towards a range of possible futures; it provides the firm with flexibility within imperfectly specified and receding constraints. (The connection with the human capital explanation of internal labour markets will only be signalled in this book.) The structure, and each element within it, is shaped – though not determined – by the past sequence of events and the responses to them within the firm; it therefore embodies the logic of appropriateness that is the working principle of Marshall's first-stage model of the brain and of the specialised adaptations that have emerged from the course of human evolution. Its orientation, however, is decided by the firm's 'productive opportunity' (Penrose 1959, 1995: 31), and this embodies the logic of consequence – of the imagined, deemed possible.

Firms vary in the relative emphasis that they place on discovery and current performance; but all construe phenomena with the aid of interpretative frameworks (Kelly 1963), which have been created and refined during the firm's history. This history is therefore reflected in the firm's current stock of direct and indirect capabilities – what each member of the firm knows how to do, and what the firm as an organisation can accomplish even though no single person can give an adequate account of how it is done. The delivery of goods and services depends on the development and co-ordination of complementary capabilities, which are likely to depend on different ways, both tacit and conscious, of organising knowledge; thus co-ordination requires compatibility of routines, frameworks, and decision premises while the continued growth of knowledge is stimulated by the differences between them.

Data constitutes information only when it is sorted into categories; thus different classification systems generate different information. All informa-tion systems assume that we know what it is that we need to know, and are liable to be redesigned in order to prevent a repetition of the most recent disaster. The significance of information depends on the context, which is formed by the organisational structure and the links that are formed with outside parties; and what receives attention within this context is influenced by such focusing devices as the management control and reward system. Some diversity of interpretation is an aid to learning: the role of the critic in drawing attention to other possibilities may avoid both misjudged novelty (Van de Ven and Grazman 1997) and the suppression of useful knowledge. The balance between expertise in productive efficiency and in labour relations contributed to the development of W. H. Smith's capabilities in managing their internal distribution system (Loasby 1973), and a major chemical company included an official 'saboteur' in the design team for each chemical plant as a means of forcing attention to safety.

However, as economists, we should always be on the lookout for oppor-tunity costs. The opportunity costs of agreement on 'how we do things around here' are twofold: the neglect of other possible ways of doing things, and the use of familiar ways where they are not appropriate. That is why methodological choices can have real effects, in business and politics as well as in academic disciplines. There are good reasons why the interpretation of organisational experience may be in error, such as the uncontrollable variability of the environment, the limited variety of the experience that is being interpreted, and the complexity of organisational behaviour which makes the identification of causality doubtful (Levitt and March 1995). As we see, firms, like people, repeatedly discover that their knowledge is false, their capabilities inadequate for the activities that they undertake, and the opportunities that they pursue fictions. The likelihood of error is inherent in evolutionary processes.

Hence the importance of variety, in academic disciplines and in the economy: an industry which meets the conditions for perfect competition is unlikely to be innovative, for it lacks the differentiation of frameworks which is normally a condition of innovation (Levinthal 1996). Within a single autonomous planning unit, seeking to allocate resources in a logically coherent manner, the preservation of variety is not easy. This is fundamen-tally a cognitive problem; very few of us are able to maintain multiple and conflicting ways of thinking, and it becomes no easier if we have to function effectively within a working group. In adding Darwin to Smith, Marshall recognised the importance of the division of labour within, as well as between specialisms; the tendency to variation which he identified as a chief cause of progress (Marshall 1920: 355) required multi-firm industries, in which entrepreneurs had different experiences and thought somewhat differently. He also recognised that in economic evolution, each firm could select from the experiences of others, especially, but not only, within industrial districts.

In practice, firms in the same industry do typically use somewhat different frameworks. Indeed, this is a common source of problems following a merger; and the resolution of these problems may destroy distinctive capabilities. Penrose explains how the particular history of each firm, as interpreted within its administrative framework, tends to maintain this necessary variety. Evolutionary economics is stronger on selection and replication than on the generation of the variety which makes selection and replication of interest; Penrose's theory helps to restore the balance. She has little to say about the selection of firms, but a good deal to say about the selection that goes on within firms. Variety generation is itself a selection process, and it is important that the criteria and processes of selection should vary between firms.

The scope of the firm

What constrains the firm's range was an important question for Coase (1972 (reprinted in Coase 1988: 63)), who reminds us that 'the costs of organizing an activity within any given firm depend on what other activities the firm is engaged in. A given set of activities will facilitate the carrying out of some activities but hinder the carrying out of others.' Coase appears to have been thinking of what are now called governance costs; but from the perspective of capability theory we should expect these interdependencies to affect production costs, through the compatibility of skills, as well. The carrying out of activities depends on both productive and governance capabilities; Williamson's 'separation theorem', that production and transaction costs may be analysed independently, looks dubious – like most separation theorems in economics outside the models of Walrasian competition.

Coase (1972, reprinted in Coase 1988: 73–4) suggested a 'direct approach' to the problem by attempting 'to discover the characteristics of the groupings of activities within firms'. This was precisely the theme of an article published in the same year as Coase's proposal, which has been increasingly both cited and used. Richardson (1972: 888) combined his experience with the UK Monopolies Commission and Penrose's work to argue, as we noted at the beginning of Chapter 4, that the grouping of activities in an economy was to be explained primarily by the relationship between the capabilities necessary to undertake them. He distinguished between similar activities, which draw on similar capabilities, and therefore offer potential economies of scope for a single business, and complementary activities, which need to be integrated. What is complementary may also be similar, and if so, the case for integration is straightforward. If complementary activities are not similar, but the relationship is standardised (the 'ideal type' is a modular system) then they are best left to separate organisations with appropriately specialised capabilities and handled by market transactions. The differentiation of knowledge implies limits to the scope of each differentiated system. (This proposition may be read in, or perhaps read into, Coase's original article.)

However, some activities are so closely complementary that they may need to be planned and managed in concert: if they are also similar, then the case for vertical integration, in order to provide a common framework for developing interdependent skills, may be very strong, even if opportunism is not an issue. But if they are not similar, vertical integration may not be a good answer, even if opportunism is a possibility. Hart (1995: 163–4) concludes his discussion of the relationship between General Motors and Fisher Body by asserting that '[o]ne thing we can be sure of is that if GM and Fisher assets are sufficiently complementary, and initial contracts sufficiently incomplete, the two sets of assets should be under common control', generalising this to the proposition that 'highly complementary assets should be owned in common'. But like other economists who are fascinated by the incentive consequences of distributed knowledge and ignore the problems of co-ordinating and developing such knowledge, Hart is solving a secondary problem. Different kinds of knowledge are differently ordered, with different frameworks and different codes; attempts to impose common standards may not only generate high governance costs but also frustrate the continued development of capabilities. Opportunism may be prevented, but the business may decay; this is not an uncommon story. Even worse, a firm which takes on a business which it does not understand may find that even the control of opportunism is impossible, as several financial institutions, who claim distinctive expertise in performance appraisal, have discovered. A working relationship between formally separate businesses, however cumbersome, may be the best available method of developing and applying closely complementary capabilities which are very dissimilar (N. M. Kay 1998). The recent proliferation of joint ventures demonstrates a willingness to incur the additional costs of managing interfirm relationships in the hope of developing important new capabilities (Zajac and Olsen 1993).

Within the confined rationality of economics, opportunism is indispensable to an explanation of firms; but Coase's visits to firms convinced him that in practice it was not (Coase 1991c: 70–72). By his account, the activities of General Motors and A. O. Smith were both closely complementary and dissimilar, and the extent of vertical integration in the motor industry has for many years been falling as a consequence of the search for improved specialist capabilities. The counterpart of integration is the separation of ways of organising knowledge that do not fit together; Arrow's interest in the problems of coding knowledge led him to recognise the degradation of performance that can so easily result from inappropriate or incompatible codes (Arrow 1974: 57–8). Knowledge should take analytical priority over incentives in explaining the organisation of industry. By respecting this priority Richardson was able to explain 'the dense network of co-operation and affiliation by which firms are inter-related' (Richardson 1972: 883) as a response to 'the need to co-ordinate closely complementary but dissimilar activities' (ibid.: 892).

Wherever its boundary is drawn, every firm will be dependent on the capabilities of other people, to provide inputs or to connect it with its eventual customers, or usually both. Richardson recognises that the distinction between market transaction and internal governance is no more than the starting point for analysis; 'what confronts us is a continuum passing from transactions, such as those on organised commodity markets, where the co-operative element is minimal, through intermediate areas in which there are linkages of traditional connection and goodwill, and finally to those complex and inter-locking clusters, groups and alliances which represent co-operation fully and formally developed' (ibid.: 887). Many of the capabilities which a firm requires must be left outside its control if they are to continue to develop. Capabilities must remain distributed; what the firm needs is access to these capabilities. Cohen and Levinthal (1989) have drawn attention to the role of research departments in identifying and importing knowledge; but all firms, and all individuals, require absorptive capacity if they are to make good use of capabilities and of information which is generated elsewhere. They need to make connections to the institutional structures which frame other systems of knowledge; and that requires an interpretative framework which is permeable to other ways of thinking (Kelly 1963: 77–82). Money may buy technology; it does not buy an understanding of technology and of the productive opportunities to which it can contribute. That was the flaw in Weinstock's strategy of accumulating cash within GEC instead of developing technologies about which he believed he could form no rational expectations.

In considering the firm as a set of capabilities (sometimes, significantly, described as an option set), some writers neglect the possibility of structuring capabilities within a network of firms. Lazonick (1992) exemplifies this neglect and the lack of balance which results. Langlois and Robertson (Langlois 1992a, 1992b; Langlois and Robertson 1995) have explored the relative advantages of control and access, and shown how the balance of these advantages may change over time, sometimes to the detriment of those who have been most effective in exploiting the existing structure. In general we would expect to find tighter constraints within a single firm than in a group of firms, which provide alternative ways of organising alternative capabilities. In those parts of an economy which most resemble a decomposable system, specialised knowledge is packaged in products which purchasers treat as black boxes and use according to familiar routines; competing producers of each product can then seek improvements according to their own ideas without requiring any change in anyone else's routines to accommodate them. Modular innovation is best served in an informally organised market (Langlois 1992a). But a substantial change in the principles of decomposition is likely to destroy the capabilities of such a market network, which in the face of such a change is likely to exhibit precisely the kind of rigidity which Schumpeter (1934: 80) attributed to a network of routines which could be modelled as the embodiment of rational choice.

The development of a new combination of closely integrated ideas – what Langlois (1992a) calls a 'systemic innovation' – is likely, as Schumpeter argued, to require the active management of a complex structure of complementary capabilities. In order to introduce moving assembly lines for the manufacture of parts Ford substituted direct control for continuing access to the routines of engineering firms which the new methods superseded. The problem was not the potential opportunism of Ford's suppliers, or the desire to secure rents from Ford's new knowledge, but the difficulty of changing the suppliers' conception of their own business, and persuading them of the obsolescence of many of their existing capabilities. Once Ford had spectacularly demonstrated the advantages of the new methods, independent parts suppliers began to adopt them; access to these suppliers then became the superior option for car manufacturers, because of the advantages of specialisation and the 'tendency to variation' which accompanies it (Langlois and Robertson 1989). The tighter constraints of integration facilitate the development of a single vision by suppressing doubts about its validity; the looser couplings of a network facilitate the exploration of an opportunity space that is widely recognised but not yet defined.

The management of transactions, within the firm, in its market relationships, and in its collaborations with other firms, is a set of activities which require distinctive capabilities. The development of such capabilities for a sub-class of such relationships – how to get things done within a particular kind of market, in a particular technological milieu, within a particular style of management – creates reserves which can be deployed to counteract a particular range of threats, or to exploit a particular range of opportunities, though what these ranges are can never be known for certain. In recent years some firms have made deliberate efforts to develop capabilities in joint venture management, which are then often used to develop further joint ventures either with the same partner or with other firms which have also undertaken joint ventures with that partner; such multiple collaborations exploit relation-specific knowledge how and also reduce the likelihood of opportunism (N. M. Kay 1997: 211–14). These indirect capabilities differ in both quality and scope between firms; and so transaction costs as well as production costs may be analysed as the product of capabilities which will be in varying degrees peculiar to each firm. Neither should be treated as technological data. In so far as they are peculiar they may be expected to provide each firm with barriers to entry, and also to exit.

The importance of developing and managing such relationships was recognised by Marshall (1920), who wrote of the capital invested in a firm's internal and external organisation, which, in our terms, reduces the costs of the chosen transaction mode and increases transaction capabilities, and emphasised the need to spend time in creating this investment. Reputations have to be earned, local institutions developed and skills practised in the varying circumstances of a trade. Learning by experimentation is continuous, and both internal and external organisations provide frameworks within which to learn. Internal organisation aids the development and application of firm-specific capabilities, and the corresponding danger of restricted and perhaps misaligned focus is mitigated by an external organisation which links different ways of understanding and provides information and ideas for continuous experimentation, thus generating a 'cross-firm economy of learning' (Nooteboom 1992: 292).

Marshall's 'industrial districts' were such cross-firm economies, and his discussion of them may be taken not only as an accurate exposition of one form of industrial organisation but also as a metaphor for Marshall's overall conception of the growth of knowledge through differentiation and integration. We can now also see the danger that interaction within a group of businesses in a single sector of industry may encourage too much integration of fundamental assumptions about the technology, markets, and organisational principles that are appropriate; a long history of successful interdependence may erect formidable obstacles to the questioning of implicit assumptions and consequential changes of framework that Argyris and Schön (1978) call 'double-loop learning'. Something similar may be true of 'industrial districts' which embrace whole economies. Eliasson (1996) presents a special case of this structure of complementary capabilities in the form of 'competence blocks' of high technology firms which are capable jointly of developing and producing highly complex products that no single firm (not to speak of a single individual) can understand, but which can be delivered by a combination of intrafirm and interfirm co-ordination, each element of which relies on locally-effective indirect capabilities. Multiple intersections of frameworks produce a network that is more heterogeneous than a single firm but less heterogeneous than a market. A successful competence block is also capable of receiving signals which indicate the need for changes both in the technology and in the patterns of co-ordination, and of responding appropriately, through a guided procedure of trial and error.

Eliasson realises that these capabilities are always problematic; the reinforcement of success easily becomes the pathway to failure (see also Levinthal 1997).

The realisation that distinctive capabilities may provide a sustained competitive advantage has provided a basis for strategy in which rent-seeking by firms takes the form of adding value rather than restricting competition. Because these distinctive capabilities are largely tacit, and embedded in idiosyncratic features of the firm's informal structures and interconnected patterns of behaviour, imitation may be difficult, even if rivals know what is worth imitating; and the causal ambiguity that is inherent in complex relationships with limited variety in behaviour is a substantial obstacle to identifying precisely where the sources of advantage lie, as was convincingly demonstrated in the lengthy debate over the characteristics of successful Japanese companies and the sustainability of their advantages. For the same reasons, it is not always at all easy even for those within a successful business to discover the reasons for this success. Strategic advice has been primarily directed at making the best use of distinctive capabilities, and has given relatively little attention to the problem of identifying what capabilities – or what combinations of capabilities – are distinctive and within what range of applications that distinctiveness matters, and even less to the problem of how capabilities can be created. John Kay (1993) explicitly confines his attention to the application of capabilities that are already established.

Even so, it is important to recognise, as Penrose (1959, 1995: 132–7) emphasises, the imperative of continued investment if the distinctiveness of capabilities is to be maintained. This investment is not only in physical capital, but also in the continuing growth of specific knowledge. 'The enterprise, by definition, must be capable of producing more or better than all the resources that comprise it....What is needed is a transmutation of the resources, [which] can only be human resources' (Drucker 1955: 12). The more diverse the areas of knowledge, the greater the difficulty both in supporting each kind of knowledge and in maintaining the kind of cohesion necessary to keep down the costs of governance, to produce sensible decisions, and to sustain a competitive advantage. We should also remember that capabilities will not yield profits unless they are continually linked to new productive opportunities. The value of a firm's capabilities is always determined in use; if no-one is interested in the goods or services that they are used to provide, they may be unique but will not produce rents. If they do not, firms may discover that their distinctive capabilities provide barriers to exit from unprofitable businesses.

It is also important to remember, as has already been noted, that every organisation depends on capabilities which it does not control; the continued availability of these capabilities should not be taken for granted. Finally, capabilities, like all other kinds of knowledge, are always conjectural, and conjectures are always open to falsification. Du Pont's postwar strategy of searching for new products that would be distinct from all its major contemporary businesses rested on the assumption that the company would be competent to develop whatever was discovered. But the company had never had such a capability. It had developed skills in product development that had given it a major advantage within certain fields, notably synthetic fibres; but these skills were not transferable to unrelated fields (Hounshell and Smith 1988). Capabilities provide a good basis for thinking about strategy, but they do not provide a golden key which will ensure that every firm will be better than all the others. We may, however, state as a general principle that governance and transaction modes should be appropriate not only to current activities but also to learning objectives.

Authority and trust

In Coase's explanation of the firm, the recognition that co-ordination within markets would require specific new contracts to be agreed at frequent intervals, in circumstances which cannot be precisely anticipated, suggests the possibility of a lower-cost alternative in a general 'agreement to agree', which includes a willingness by those accepting a contract of employment to accept the authority, within limits, of their employer; and Penrose, as we have noted, described the firm as an area of authoritative communication. To understand firms, we need to understand authority. Barnard (1938: 163) defined authority as 'the character of a communication in a formal organiza- tion by virtue of which it is accepted by a contributor to or "member" of the organization as governing the action he contributes', and reinforced this definition by declaring, as we observed in Chapter 3, that 'the decision as to whether an order has authority or not lies with the persons to whom it is addressed' – and not least, as he notes with a supporting quotation, in an army. Inducing contributors to accept one's authority is for Barnard one of the most important functions of a Chief Executive, as of a commanding general. His conception of a 'zone of indifference' within which communi- cations will be accepted as authoritative (Barnard 1938: 163) gives substantive content to Coase's (1937 (reprinted in Coase 1988: 40)) recognition of a range of acceptable instructions.

Ménard (1994) has pointed out that authority, in Barnard's sense of accepting a communication as governing one's action, is not necessarily associated with hierarchy, even within a formal organisation; and Barnard's definition explicitly includes those outside the organisation who contribute to its effective performance. People have authority within a certain sphere if others are 'prepared to take their word for it' within that sphere. It is not unknown for subordinates to ignore or evade messages from superiors; but nor is it unknown for people to accept without question messages from people with whom they have no formal relationship, or who indeed may be subordinates – to treat these messages as authoritative.

In organisations of any complexity, the quality of performance depends on the knowledge and skills which are distributed within that organisation, and which cannot be encompassed by any single member, or group of members, whatever their formal status – just as the performance of a market economy depends on the knowledge and skill distributed within that economy. This knowledge and skill cannot be effectively harnessed unless everyone, including the Chief Executive, is willing to accept without question most of what they are told by people in other parts of the organisation, and even by their own subordinates. As Ménard argues, organisational cohesion is heavily dependent on the flow of authority, in this sense, across and up, as well as down, the hierarchy, which requires intersecting zones of indifference. Credible messages are vital to the efficient functioning of a business; they allow people to focus on the performance of specific activities, and on the improvement of that performance.

Economies are stabilised by their institutions, and each firm is stabilised by its interconnected structure of procedural rationality (Simon 1982, vol. 2: 389–91), which is a network of communications that are generally accepted as authoritative by their recipients. Only by accepting the authority of most communications can each contributor to an organisation keep the cognitive load within bounds. Some questioning is essential to innovation; much questioning leads to individual disorientation and organisational collapse. In formal organisations, each member is assigned to a role which 'is a social prescription of some, but not all, of the premises that enter into an individual's choice of behaviours' (ibid.: 345). Shared decision premises encourage people to close their models in compatible ways, and thus facilitate the co-ordination of activities and the growth of knowledge. The degree of freedom that is left to the individual, of course, varies greatly between prescriptions; and it is one of the most important tasks of those in charge of a business to achieve a set of prescriptions which is appropriate to that business in its particular environment.

We should note that the willingness to accept such a role depends not only on the inducements which are offered but also on the perceived convenience of a ready-made framework for defining problems and seeking appropriate solutions. As we have seen in Chapter 3, it is often much less trouble to accept someone else's framework rather than invent one's own, and so accepting the authority of communications within a firm, whether from a superior or from someone who may be presumed to have relevant specialist knowledge of another part of the business, requires no distinctive explanation. Simon (1992: 6) has suggested that people may be encouraged to join an organisation because they can then accept the organisational definition of problems as their own and consequently know, without deliberation, what they should be thinking about. Their motivation is derived from their cognitive needs. We should not be surprised at the willingness to accept authority that has often been demonstrated in experimental and practical situations, since the acceptance of authority is an essential element in the solution of our personal problems. It is a response to the limitations of human knowledge and human cognition. The division of labour, by reducing the scope of our direct access to knowledge, aggravates these problems, but it does not create them.

The cognitive attractions of organisation membership not only tend to enlarge each individual's 'zone of indifference'; as Barnard (1938: 169–70) points out, they give each person an interest in the general acceptance of authority within the organisation in order to preserve the familiar institutional structure. This tacit agreement to preserve a tacit coalition, Barnard claims, explains the widespread acceptance of 'the fiction that authority comes down from above'. A beneficial consequence is that the attractions of opportunistic behaviour are often outweighed, or simply crowded out, by the attendant inconveniences. In a study of a maintenance workshop, Reynaud (1996a) reports that workers generally followed rules even when this conflicted with their individual interests (as conventionally defined, without reference to cognition costs). We often act in the interests of others when we might at little risk have pursued our own different interest simply because it is so much easier to follow familiar procedures. The pathology of this acceptance of authority is 'x-inefficiency' (Leibenstein 1976). In order to maintain the organisational truce, people are willing to accept communications, even from subordinates, which they know very well are obstacles to effective performance. They will be careful not to draw attention to these obstacles, and they will avoid any suggestion that there is a deficiency in the system. The undiscussability of the pathology becomes itself undiscussable. As a consequence, programmes for fundamental change, such as total quality management, may become useful routines for detailed improvement, but inhibit the transformations which they are (sometimes) intended to deliver (Argyris 1994).

It is not only within formal organisations that we cannot escape the necessity of allowing other people's conventions and other people's communications to constrain and direct many of our actions; we may decline to accept the authority of many such conventions and communications, but to deny authority to all is hardly conceivable. Even those whose professional business is the discovery of new truths, and the discarding of currently accepted ideas, must accept the authority of much established science. Academic disciplines develop categories for phenomena, methods of structuring problems and analytical techniques; and academic education is largely designed to induce students to accept these, in the dual belief that these decision premises will provide sufficient closure to focus attention and sufficient commonality to make communication easy. By operating within the shared routines of 'normal science', well-educated members of a discipline can therefore develop their capabilities, improving their objective knowledge and their know-how, and their knowledge of how to gain access to the objective knowledge and know-how of others. Much the same is true of a highly capable business.

The acceptance of authority is always provisional; but it does not depend only, or even mainly, on the terms of the contract. The authors of communications must, consciously or unconsciously, be continually acting to renew it; by the rhetoric of their actions as well as their words, collaborators and subordinates, even more than nominal superiors, must generate an adequate degree of trust among the recipients. In the co-ordination of human activities, trust is often not an alternative to authority but a precondition for its acceptance. Because North American economists have been so ready to assume that people will be opportunistic unless there is a clear incentive not to be, it seems natural to construe trust as the absence of any malicious intent or the discounted net value of creating or maintaining a reputation for fair dealing. Neither is relevant in the face of the immediate penalties of a perfectly competitive market; as Casson (1997: 121) observes '[c]ompetition is a low-trust mechanism'. But perfect competition is an analytical fiction, and Casson has been so impressed by the economic advantages of high-trust regimes, which do not have to bear the costs of constraining a perpetual search for opportunistic advantage, that he has given increasing attention to the effects of organisational culture on economic performance and to the role of the entrepreneur in developing appropriate cultures (Casson 1990, 1991, 1997).

Casson's 'high level entrepreneur' seems to combine two activities to which Adam Smith gave much attention: the imaginative creation of new connections which, in both science and industry, is the work of 'philosophers or men of speculation', and the reinforcement of moral sentiments. Casson (1997: 118) defines trust as 'a warranted belief that someone else will honour their obligations, not merely because of material incentives, but out of moral commitment too'. This, he claims, is a 'strictly rational approach to trust': rationality is preserved because moral commitment generates emotional rewards. Since economists abjure any enquiry into the sources of preference, they can have no rational objection to such a proposition; but many will not like it. What others may find somewhat disturbing is Casson's instrumentalist approach to trust, and indeed to the moral principles which underlie it. Casson (1997: 139) argues that 'the engineering of trust requires investment in moral rhetoric and social bonding' and that 'leadership can be employed as a form of intermediation to create...trust'. Adam Smith's theory of moral sentiments was not a prescription for the engineering of morality; and Arrow's (1974: 23) recognition that trust has 'a very important pragmatic value' is matched by a warning that it cannot be bought or secured by contract (ibid.: 26). Though Casson tries to adhere to the principles of efficient allocation, he is

ECONOMIC ORGANISATION

clearly uncomfortable about his engineering approach; he recognises the importance of character, and clearly believes that some people are more admirable than others, but finds difficulty in squaring his own beliefs with what he perceives to be the requirements of economic theory (Casson 1997: 98–9).

Whereas conventional economists argue that the lack of explicit knowledge makes opportunism possible, Dibben (1997) insists that this lack of knowledge makes trust indispensable. Moreover, since incompletable and ambiguous knowledge is the normal state, the need for trust is pervasive for anyone not living in complete isolation. The gaps in our knowledge can be filled only by making inferences about the quality (or authority) of the communications that we receive and making appropriate selections from them, and by formulating expectations about the future behaviour of other people. Dibben distinguishes between the basic disposition of a specific person to trust others, the general tendency to trust at a particular time, which is 'indirect knowledge that', based on the interpretation of past events, conjectural and fallible, and situational trust, which is a subjective perception, influenced both by general trust and by the history of a particular relationship, that helps to fill the gaps in an individual's knowledge on a specific occasion. The acceptance of another's good faith is an important way of simplifying decisions. Trust is an intrinsic part of cognitive processes, and cannot be completely understood outside that context.

Whether someone is to be trusted to do what is required does not depend only on incentives and moral principles; it also requires a judgement of capabilities. The first requirement for relying on other people's knowledge – before any consideration of opportunism becomes relevant – is evidence that this knowledge is both adequate and appropriate for one's particular purposes, and a firm provides a selection environment within which this evidence can be collected and assessed. The formal institutions of a firm also provide a basis for the development of informal relationships (or indirect capabilities), on which every organisation depends both for daily performance and for group learning. Casson recognises both the importance of capabilities and the difficulty of judging the capabilities of other organisations when explaining why a market-maker, who reduces transaction costs by creating a chain of trust which links customers with suppliers (Casson 1997: 88), may be unwilling to contract out production: 'even if he trusts the supplier's integrity, he may not trust in his competence' (ibid.: 94). We have emphasised in Chapter 4 that neither the quality nor the scope of any capability can be guaranteed; and decisions to extend or reduce the degree of vertical integration all involve some degree of novelty. As Langlois (1992a) observes, changes in industrial structure may be a response to changing distributions of relative capabilities: new activities may be internalised because established suppliers are not trusted to perform them satisfactorily, however conscientious they may be, or they may be externalised because outsiders are trusted to perform them better.

Trust is developed, or destroyed, by experience of other people's behaviour in situations which have not been anticipated, and for which therefore no prior provision has been made. Organisations typically provide a setting in which such experiences can be readily accumulated and assessed. A firm is a social system as well as an economic system, and social as well as economic capabilities are developed in the process of carrying out the firm's activities. In Levinthal's (1996: 9) words, 'governance mechanisms are important in their ability to *induce* relation-specific attributes, rather than their role in controlling for the dependency relationships that these relation-specific attributes imply'. Some organisations generate very high-powered incentives, thus dissolving the problems of opportunism; others rather obviously do not, and may even dissolve the organisation. 'Ultimately there is no substitute for a high degree of trust between the major partners in a firm' (Casson 1997: 106).

Levinthal's principle may be extended to interfirm collaboration. Neil Kay (1997: 215) argues that 'firms do not cluster agreements in particular alliances *because* they trust their partners, but *in order to* trust their partners': the multiplicity of ties provides a strong inducement to forgo opportunistic advantages in any single collaboration. But the process of working together on several projects may help to develop a warranted belief in the capabilities of one's collaborators, while the governance systems may encourage the development of relation-specific institutions which ease the cognitive burdens of both parties. Indeed, it is precisely when it is impossible to devise mechanisms that can provide guarantees against opportunism or that one's co-workers will have the ability to cope effectively with unforeseen events that people can make well-informed judgements about the trustworthiness of others – both their attitudes and their competence – on which they can base their willingness to invest in relation-specific attributes.

Long-term relationships between firms, and the multiple interactions within an industrial district, have similar advantages over the anonymous contracting which implicitly precedes competitive equilibrium. Though the discovery of knowledge may be guided, it cannot be prescribed; it requires exposure to error, and to other people's errors as well as one's own. New distributions of knowledge, with new patterns of dependence, require voluntary exposure to unpredictable contingencies, which is hardly to be expected in a low-trust environment. Differences in interpretation can be advantageous if there is a shared interpretation at a higher level – for example of the objectives and of the process of learning – and a readiness to trust the quality of each person's interpretation. Thus learning in complex environments entails a generous willingness to accept the authority of others within their own areas of expertise and trust in their competence and goodwill. The importance of such trust, and the ways in which it can be developed, have been demonstrated in a number of studies, especially in France, of learning in organisations (e.g. Lazaric and Monnier 1995).

Since we adopt, or accept, other people's conventions and decision premises because we believe that they will help us to behave sensibly, if we begin to suspect that they will not do this, then we begin to withdraw our acceptance – whatever the formal relationship may be. Keynes (1936: 148–9) observed that the state of business confidence was a major determinant of investment; the state of confidence in the quality of one's managers, and of one's fellow workers, is a major influence on the performance of every business. The credibility of macroeconomic policy frameworks matters precisely because economic agents are expected to base their decisions on the decision premises provided (though it is unfortunate that economists discuss credibility in terms of policy-makers' incentives far more than in terms of their competence – for which economists themselves have some responsibility). In all these cases, if one cannot trust the premises on which one is asked to act, it becomes very hard to take any effective action.

Economists typically seek to explain co-ordination by efficient contracts, but people know more than their contracts can tell, or than their contractual partners can understand, and at the same time less than is necessary for contracts to cover all possibilities. When hierarchy appears in economic analysis, the right to command is usually assumed to encompass the power to secure obedience, just as the explicit terms of any contract are assumed to be readily enforceable, with little thought to the limits of any decision maker's knowledge – which depends substantially upon other people. The growth of knowledge and of productive capabilities depends on the division of labour, and is therefore accompanied by increasing interdependence. The quality of our actions thus depends substantially upon the authority which we grant to communications from others, and that depends on our willingness to trust both their integrity and their competence. Authority and trust are not alternatives to rational choice but preconditions.

7

UNDERSTANDING MARKETS

Exchange and markets

It is not surprising that both Coase and Williamson began their analyses of firms by assuming that markets constitute the default case of economic organisation, for neoclassical economics is normally presented as the theory of a market economy. But in these presentations even careful theorists introduce 'markets' as a primitive concept: 'these markets are conjured up but not analysed' (Hahn 1993: 203). As Coase (1988: 3) observed, microeconomics offers us models of 'exchange without markets'; what is called a market is simply a label for an intersection of supply and demand correspondences, from which equilibrium allocations may be deduced. If these correspondences fail to intersect, there is no possibility of mutually beneficial exchange, and therefore no 'market'. Even Schotter (1994: 8), in a textbook which is intended to reorient the presentation of economic theory by placing much greater emphasis on institutions, promises to explain 'the emergence of markets' but then actually writes about exchange.

To confuse markets with exchange is a category mistake; it is a confusion of institutions and activities. An exchange is an event – or if, as price theorists rarely do, one wishes to include all the preliminaries, it is a process; it is something that happens. A market is a setting within which exchanges may take place – a setting which refers to 'a group or groups of people, some of whom desire to obtain certain things, and some of whom are in a position to supply what the others want' (Marshall 1919: 182). The relationship between markets and exchange therefore requires some analysis. But not all exchanges take place in markets; and therefore we need to explain why some do. Why and how do these groups come together, and how do they interact?

Consumer preferences and production functions may suffice for price theory, which is usually interpreted as explaining a continuous process of exchange (even though this is not often made explicit); but continuous exchange is not sufficient to explain the persistence of markets over time. This is clearly demonstrated in the most comprehensive account of a decentralised economy that has yet been produced, the Arrow–Debreu model in which the co-ordination of economic activities is secured by a full set of contracts for every date and every contingency. As careful expositors have made clear, in the Arrow–Debreu system all markets open simultaneously, and once only; when a complete set of equilibrium contracts is in place, they all close – forever. All that is necessary thereafter is for each person to carry out precisely the programme which is defined by the contracts into which that person has entered, including the pre-specified contingent responses which have been agreed. Not only is routine behaviour sufficient; any departure from routine is a threat to equilibrium. Thus our most complete model of a decentralised economy allows for market activity as a preliminary, but explicitly not as an accompaniment, to economic activity; when the economy is operating, the markets are not. Since money is of little use if all markets are permanently closed, there is no role for money either, as is well known (e.g. Hahn 1984: 78–9).

Now it cannot be denied that, within the parameters of the Arrow–Debreu model, no individual can be sure of constructing an optimal plan unless it has been adjusted to everyone else's optimal plan, where optimality (it hardly needs saying) is defined by reference to the complete data set. Only when this adjustment has been completed can the optimum set of trades be known. It is not therefore surprising that the contents of these individual plans correspond precisely to the contents of a centrally compiled optimal plan which is based on individual preferences; for the set of 'markets' in which these plans are brought into alignment is a planning structure. Whether the contents of these plans appear as instructions or as contracts – which are mutually agreed instructions – is a secondary issue. So it is entirely consistent with the modelling strategy to require the completion of all market activity, or alternatively of all planning activity, before either production or exchange begins. But is it not somewhat misleading to refer to the 'decentralised' version of this model as a market system?

Nevertheless, in identifying 'markets' as the setting in which the arrangements for exchange are worked out, and not as the setting for the exchanges themselves, the Arrow–Debreu system provides the foundation for our analysis: markets are valuable precisely when there is a need to change established patterns. Markets, like money and the firm, are consequences of uncertainty. Since an Arrow–Debreu equilibrium defines a complete programme which requires no change, within that equilibrium markets have no value, and therefore do not operate. This analysis shows what the world would have to be like if there were to be no need for continuous markets – as, not coincidentally, it shows what the world would have to be like if there were to be no Keynesian problems (Hahn 1984: 65). But in an economy in which knowledge, capabilities and perceptions are continually changing, there is a perpetual need for new arrangements in response to these changes. Markets can provide a setting, though not of course the only setting, for such arrangements.

Because the 'markets' in standard microeconomics lie outside the economy, and also outside time, they lie outside the scope of economic analysis: the creation and operation of markets absorb no resources that are relevant to the 'real' economy, and therefore impose no costs upon it. All that matters is the rational choice equilibrium which corresponds to the initial specification; markets and rationality are free goods which provide a costless transition to that equilibrium, and this transition does not therefore need to be modelled. Just as there is no competitive activity in perfect competition, so there are no active markets in standard market theory; and since markets have cleared, there is no need to explain how they clear. However, because economists assume that market success is thoroughly understood, they often produce illegitimate analyses of market failure, as Coase has pointed out (see Chapter 5). Despite their concern to identify system optima, economists commit themselves to sub-optimisation because they close their models by ignoring the simple economic imperative to recognise all relevant costs. The costs of using markets and the costs of rationality never appear.

The theory of 'exchange without markets' (Coase 1988: 3) is a theory which ignores relevant costs. Production is a process which converts inputs into higher valued outputs, and any particular productive activity is profitable if the value added exceeds the cost of conversion; exchange is a process which transfers commodities to those who value them more highly, and any particular exchange increases welfare if the value added by the transfer exceeds the costs of arranging and carrying it out. But the production function which is supposed to represent the technology of production is not matched by a function which claims to represent the technology of exchange, and so the standard assumption is that production incurs costs, while exchange does not. However, by this stage in this book, no one will be unaware that transactions are costly; and the costs of arranging exchanges is the second element in our explanation of markets. As in our analysis of firms, however, we shall look beyond these costs to the capabilities of the transactors. For almost all economists, including Coase and Williamson – but not Casson – markets are not quite treated as natural givens, but they are assumed to be directly deducible from natural givens: for each economic good there is a market. Hahn (1993) does not question this basic model, but recognises that transaction costs may explain why markets are incomplete; he even recognises the importance of mediators, who have to earn a return if they are to stay in business, but, presumably because he is seeking to modify an analytical system in which markets are not problematic because exchange is costless, he does not follow Casson (1982, 1997) by considering the role of mediators in creating markets, thereby reducing transaction costs below the level that would be experienced in a world of exchange without markets. Nevertheless, Hahn's emphasis on intermediation and his recognition that 'mediation only makes sense in a monetary economy' (Hahn 1993: 214) provide important guides to the analysis that follows.

Defining a market

If conventional market theory does not provide a very good explanation of markets, at least it claims to define them rigorously. It does so indirectly, by defining commodities. Each 'market', as we began by noting, is an intersection of supply and demand correspondences, and must therefore refer to a homogeneous commodity. A general equilibrium system encompasses a heterogeneity of homogenous commodities, and there is no direct limit to this heterogeneity. There is, however, an indirect limit if markets are to be perfectly competitive, because perfect competition requires the quantity of each commodity to be sufficient to make the economic significance of each transactor zero. It is important, therefore, that commodities (and therefore markets) should be defined in such a way that each category is internally homogeneous, externally distinctive, and well populated. It is now well understood that this requires a definition which includes the commodity's characteristics, its location, the date of delivery, and the state of the world at that date. But, although such a precise and comprehensive specification is easily supplied in an abstract model, where indexing is sufficient, it presents formidable difficulties in very many applications.

Let us take a convenient example once offered by Hahn (1984: 73): umbrellas in Cambridge on May 15, 2006, if it rains. (I have changed the date to keep it in the future). Now Hahn recognises that the market for this class of goods may be missing; my question is whether the class is properly defined. Even a simple object like an umbrella comes in many shapes, sizes, colours and configurations; how narrowly must we specify the bundle of characteristics if we are to meet our criterion of homogeneity? Then Cambridge is a large town: umbrellas in Mill Road are not likely to be of much interest to anyone caught in a downpour on King's Parade; umbrellas in Regent Street are better, but perhaps not much better; how about Sidney Street? Next, a day can be a very long time when it is raining: an umbrella at 5 p.m. is not a very good substitute for an umbrella at 9 a.m. – unless, of course, the prospective purchaser does not wish to go out until the evening; but that qualification suggests that, rather than using the market specification as a framework for investigating demand, we might need to think about the variety of intentions among potential purchasers in order to specify the market correctly.

Contingencies open up a very wide field. Rain on May 15, 2006 certainly matters, but so does rain on May 14, since this is likely to bring forward some purchases, and therefore to affect both supply and demand on May 15; in general, the stock of umbrellas already owned by those who might otherwise be prospective purchasers is likely to depend on the particular pattern of rainfall over several years, and its interaction with their particular pattern of activities. In fact, it would be better, if we are to be rigorous, to replace states of the world with histories of the world, each of which would include particular histories of each potential participant in trade in the commodity – and therefore the market – that we are seeking to define.

Now this set of difficulties in specifying the commodity and the market is not just a theoretical inconvenience which suggests that relatively few markets will be large enough to be perfect and that markets for differentiated products may be difficult to specify in econometric models – though they certainly justify Hahn's (1993) concern for a much more extensive and careful treatment of incomplete markets; they are of immediate relevance to shopkeepers offering umbrellas for sale in Cambridge, and to umbrella manufacturers deciding which Cambridge shopkeepers to include in their promotional activities. Moreover, they are of relevance not only because they present difficulties; it may be possible for particular shopkeepers and manufacturers to turn these difficulties into opportunities by redefining the markets which they serve. The third element in our analysis of markets, in addition to provision for change and the costs of making arrangements for change, is the ambiguity of definition of many products, and the importance of a framework, such as an incompletely specified market, in which this ambiguity may be both contained and exploited.

New entry typically entails some redefinition of the relevant market; and every definition is a conjecture. Conjectures matter. Walls, the leading firm in the British ice cream market, continued to assign ice cream to a distinctive market category while Mars redefined it as part of the snack market, in which they had formidable capabilities; consequently Mars began to compete with Walls in Britain, rather than the other way round. The prior introduction of Mars' new ice cream product in the United States, where Unilever subsidiaries were operating, did not save Walls from this error. The neglect of what turned out to be relevant information may have been due to a belief that these markets should be differently defined in the two countries, and therefore that the information was not relevant (a judgement which has been justified for some products) or because the organisational and communication systems in Unilever were ill-adapted to such information. Organisation and communication systems are based on conjectures about the problems that are likely to be encountered and the most effective way of handling them (Egidi 1992: 166–8); once corroborated by successful performance, such conjectures are likely to be resistant to falsification.

Economists who are ready to recognise the inherent ambiguities of market definitions may correspondingly be able to analyse the market-modifying activities of manufacturers, retailers and providers of services, and, more generally, the role of market organisation and market relationships in the continuing creation of products. The creation of telephone markets for many kinds of insurance exemplifies the interconnection between creating a product and creating a market, and reminds us that neither fit very comfortably into the conventional categories of economic analysis, which may also be ripe for redefinition. Where there is more than one way of closing the model there is scope for variety and evolution.

The rationale of markets

It seems clear that what is called 'market theory' tells us rather little about markets; and because it tells us rather little about markets the conclusions of this theory may be unreliable as a guide either to understanding or to policy. Markets are much too important, and much too amenable to economic analysis, to be treated as primitives. In this chapter we will try to explain markets; and in doing so we will see why this explanation comes towards the end of this book. Now if we wish to endogenise markets, we have to start somewhere else; and we will start with what some people might be surprised to learn is an Austrian assumption: in the beginning, there was a plan. However, this is neither the plan for an efficient allocation of resources across an economy nor the plan of an individual, formulated as a complete set of contracts, which is optimally adjusted to the fundamental data of the economy and to the optimally adjusted plans of everyone else – though such concepts serve as a foil to Austrian ideas. It is the plan of an individual who is trying, intelligently but not 'rationally', to meet human needs, and it may therefore be treated as a conjecture in an evolutionary process. We will follow Carl Menger's (1976 [1871]) sequence of increasingly elaborate plans, until we reach markets of a kind which incorporate the three elements – the desire for change, the cost and capabilities of making fresh arrangements, and the inherent uncertainty – that have already been identified.

The sequence begins with goods; but goods are not part of the data. A good is something which an individual perceives can be used to meet a human need and which that individual is able to use for this purpose (ibid.: 52). Goods are means, not ends. Menger emphasises the causal connection; we shall be more concerned with the 'knowledge how' to meet the need. This is a very wide definition: money, firms, and markets are all goods, and the definition serves to draw attention to what they have in common. It is also, at least in origin, a subjective definition, and explicitly does not depend on correct perceptions; people can be partly or wholly mistaken about the ability of particular items – from, perhaps, powdered rhinoceros horn to nuclear power stations – to meet human needs. Menger (ibid.: 53) believed that the progress of knowledge would steadily reduce the importance of 'imaginary goods', and therefore had little to say about them, not perhaps appreciating the ease with which all kinds of new imaginary goods (not excluding economic policies) can be created.

Economists who wish to use the concept of 'merit goods', which relies on the opposite failure of perception, might find Menger's approach congenial.

Menger's assumption of increasing knowledge implies that people will find increasingly indirect means of meeting their needs; and the principle of increasing roundaboutness is used to structure his logical sequence, which is not to be taken as a historical hypothesis. Starting with direct consumption of what lies to hand, this sequence continues with the use of what lies to hand to produce consumption goods, then to produce goods with which to make consumption goods, and so on into more complex production sequences which depend on structures of complementary capital goods – and also on elaborate patterns of capabilities, which need to be correctly sequenced. Roundabout methods, structures of complementary capital goods, and direct and indirect capabilities have already been used in this book; we shall need them again in our explanation of markets.

Hitherto, we have seen no more than an increasing complexity of planning, but still at the level of the individual. We have not yet departed from self-sufficiency – though we may have a division of labour between members of a family, and perhaps servants, within a miniature planned economy (ibid.: 236). In Menger's logical sequence of increasing knowledge and increasing complexity, it is only after exhausting the recognised potential of what is already owned that people consider the possibility of satisfying needs by exchanging goods with someone else. Using goods by parting with them introduces a new dimension of roundaboutness.

Menger (ibid.: 192–3) insisted that such exchanges must be exchanges of unequal values, even at the margin. That was not simply because, contrary to Walras, his base case was not perfect competition but bilateral exchange; he noted as a general principle that, even in well-organised markets, the price that one pays as a buyer always exceeds that received as a seller. A moment's reflection on the pricing structure in the most efficient of financial markets will confirm that Menger was factually correct; he was analytically correct too. Because, as Menger (ibid.: 189) points out, there are costs in the process of exchange, the standard 'equations of exchange indicate states where no exchange takes place' (Woo 1992: 41); the assimilation of buying and selling prices which is a defining characteristic of perfect markets conceals what Menger regarded as an important feature of economic activity. Many potential gains from trade are not realised because they do not match the costs of trade. Ignoring transaction costs is analytically extremely convenient; but what, as Coase asked, is the value of this analysis?

An exchange of some part of the initial endowment can happen only once; however, the growth of knowledge which Menger regarded as the driver of economic development might be expected to reveal new possibilities of mutually beneficial exchanges of initial endowments from time to time, and therefore to suggest the desirability of creating systems of exchange which would reduce the direct cost of single transactions. But Menger (1976 [1871]: 236–9) ignores this step, and focuses on the stronger incentives to create such systems which result from the recognition of an even more indirect route to the satisfaction of needs: the use of initial endowments to produce goods for the specific purpose of exchange, and then the acquisition of inputs in order to perpetuate the production of such commodities. What makes commodity production attractive within Menger's analytical system is presumably new knowledge about the possible advantages of specialisation; but at this stage in our own analysis we may invoke the benefits of developing and applying clusters of productive capabilities, which we have already discussed, and which, as we noted in the preceding chapter, might often be expected to outweigh the costs of exchange.

It is the establishment of a continuing flow of exchanges as a concomitant of commodity production that leads Menger (ibid.: 241–56) into the discussion of markets as goods. They are goods because they facilitate exchange, by providing 'points of concentration of trading and price formation'; in other words they make it easier for those wishing to trade to discover the possibilities and to engage in negotiations. Menger's world, we should remember, is one in which all human action takes place in time and in conditions of limited knowledge; there is a recurrent need to make new arrangements. Whereas Coase started with the costs of using markets, Menger recognised the costs of exchange in the absence of markets, and was therefore able to identify the role of markets in reducing transaction costs from their level in an economy without markets. The value of markets in this role is derived immediately from the value of the exchanges that they facilitate, and ultimately, like all goods of higher order, from the needs which they indirectly help to satisfy. What is significant for our present purposes is that the value of markets is substantially dependent on the superior and differentiated capabilities that can be developed by organising production in firms; instead of relying on market failures to explain firms, Menger in effect relies on the productive success of firms to explain markets – as, less explicitly, does Smith. But, as we shall see, his explanation is not complete.

Menger directs his attention less to the markets themselves than to the explanation of which goods become commodities; that depends on their marketability, which may be thought of as the inverse of the transaction costs which are associated with them. A good which is of high value to consumers may not be worth making if the cost of demonstrating that value is also high – whether that cost is borne by the customer in expensive search, or the producer in expensive information and persuasion. If we ignore such costs, we may very easily believe that we can identify opportunities for mutually beneficial exchange which are rejected in apparent defiance of simple rationality; in particular, some commodities with a high margin between price and cost of production, narrowly defined, may appear to be underproduced in relation to some other commodities with a much lower margin. Menger's extensive discussion of the factors which affect marketability contains much of relevance to markets; but his own interest lies elsewhere, in explaining how the most marketable of commodities may become acceptable in exchange even by those who have no use for them, because these commodities are easily disposable in exchange for goods which they do wish to use; they thus acquire the attributes which we ascribe to money. We shall reverse Menger's emphasis by concentrating on the role of money in reducing transaction costs (not least through its function as a store of value, which allows customers to await better information), and thus increasing the marketability of goods.

Menger (ibid.: 242–53) offers a typology of markets, depending on the number of potential customers, the area, the quantitative limits to consumption within a time period, and the significance of both calendar time and storability, explaining that the particular incidence of these elements must be considered in seeking to understand any particular market. Marshall also indicates the importance of studying particular cases, but introduces the analytical core of his *Principles* (Book V) with 'a short and provisional account of markets', warning his readers that 'a full study of [the organisation of markets] must...be deferred to a later volume' (Marshall 1920: 324). The context even for this theoretical analysis is an economy in which most markets are intermediate between the general 'markets for things which satisfy in an exceptional way [the] conditions of being in general demand, cognizable and portable' and the specific markets for goods which are made to order, perishable, or bulky (ibid.: 326–9). It is easy in retrospect to associate this range from general to specific with decreasing marketability, or alternatively with increasing transaction costs. What is common to all categories is the importance of the arrangements for using each market.

Market institutions

One theme of this book is the ubiquity of conventions, routines, and procedures which help to fill the gaps in our knowledge and make it possible to act intelligently – and sometimes rationally. In providing a setting for exchange which enables people to close their models of search and decision making, this is what markets do: 'a *market* is a specific institutional arrangement consisting of rules and conventions that make possible a large number of voluntary transfers of property rights on a regular basis' (Ménard 1995: 170). Since there is a considerable variety of such institutional arrangements, those who are familiar with each market typically face lower transaction costs than those who are not. Hahn (1993: 217) thinks it important that 'markets do not provide a sufficiently rich language by which agents can communicate', and he observes that the inadequacy of communication is a source of Keynesian problems; but one of the research topics awaiting attention in the study of markets is the range and content of communication which each particular set of institutions makes possible. A market may provide opportunities for efficiency-enhancing arbitrage (Kirzner 1973) by encouraging specifically oriented alertness, it may encourage social learning (Choi 1993: 143), and it may provide a competitive setting for a particular kind of evolution, while the variety of market institutions provides the material for evolution at another level of the system.

The institutions of a market provide the rules of competition within that market – though they do not exclude competition to change those rules, as has been amply demonstrated in food retailing and financial services. As Hayek (1948: 103) pointed out, competition 'is more important when objective conditions are imperfect'; it is a 'process of formation of opinion' (ibid.: 106). Competition within the provisionally accepted set of institutions shows which plans are false (though it does not reveal which are the false elements in those plans) and therefore encourages convergence; at the same time it provides the partial closure within which new variants may be imagined. Competition shows who will serve particular needs well – whose capabilities we may provisionally trust to deliver what we may want in the future, and which knowledge we may reasonably reuse. As Mises rightly perceived, in the absence of market processes there is not enough reliable knowledge on which to base a plan.

The most important of all institutions for reducing transaction costs is money; that is why, as Clower (1969: 13–14) emphasised, 'goods buy money and money buys goods – but goods do not buy goods in any organised market'. The model of a market economy without money is a false and misleading ideal, for it is money which makes possible the calculations on which the efficiency of markets depends. If 'the market process is a process of dialogue, [then] money is the language from which that dialogue is formed' (Horwitz 1995: 168). The price system is a monetary system: a multiplicity of bilateral exchange ratios, however complete and coherent, is a quite different institutional setting, far less appropriate as a guide to choices than the measuring rod of money. In consumer theory, Marshall saw this far more clearly than those who devised the more elegant preference orderings of the 1930s and 1940s, as Hicks eventually came to realise.

Woo (1992) explains how the current set of prices provides the shared conventions on which most of us rely, most of the time, as a measure of values against which to judge the alternatives which are presently being contemplated, and indeed to decide for or against a purchase without comparing it directly against any alternative. In an evolutionary economy, the role of prices as conventions which simplify decisions may be no less important than their allocative function (Shackle 1972: 227–8). It remains true, of course, that prices have to be interpreted, and that any interpretation may be mistaken; indeed, the standard assumption that everyone correctly assesses the significance of a change of price is one of the most extraordinary elements of a theory which has no adequate means of explaining any behaviour out of equilibrium. Price fluctuations for a single good increase search costs, and inflation makes interpretation far more difficult, and may raise the costs of transacting to levels which severely impair the ability of consumers to make reasonable judgements (Leijonhufvud 1981).

The institutions of a market, like other institutions, help us to behave intelligently despite pervasive uncertainty. Uncertainty therefore does not mean an end to planning; indeed it makes planning more important, because now, instead of being a prelude to action, it becomes a part of the process of managing a business, or one's life. In this context, moreover, we find a new objective of planning, and a new good, identified by Menger and introduced in the preceding chapter: reserves. Reserves provide a capacity to deal with contingencies which have not been anticipated in detail. Many kinds of reserves can be useful, and a sensible plan for an uncertain world includes the creation and maintenance of a carefully judged portfolio, as Ansoff (1965) pointed out in his pioneering study of business strategy. If we are to understand the role of money, we must recognise that people who wish to hold money will also wish to hold stocks of many other things – most of which will not be financial assets. If money influences the behaviour of the real economy, the real economy influences the behaviour of money.

As we have already seen, the firm, as described by Coase, offers control over a particular range of capabilities rather than access to many more – some of which, however, the purchaser may not know how to use effectively. We now have to consider the set of institutions that we call a continuing market, which not only provides access to the capabilities of those who transact in that market but also provides a setting in which supplier and customer may develop some mutual understanding of problems and possible solutions. Firms and markets are clearly partial substitutes; but it is no less important to recognise that they are also complements. Firms need markets because of the large volume of transactions that they undertake, both as buyers and as sellers; and that is an important part of our explanation of how markets come into existence. 'It seems improbable', observed Coase (1937, reprinted in Coase 1988: 40), 'that a firm would emerge without the existence of uncertainty'; and it is clear from the context that it is Knightian uncertainty that he has in mind. But neither would we have continuing markets without uncertainty. Both firms and markets are devices for creating and preserving the possibility of future transactions; they are intangible and complex capital assets which are valuable precisely because the future is not predictable enough to justify present commitments. This, in different phraseology, is Coase's (1937) explanation of firms; his brief account of the cost of using markets suggests that it is also his implicit, if unconscious, explanation of markets.

Markets are valuable to many people even when they are not using them, because they allow the formulation of plans which assume that particular markets will be available if and when they are needed, providing access to other people's capabilities and so encouraging people to develop their own capabilities. Instead of the contracts for future options which define Coase's firms, continuing markets provide options for future contracts. Shackle is the supreme exponent of the view that 'money is the means by which choice can be deferred until a later and better-informed time' (Shackle 1972: 160); but so are markets (and, as we have previously noted, firms); indeed, without continuous markets money could hardly be used to make later choices. Firms, markets and money provide reserves which allow people to respond to threats and opportunities in a world of uncertainty.

Making markets

Markets, as we have seen, are goods. But they are not natural givens; they are goods which are created by economic activity. How, then, do they come into existence? Our understanding of this question has not been helped by the orientation of Coase's original article, for in his focus on the need to explain the existence of firms he failed to realise that by basing his own explanation on the cost of using markets he was calling into question the adequacy of the contemporary treatment of markets, in which – apart from Chamberlin's (1933) misunderstood work – such costs were ignored. It is also unfortunate that the long-delayed emergence of a body of theory which seeks to explain the choice between the alternative governance structures of market and hierarchy has been based on the convention of taking the transaction as the unit of analysis. For this naturally, if not inevitably, leads to a focus on the costs of individual transactions; but these costs, as Coase (1972) noted, often depend on the way in which transactions are grouped, and in particular on the amount and kind of investment in transaction technology, which may drastically reduce the cost which is directly incurred in each particular transaction. Marshall explicitly extended his principle that '[t]he cost of production which controls value relates to whole processes of production rather than to any particular parcel of products' (Marshall 1919: 190) to the costs of marketing: 'the marketing side of the work of a business is an integral process, and not a series of independent transactions' (ibid.: 270). Casson's (1982: 179) recognition that 'the set-up cost of a market organization is likely to be quite high compared with its recurrent costs' is the key to his theory of market-making, which is both closely complementary to and highly compatible with Penrose's theory of the developing firm.

Now there are at least two parties to any transaction, and we should not be surprised to find that many investments in transaction technology reduce costs for the party which does not invest. Arrangements which facilitate transactions often create externalities. They will almost always do so when the arrangements are designed to create a continuing transaction capability – in other words a market – which is accessible to many. Indeed, since the objective of such arrangements is precisely to make it accessible to many, so that the creator of this capability can attract many transactors, then one might say that the purpose of the investment is to create externalities. A market is a kind of public good. But who will have sufficient inducement to invest in a public good? Such investment will appear attractive only to someone who expects to undertake a great many transactions, and who values the private benefit above the private costs, or who expects to be able to charge traders for the transactions which they undertake.

The latter is the practice in the great exchanges, and in the classified advertisement columns of newspapers; it is exemplified both in the market which Walras chose for his *tâtonnement*, which was modelled on the Paris Bourse, and in the corn-market of a country town, which Marshall chose for his illustration of the emergence of a market price. Neither Walras nor Marshall, in the *Principles*, bothered to explain how these markets came into existence, and how their costs were met, and neither drew explicit attention to the fact that they were populated by regular traders, whose bids were based on long experience, including experience of each other – though Marshall seems to have been well aware that this particular setting, which hardly conforms to the requirements of perfect competition, was essential for his argument that the bargaining process would lead to something very close to the equilibrium price which could (in principle) be directly computed from the data.

In his extensive survey of business practices in *Industry and Trade*, Marshall (1919: 256) describes an organised market as one that is formally regulated, normally by its participants, who have a clear interest in devising a set of regulations which will allow deals to be quickly and easily made, in full confidence that they will be carried out. The institutional structures, both formal and informal, of such organised markets minimise the transaction costs of price flexibility: it is not therefore surprising that they appear to offer the closest approximation to perfectly competitive markets.

The general case, however, on which we shall focus in this chapter, is that in which the market is created by the market participants themselves, but predominantly by those who are the major transactors; and here Marshall is much more explicit, especially in *Industry and Trade*, where one can find an elaborate discussion of market-making. It is the trading partner who expects to engage in most transactions, and therefore is likely to gain the greatest individual benefit from being able to reuse the knowledge that is embedded in the market institutions, who normally has the greatest individual incentive to bear the capital costs of organising the markets for those transactions. Young (1928: 536) declares that 'the finding of markets is one of the tasks of modern industry', and explains 'the new importance which the *potential market* has in the planning and management of large industries' by its implications for the continued pursuit of increasing returns, as Chandler was later to do. Thus merchants and manufacturers usually take the initiative, both as suppliers and customers (Marshall 1919: 271–4), though Marshall devotes a chapter to the development of large-scale retailing, which entailed – as it still does – competition in market organisation between businesses which operate at different stages of the productive sequence. The significance of this kind of competition was recognised by Andrews (1950), but was no better appreciated than his other insights into the working of a competitive economy. The rivalry between manufacturers and retailers for primacy in the organisation of retail markets has been a major feature of advanced economies; but it has received more attention in business schools than in economics departments.

> Everyone buys, and nearly every producer sells, to some extent in a *'general'* market, in which he is on the same footing with others around him. But nearly everyone has also some 'particular' markets; that is, some people or groups of people with whom he is in some-what close touch: mutual knowledge and trust lead him to approach them, and them to approach him, in preference to strangers.
>
> (Marshall 1919: 182)

As Marshall makes clear, the creation of these particular markets is no trivial matter: it necessarily takes time (Marshall 1920: 500), because it includes the building of a reputation and the development of understanding with trading partners, and it requires a substantial commitment of resources, amounting in some cases to as much capital as is embodied in fixed plant (Marshall 1919: 270). The transaction is not the appropriate unit of analysis: a firm's market is an institutional framework which is intended to facilitate a continuing series of transactions, and the routines that constitute that framework, though initiated by specific investments, evolve through the sequence of transactions themselves, like the routines of the firm's internal organisation, as portrayed by Nelson and Winter (1982). Like other institutions, it is a source of increasing returns.

This perspective resembles that of the organisational ecologist, who 'views the market as much the consequence of organizational actions; in other words, as endogenous' (Carroll 1997: 120). It may indeed go a little further by insisting on thinking, not of 'the market' but 'the markets', and perhaps even dramatising this stance by adopting Levitt's (1980: 83) slogan 'There is no such thing as a commodity', which could be the moral of our enquiry into the 'market' for umbrellas in Cambridge. Penrose (1959, 1995:

80–5) explicitly treats the demand faced by each growing firm as something the firm can expect to do something about, by its production as well as its marketing decisions. As Drucker (1964: 85) declared, 'the purpose of a business is to create a customer'; each business seeks to develop its own particular set of connections, within which it can trade much more readily – or, as we should now say, at much lower incremental costs for each transaction. Regular trades reduce the transaction costs of both parties, not least because they allow the development of reliable expectations, especially in a competitive environment; as Hayek (1948: 97) observed, 'the function of competition is here precisely to teach us *who* will serve us well', thus reducing both the costs of search and the chances of making mistakes, which – outside our perfectly competitive models – are often expensive, and sometimes impossible, to retrieve.

In order to create a customer, a firm must not only make the transaction easy but supply reasons why it should be worth while. Rogers' (1983) list of factors influencing customer selection, though presented as an analysis of the diffusion of innovations, offers a helpful classification. In addition to the relative advantage of what is being offered, the categories include the complexity of the product, its compatibility with each customer's patterns of behaviour and ways of thinking, the ease of communicating the message, and the scale of initial commitment required. What matters is each customer's subjective perception of each of these factors, not any supposedly objective assessment by the seller; the customer may not be right, but it is the customer who makes the decision. Relative advantage is not easy to establish if, as Drucker (1964: 87–8), claims, '[t]he customer rarely buys what the business thinks it sells', and both compatibility and communicability are problematic if the customer classifies goods and services in ways that the supplier fails to recognise. An interesting current example of a campaign to create customers is the effort by British Telecom to 'change the way we work'; one theme in this campaign is the offer of new decision premises which are intended to lead to the conclusion that there is no longer any reason for working in offices.

The costs of creating a customer can be very high – as indeed can be the costs of deciding which supplier should be the recipient of one's custom; the latter costs are often subsidised by suppliers, which naturally increases their own outlay. While it is seeking to develop its own market each business may therefore be faced by the kind of 'very steep' demand curve described by Marshall (1920: 458) which has attracted some comment: most commentators have failed to notice that in the text to which this footnote is attached Marshall reminds us that the required return on the capital cost of developing its external organisation is 'a large part' of a firm's supplementary cost, which explains why it is usually both eager and able to cover at least some of those costs even in the short period. By reducing the transaction costs incurred by those who become regular customers through its own investment in transaction technology, it increases the quantity which these customers are willing to purchase at a given price – and unless it succeeds in doing so, it will not survive.

Since Allyn Young was his thesis supervisor, it is perhaps not surprising that Chamberlin (1933) produced an analysis of market organisation by producers who have to 'hunt up their own customers' (Robinson 1970: 33). Chamberlin's (1933) emphasis on product differentiation recalls Marshall's (1919: 181) insistence that '[p]roduction and marketing are parts of the single process of adjustment of supply to demand': the distinction between production and selling costs is strictly valid only if selling costs are unnecessary. Product design may have a major impact on the transaction costs faced by potential users, or, in Menger's terms, on the marketability of a product, most obviously through its effects on the compatibility of the product with other equipment, or with established habits. But the costs of market-making, which are excluded by assumption from perfectly competitive models, were readily interpreted as costs of market failure despite Chamberlin's justified protests; in relation to costless exchange, every market cost is necessarily an imperfection.

It is unfortunate that Marshall did not spell out the process by which the efforts of many firms to develop similar markets for similar products interact to create a wider market area in which the transaction costs faced by buyers are reduced, and their demand prices thereby increased. Since, as we have already observed, new entry changes the market, it may be better to think of an intersection of markets, all of them imperfectly specified in the space of representations. We may take supermarkets as an example. These are aptly named, for each store is itself a complex market, with its own range of products and its own routines which keep down the transaction costs of regular shoppers (except, as supermarket directors do not always seem to recognise, when the routines are changed). But since the product ranges and routines of the rival companies, though similar, are not identical, each is a different market. How similar they should attempt to be is an important strategic issue; the food section of Marks & Spencer is, by design, noticeably different from the food sections in supermarkets.

Nevertheless the efforts made by each firm to improve its own external organisation tend to generate external economies for its rival firms and their customers; that is why transaction costs are often low enough for a firm to compete outside its own particular market. Variations in the degree to which this is possible receive sufficient attention in Marshall's *Principles* to scotch the notion that he thought he was analysing perfect competition. The integration of particular markets into a general market will be particularly marked if rival firms develop similar market routines on such matters as standard sizes, labelling symbols, credit terms, and after-sales service, thereby creating network externalities. There are often, but not always, strong incentives to do so. This topic has received some attention from industrial economists, and deserves more.

Thus a 'market' (or a market cluster) populated by many firms may be seen as an example of those many institutions which, as Menger (1963 [1883]) pointed out, develop through a sequence of deliberate human plans which have consequences beyond those that were explicitly intended. They are complex structures of human capital which provide public goods to those who have made appropriate investments and developed appropriate indirect capabilities. Menger and Marshall both emphasised deliberate choice; but neither expected even the most determined seekers after improvement to have a complete knowledge even of the possible conse-quences of the choices that they made.

What they did expect was that new opportunities would be continually revealed by the growth of knowledge. Marshall went further in arguing that the growth of knowledge was itself partly a product of the various kinds of organisation within the economy. The creation of capabilities not only helped each firm to react to events but also to shape events. Each firm's investment in the organisation of its particular market was both a source of information which could be used as a basis for new ideas and also an environment in which these ideas could be tested, and discussed and improved before testing; and the intersection of the external organisations of rival firms helped to distribute knowledge within the larger market. Essential to this process, as Marshall observed, were the differences among market participants in their capabilities, experience, and perception, which together generated the variations from which new combinations of ideas could be formed.

The role of markets in fostering, and shaping, the growth of knowledge is not easy to incorporate into a method of analysis in which all possibilities are included in the original specification. It has received surprisingly little attention even from Austrian economists, who have been predominantly concerned with the effectiveness of market processes in mobilising the existing fragments of knowledge which are scattered among people, and which, it is argued, are most likely to be made available to others if each person can see some benefit from using private knowledge as a basis of market transactions. Nor have Austrian economists given much attention to the investment in transaction capabilities that is required. Indeed, the only economist who has given substantial emphasis to this (one might think) natural corollary of Austrian theory is Casson (1982: 163–4), who discusses in some detail the obstacles to trade when markets are missing. He lists six obstacles: no contact between buyer and seller, no knowledge of reciprocal wants, no agreement over price, the need to exchange custody of goods, no confidence that the goods conform to specification, and no confidence in restitution. It is because of the capital commitment needed to overcome these obstacles that Casson associates market-making with the creation of firms, as it is only by attracting custom over a reasonably lengthy period that an entrepreneur can expect to make an appropriate return on this investment. Casson is here much closer to Marshall than he acknowledges, or perhaps realised at that time. Nor does he appear to recognise that his analysis is not just applicable to entrepreneurship – important though that is – but raises fundamental questions about our conventional theories of markets and of market failure. Anyone who wishes to understand markets should read Casson on market-making.

A market, like a firm, is an institutional structure which channels processes. All processes require structure – a relatively stable framework within which changes can be made. Frameworks may change too, but they must change more slowly – or they cease to act as frameworks. The difference between a firm and a market lies in the extent to which the institutional structure is the result of a single plan. This is a difference of degree; no firm of any size, and with any history, operates in the way that any one person – or any board of directors – intended, while many markets bear significant traces of deliberately imposed organising principles. In both, the institutional structure at any time is a product both of deliberate investment and of learning by doing – or rather, by contrast with standard economic models, of learning by interpreting the apparent results of doing, a process which is itself structured by a set of connecting principles. Structures both enable and constrain; indeed, they enable because they constrain.

Switching costs

The importance of investment in market-making provides a neglected insight into the important phenomenon of switching costs. When the minimisation of long-run transaction costs requires a substantial and non-recoverable initial investment in a particular transaction technology or trade connection, any shift between technologies or connections necessarily entails switching costs, just as does a shift between production technologies. Some level of switching costs is inherent in the nature of transactions, as in any form of capital-using technique, or indeed any kind of commitment to a particular way of closing a system: it is the cost of abandoning established routines and finding replacements that explains why major innovations are so disruptive in Schumpeter's theory. Now the initial investments in developing a set of market institutions which reduces the cost of individual transactions, as has been seen, are almost always made by those who expect to be undertaking many transactions, notably the producers and retailers in consumer markets; and their willingness to undertake them will be increased by greater assurance that they will indeed be able to undertake many transactions – that they will keep their customers. But since a major part of their investment is designed to reduce the transaction costs faced by the customer, there is often a danger that the customer will go elsewhere; for example, customers provided with extensive showroom displays and detailed advice, which make it easier for them to decide precisely what they want to buy, might then make their purchases from a rival who simply takes orders for delivery from a warehouse and offers a lower price. Firms cannot charge customers directly for all the benefits that they provide, and therefore cannot survive unless some of these benefits can be sold at a price which exceeds their cost.

Therefore it is not surprising that many firms which make substantial investments in overcoming obstacles to trade then create obstacles to the transfer of that trade to their rivals. The imposition of such switching costs on customers may have the effect of charging them for the benefits they have received, and may therefore internalise an externality and so improve allocative efficiency. That the success of such switching costs in retaining customers may encourage the creation of additional costs which simply create monopolistic advantages for no public benefit should not be surprising, and indeed most of the switching costs that we observe may perhaps be thus explained; but we should not begin by assuming that switching costs are necessarily barriers to efficiency. Such a universal assumption could be appropriate only in a world without transaction costs, but as Coase (1988: 14) has observed, that is a world with 'very peculiar properties'. Switching costs are an inevitable consequence of uncertainty; but like so many natural phenomena in an economy, they have their own pathology.

Markets and consumption

Because markets provide access to other people's capabilities for those who know how to use those markets and those capabilities effectively, it is important to consider the consumers' perspective. People who expect to engage in a long series of transactions, such as developing a major recreational activity, or in a single transaction of great importance, such as the purchase of a home for retirement, may think it worthwhile making a substantial investment in developing the indirect capabilities which are relevant to their particular needs, rather than relying on the more general transaction technology which has been developed by producers. But for most of the time they will take advantage of what exists, and use the resources, including the cognitive resources, that are thus released for other purposes. What is of especial interest in our present enquiry is the use of such resources for the development of consumer capital. If we do not need to think about how to transact, we can think more carefully about what to transact, and what uses to make of what we buy. We thus develop both indirect and direct capabilities which are complementary to the direct and indirect capabilities of producers.

Preferences are discovered partly in the process of choosing, and partly in putting to use what has been chosen. Household production functions, like the production functions of firms, abstract from the knowledge and skills that are required for successful performance, and from the processes by which performance is improved. Economic evolution is shaped by consumer capabilities as well as by capabilities in production. This is not only because market selection depends on consumers' interpretations of what is being offered; we should not forget that consumers are also generators of variety, through their abilities to make use of the characteristics of products and services to solve their own problems, perhaps in combinations that no producer has ever imagined. The most striking example is the development of the personal computer, which originated with hobbyists, and has resisted all attempts, even by the most expert producers, to turn it into to a well-defined product; but no-one who has ever observed how young children can create goods from unlikely materials should doubt the potential of consumer innovation.

Marshall recognised the importance of new products and of new wants; his suggestion that once economic development is under way new wants would tend to follow new activities suggests a line of research that is not well represented in economics, but which should be incorporated in any comprehensive endogenous growth theory (Swann (forthcoming)). Another of Marshall's underdeveloped ideas, that of a ladder of consumption, has appeared from time to time in economics, in discussions of motivation: for example in Knight's (1921: 369) observation that people look for challenges, and in Schumpeter's (1934) account of entrepreneurial ambitions. Maslow's (1954: 35–46) hierarchy of wants clearly implies a substantial change in the character of goods as people move up the hierarchy, with the nominal use becoming less important to the consumer; Maslow (ibid.: 37) also suggests that a movement between levels implies a substantial change of cognitive framework, and thus both in the criteria for selection and in the process by which new goods might be generated.

Consumers make conjectures, using their own mental frameworks against a background of institutions. Market institutions, including the price system, can provide the stability which allows the time and mental energy to make and evaluate such conjectures. Sometimes consumers just do what seems best, and sometimes they deliberately experiment; but in either case it is as true for consumers as for producers that 'imagination, rather than information in any ordinary sense, is what entrepreneurs require in order to discover new ways of combining resources in order to meet consumers' desires' (Richardson 1960: 105). We should remember Menger's warning that 'goods' may be wrongly identified, either because the supposed causal connection does not exist or because the supposed human want is not genuine; and the whole process is complicated by the difficulty of interpreting both the initial information and the outcome. Consumers make plenty of mistakes, but so does everyone else in an evolutionary process. The evolution of demand is at once a major influence on the working of market processes and channelled by market institutions, and its analysis requires something more than conventional consumer theory. (Some contributions to this analysis are to be found in Bianchi 1998.)

Markets and evolution

Economic efficiency, as that is usually understood in conventional economics (including transaction cost theory), depends on the best use of the knowledge that is already contained somewhere within the economy; but economic progress depends on the generation of new knowledge. It is tempting to think of the market (or, unfashionably, planning) as the mechanism for achieving the former, and the firm as the prime source, within the economy, of the latter. Schumpeter (1943), Chandler (1990), and Lazonick (1992) might all be cited in support of this view, at least in a general way. If one adds a Darwinian twist, one might think of markets as selection environments in which firms' plans, based on what they believe to be new knowledge, are tested. We should then expect most plans to fail, at least in part; a market which exhibits no market failures, in the conventional sense, is a failure as a market.

However, markets are both less and more than selection environments. They are less because market institutions are the product, in substantial part, of firms' investments in making markets, and are to that extent selected rather than selecting; they are more because the interactions between firms, and between firms and their customers, are often the trigger to new ideas. Thus the pattern of supply and demand in a market may be, in part, a consequence of the institutions of that market. Dubuisson (1998: 86) takes a similar view, and traces the evolution of supply and demand within a specific market for industrial catering. Nor should one forget that firms often provide a fierce internal environment for the selection of new ideas. So it may be better to think, as Marshall did, of firms and markets as alternative, and often complementary, forms of organisation which aid the growth of knowledge and its effective use, through various combinations of specialisation and integration, in which new ideas are generated, tested, modified, and tested again, in a continuing process. Firms and markets are both investments in the future, investments which are made because the future is not predictable. It is because we cannot plan the future that we need to plan for the future, by creating capabilities.

In the beginning there was a plan, a plan by an individual or small group to use goods in ways which were thought likely to satisfy needs. In our world of Knightian uncertainty, every plan is necessarily based on a conjecture about the properties of these goods; the outcome may call for a revision of both plan and conjecture. A plan to inaugurate a complex productive process, employing structures of complementary capital goods, is based on a complex conjecture; an unsatisfactory outcome might be difficult to interpret unless most parts of that conjecture are deemed to be beyond question. The system of thought must be almost completely closed if evidence is to be interpreted. A plan to make a market for a new product, or to make a new market for an existing product, also involves a complex conjecture, and the outcomes of that conjecture may also be difficult to interpret. The reluctance of Casson's (1982) entrepreneur to change price makes it easier for him to assess the results of his marketing policy.

The interaction between plans and the interpretation of their outcomes leads each individual or firm down a particular path of knowledge, which cannot be anticipated in detail – since no-one can know what they have yet to discover; but what can be anticipated, as Penrose (1959, 1995) recognised, is that, even from a common starting point, individuals and firms will tend to follow somewhat different paths. If they respect the institutions of their community or market, they will not drift out of touch with their group – though both individuals and firms sometimes do; but they may well have different ideas, for example, about the market for umbrellas in Cambridge. Since the characteristics of that market (or should it be those markets?) cannot be established for certain, and are liable to change, these different ideas may be beneficial. Models of exchange may be defined by theorists, but real-world markets are defined by the conjectures of market participants – like all scientific phenomena.

The argument for variety, as a response to uncertainty, can be greatly widened. Where substantial investment is required to establish a transaction technology, in firm, market, or knowledge community, then switching costs, as already noted, are likely to be high, and speedy movement between institutional patterns almost impossible. Since we do not, and cannot, know what threats and opportunities will face us, it seems desirable to create and maintain a range of capabilities each designed with reference to a particular range of conjectures; and that is best done by encouraging a variety of organising principles, which are not easily incorporated within a formal institution. Conjectures about the market, and about the capabilities of a firm, or a strategic business unit, may be no more than working assumptions; but if they are to work effectively they must provide focus, and that requires them to be resistant to change. Markets also require an institutional structure, and the more highly organised the market (and the lower therefore the direct cost of each transaction), the tighter its constraints are likely to be; yet there is some evidence that markets, if appropriately organised, may be able to accommodate a greater range of capabilities than is possible even within the most successful firm.

We can access more than we can control. The most striking contemporary evidence for this proposition is to be found in the computer industry, the major capabilities in which now appear to be distributed in its network of markets. The enormous investments which have been made in creating the much admired internal and external organisation of IBM, on the other hand, can now be seen to have imposed on that company switching costs of a magnitude unprecedented within a private firm. Indeed, IBM's current emphasis on the provision of complex business services may be interpreted as a realisation that their distinctive competence always lay, and still lies, in such services; even when their revenues came from sales of equipment it was the services, and the assurance of services, which they offered that generated these revenues. But the problems faced by IBM are as nothing compared with the switching costs imposed on Russia by centuries of authoritarian planning.

8

THE DIVISION OF LABOUR AND
THE GROWTH OF KNOWLEDGE

In this final chapter we will revisit topics already discussed, in the course of providing a historical perspective on the conception of the economy as a system for generating and using knowledge through the division of labour. Human knowledge is necessarily fallible and incomplete, but the knowledge available in human society can be increased, not only through individual effort but through the better organisation both of existing knowledge and of the search for better knowledge. In order to construct a logical argument or to develop an effective sequence of actions, it is necessary to close the system of thought or the domain of activity against many possible complications. Among the most important means of closure are the neural networks within each person's brain and the institutions on which we all rely, which we may call, adapting Marshall's phraseology, the internal and external organisations of each individual. The human brain is not a general purpose problem solver, for there is no evolutionary pathway which could have produced such a biological system, which would have been very inefficient in coping with the specific problems of our ancestral environment. Our logical capacity is therefore limited, and may be domain-specific, but our neural systems are capable of acquiring new specialist skills, including skills in developing new 'knowledge that', by making new connections: the development of human knowledge, though utilising logic, is structured by non-logical processes.

Because different people can develop different skills, a knowledge-rich society must be an ecology of specialists; knowledge is distributed within each human brain, within each organisation, and within the economic and social system; and being distributed it can grow, provided that it is sufficiently co-ordinated to support increasing interdependencies. Co-ordination cannot be guaranteed, and, as Schumpeter insisted, new knowledge may be extremely disruptive. A systematic exploration of co-ordination failure is beyond the scope of this book; so we will conclude by reviewing the relationship between industrial organisation and the growth of knowledge, drawing primarily on a distinguished economic tradition, and beginning with the most distinguished of all writers on economics.

Adam Smith's principles of economic development

In the opening chapter, we drew attention to Adam Smith's psychological theory of the growth of science as a human response to the problem of knowledge, and we have since made frequent reference to the significance of pattern making and pattern matching, which is often guided by the institutions of a particular community. Smith's recognition of the universal appeal of connecting principles inspired his advice on didactic writing, which was to 'lay down certain principles...from which we account for the several phenomena, connecting all together by the same chain' (Smith 1983: 146). In the first chapter of Book 1 of his *Inquiry into the Nature and Causes of the Wealth of Nations* Smith follows his own advice to use this 'Newtonian method'.

Smith opens this chapter with a paragraph of a single sentence which encapsulates his fundamental principle of economic development. 'The greatest improvement in the productive powers of labour, and the greater part of the skill, dexterity and judgment with which it is anywhere directed or applied, seem to have been the effects of the division of labour' (Smith 1976b: 13). Smith immediately follows up his Newtonian assertion with a rhetorical masterpiece, in which he leads his readers from the workers in his celebrated pin-factory, chosen because their activities can be 'placed at once under the view of the spectator' (ibid.: 14), through the 'separation of different trades and employments' (ibid.: 15) in a single country, to the complex patterns of international specialisation (ibid.: 22–4). In thus emphasising the common principle underlying these various forms in which the division of labour appears, he diverts attention from any explanation of the distribution of activities among them; this question was left for later economists to discover, but it is a question which can be accommodated easily within Smith's analytical framework – and indeed may be best accommodated there, since a comprehensive answer requires consideration not only of transaction costs, on which most modern analysis of this question is based, but of production costs, and, even more, of the possibilities of reducing these costs.

That productivity may be increased through the division of labour was hardly a new idea in 1776; but no-one had ever before assigned it the primary role in promoting economic growth. Smith's justification for doing so was his belief that a prosperous economy grew, in Schumpeter's (1934: 6) phrase, 'by its own initiative, from within'. His account of this growth, however, differed from Schumpeter's theory of development. What Smith did was to reverse the long-recognised causal sequence, in which specialisation allows the best use to be made of distinctive skills, arguing instead that 'the very different genius which appears to distinguish men of different professions, when grown up to maturity, is not upon many occasions so much the cause, as the effect of the division of labour' (Smith 1976b: 28).

The division of labour thus results not only in an 'increase in dexterity' and 'the saving of time in passing from one species of work to another' but in the creation of capabilities.

The division of labour may be seen as Smith's solution to the problems posed by the scarcity of individual knowledge and, perhaps even more constraining, of human cognition. The total resources of 'knowledge that' and 'knowledge how' available to any community, and the consequent productivity of that community, could be enormously increased by distributing these resources throughout the community. The dispersion of knowledge, which when taken as a datum appears to be the source of co-ordination problems, is actually by far the most effective solution hitherto discovered to the problems caused by the limitations of human cognition. Smith thus complements his psychological theory of the development of science as a means of economising on cognition (Smith 1980), which anticipates and in some ways improves on modern conceptions of paradigms and research programmes, with what might be called a psychological theory of the origin of species of knowledge which, as we saw in Chapter 3, is consistent with current ideas about functional specialisation within the human brain. The fundamental institutional setting for both processes is explained in his *Theory of Moral Sentiments* (1976a). This triple response to uncertainty is not a prominent feature of contemporary neoclassical economics.

An indication of the scope for improvement which is opened up by the division of labour is to be found in Smith's third means of such improvement: 'the invention of a great number of machines which facilitate and abridge labour' (Smith 1976b: 17). Smith distinguishes three sources of such inventions. First, as the division of labour within a trade becomes finer, each workman's 'attention comes naturally to be directed towards some one very simple object'; thus he becomes increasingly familiar with the details of his task and may develop the capabilities which allow him to find ways of making it easier (ibid.: 20). Second, if the division of labour between trades leads to the emergence of specialist machine-makers, we may expect to see a sequence of improvements which are complementary to the first, being based on a detailed understanding of particular machinery rather than of the operations which that machinery may be required to perform. Third, the differentiation of focus between trades creates an opening for

> those who are called philosophers or men of speculation, whose trade it is, not to do any thing, but to observe everything; and who, upon that account, are often capable of combining together the powers of the most distant and dissimilar objects.
>
> (ibid.: 21)

(This third category, and the language used to describe it, is adapted from Smith's *History of Astronomy*). By dividing up the knowledge requirements of an economy, the complexity of each person's task is greatly reduced, and so it is easier to develop a set of conventions which is specific to that task. Moreover, since there are likely to be many other people engaged in similar tasks, those who are most proficient become a natural source of authority on the best ways of working effectively and of generating improvements. There is thus a natural tendency for those working in a trade to adopt similar conventions to guide the development of capabilities.

In Rosenberg's (1965: 131) words, Smith envisages 'a hierarchy of inventions involving varying degrees of complexity, and requiring different amounts of technical competence, analytical sophistication, and creative and synthesising intellect'. As Rosenberg points out, the multiplication of distinct trades, and the distinct capabilities and patterns of thought which are thereby generated, increases the scope for 'philosophers' to create what Schumpeter was to call 'new combinations'. Not only is the amount of technological development substantially attributable to the division of labour; the form of this development reflects the particular ways in which labour is divided.

Smith does not emphasise the role of businessmen, but it is not ignored.

> It is the stock that is employed for the sake of profit, which puts into motion the greater part of the useful labour of every society. The plans and projects of the employers of stock regulate and direct all the most important operations of labour, and profit is the end proposed by all those plans and projects....Merchants and manufacturers...commonly employ the largest capitals...[and as] during their whole lives they are engaged in plans and projects, they have frequently more acuteness of understanding.
>
> (Smith 1976b: 266)

In his *Theory of Moral Sentiments*, Smith (1976a: 213) had included 'real knowledge and skill in our trade or profession, assiduity and industry in our exercise of it' among the attributes of the 'prudent man', and commented that if 'he enters into any new projects or enterprises, they are likely to be well concerted and well prepared' (ibid.: 215).

If we redefine Smith's third cause of increasing productivity to include all kinds of improvements, then the contributions of the prudent businessman may be grouped with those of the workman in a general category of improvements which arise from detailed knowledge within a single business. Then the division of labour within a firm becomes a means of developing specific operating, managerial and entrepreneurial skills, which is especially effective when these skills have to be exercised in a competitive environment. (It is important to remember that Smith uses the word 'competition' to denote a process of active rivalry, which is essential to his analysis of economic progress.) The second category of improvements may also be enlarged to include the suppliers of all complementary goods and services which have become distinctive trades as a result of the division of labour between firms, and the third to include the introduction of all kinds of 'new combinations' of improvements which have been generated in the other two categories. This multiple development of machinery and skills available within each industry enlarges the size of the market for its products, thus permitting an extension of the division of labour, and also generates profits which allow merchants and manufacturers to augment their capital stock. The combination of this extended division of labour and increased capital stock in turn leads to further improvements in skills and machinery. Smith's account of the generation of inventions thus provides the basis for a comprehensive theory of the generation of productive knowledge.

Smith's cumulative process is at least a proto-evolutionary theory, as Marshall (1920: 241) pointed out in combining Smith's ideas of development with those of Darwin into a unifying principle of biological and economic evolution through a cumulative interaction between differentiation and integration, thus connecting previously separate spheres of knowledge as Newton had connected terrestrial and cosmological phenomena. Marshall was well aware that this unifying principle required both biological and economic systems to be permanently open, and was correspondingly cautious about the applicability of equilibrium analysis, restricting his own use of it to limited dimensions of time and space within which models could be plausibly closed. The concept of general equilibrium he dismissed as of little practical value, because the continual generation of unforeseeable novelty would frustrate the attainment of any general equilibrium that could be calculated.

We should remember that Marshall's enthusiasm for the consequences of evolution was not unrestrained. Neither in biological nor economic systems is natural selection an optimising principle: many organisms or arrangements which would be highly beneficial may fail to come into existence, and many which are harmful to other organisms or other people may flourish. Even characteristics which are harmful to their hosts may survive if they are associated with other characteristics which confer substantial advantages, especially, Marshall (1920: 245) noted, 'in matters of organization'. Though Marshall clearly believed that evolutionary processes were the principal factors in improving the human condition (and not only in the narrowly economic sphere), he had no intention of abjuring the possibility of intervention in order to remedy, or perhaps avoid, undesirable consequences – even though the ethical principles on which such intervention would be based would themselves be the product of evolutionary processes.

For, as Marshall realised, there is one crucial difference between the evolution of species and the evolution of human societies: human beings are purposeful, and at least some of the novelties which they introduce into the selection process are designed; so too are some of the selection processes themselves. (Consider, for example, Marshall's (1920: 6) assertion that 'It is deliberateness, and not selfishness, that is the characteristic of the modern age.') Within some poorly defined limits, the processes of economic evolution may therefore be guided by human initiative; and Marshall wished them to be so guided, through individual, group, and state activity. It was particularly important that the means by which specialised activities were integrated should encourage further development; what had to be co-ordinated was not only dispersed knowledge but the continued growth of knowledge, including knowledge of methods of co-ordination. We have previously observed, in Chapter 2, that the role of human purpose was invoked by Penrose (1952) in her criticism of Alchian's (1950) pioneering, and moderately cautious, attempt to provide an evolutionary, but non-purposeful, justification for standard non-evolutionary economic theory. Thus neither the generation nor the reduction of variety within economic systems can be satisfactorily explained by a simple application of the biological model.

The Darwinian component that Marshall added to Smith's account of economic development was an emphasis on the generation of variety within each activity. It is a matter of emphasis only, for variety within specialised activities is implicit in Smith's analysis: new machines are constructed, enhanced skills emerge, and new combinations are created, all in particular places, and each stimulates 'a competition' within a particular trade. But the variety to which Smith's exposition gives emphasis results from the differences between activities in their focus of attention, and the corresponding differences in the kinds of improvements which each is likely to deliver. The effects of the division of labour in generating different kinds of variety, and the generation of variety within each kind, both deserve greater emphasis within evolutionary economics; both are major elements in the extension and refinement of Smith's analysis to which we will now proceed.

The division of knowledge

In his presidential address to the London Economic Club in 1936, Hayek (1937: 49) drew attention to 'a problem of the *Division of Knowledge* which is quite analogous to, and at least as important as, the problem of the division of labour'. But the relationship is much more than an analogy. The division of labour is the primary means of increasing the division of knowledge, and thereby of promoting the growth of knowledge. Knowledge grows by division; each of us can increase our knowledge only by accepting limits on what we can know. A loosely defined framework of scope and methods, which we might call the institutions of learning, is necessary for any of us to increase either our skills or understanding, and a framework which is substantially shared with others permits the kind of competitive collaboration in the development of knowledge that can be observed within an industry or an academic discipline. What framework is appropriate depends on the way in which labour is divided, and the particular set of activities or problems about which one wishes to know more. The organisation of industry is an organisation of knowledge, and the way in which knowledge is organised shapes the content of the additional knowledge that is produced.

Economists should not be surprised to discover that this process has its opportunity costs. We shall here note two related kinds. The first is that what cannot be accommodated by the framework will not be considered; in any academic discipline, and in any organisation, many phenomena are invisible. Thus a major source of error in the conclusions of academic analysis is the omission from the premises of what turns out to be a crucial factor, or the absence from the experimental design of what turns out to be a crucial control; and such errors may be due to 'good practice' rather than bad. As Wittgenstein (1922: 188) observed, 'Wovon man nicht sprechen kann, darüber muß man schweigen.' ('Whereof one cannot speak, thereof one must be silent.') Within the bounds of any academic discipline, there is much of which one cannot speak, many phenomena are invisible, and many kinds of analysis are never used; and the major crises in business are likely to result from events which are outside the terms of reference which are agreed, explicitly or tacitly, within the firm, or even within a whole industry.

The second cost is the aggravation of the co-ordination problem with which Hayek was concerned. In Marshall's unifying principle, integration was the obverse of differentiation. A single-cell organism or Robinson Crusoe before the arrival of Friday has a very simple problem of co-ordination; a complex organism or a complex economy has a much greater problem. In an economy there is an extra dimension of difficulty, because there is no single brain to supervise the co-ordination. It was Hayek's contention that no equivalent to a single brain could be contrived for an economy; thus, he claimed, to speak of an individual being in equilibrium was not problematic, but to speak of an economy being in equilibrium certainly was (Hayek 1937: 37–8). A 'representative agent' may sometimes serve for the study of individual behaviour, but not, as has been the recent fashion, for the interactions between individuals. The problem becomes increasingly complex as the division of labour increases: each person's knowledge is a diminishing fraction of what is required to meet that person's needs and the bases of these different kinds of knowledge become more and more diverse; efficient communication therefore becomes more and more difficult. Smith (1976b: 26) clearly defined this problem as one for each individual to solve; and we have considered the contributions of indirect capabilities, institutions, and evolutionary processes to the search for solutions in earlier chapters.

Evolutionary cognition

We sought an evolutionary explanation of the characteristics of human cognition in the work of Marshall and Hayek, who both became interested in psychology at the beginning of their academic careers. Both suggest that the survival of the human species required the clustering of neural connections to allow rapid perception and rapid response rather than the linear sequences that we associate with logical thought. This is a path-dependent process, which generates variety among the ways in which individuals interpret situations and the actions that they take. The basic architecture of the human brain sets limits to what is possible; these limits allow for a great variety of different skills embodying the same basic neural tissue, but restrict each individual to a small subset of these possibilities. There is thus scope for a great variety among individuals in the ways in which they organise knowledge, especially 'knowledge how' or capabilities, and therefore a great variety in the accessibility of that knowledge to others. It is precisely this combination of a wide potential range and severe constraints on the selection that may be made from it, that makes the division of labour so important.

This account of the development of patterns of behaviour, which is consistent with present knowledge about the human brain, provides an appropriate psychological foundation for Smith's proposition that differences in ability are more often the consequences than the stimuli to the division of labour; people in different specialisms make different selections from the repertoire which is implicit in the architecture of the brain, and in doing so are continually closing off other options. Smith's (1980: 38) argument in his *History of Astronomy* that those who take a particular interest in a topic will be more sensitive to detailed anomalies than those whose interests are more general, although presented in the context of the development of 'knowledge that', suggests how the performance of more narrowly limited tasks stimulates the development of a more finely structured network both of perceptions and actions, and incidentally produces the selective alertness that is characteristic of Kirzner's (1973) entrepreneurs. Thus the development of proficiency within a task is difficult to separate in principle from the introduction of improvements; and Marshall did not separate them. Capabilities are not static; as Cratylus declared, you cannot step into the same river, even once.

What is of particular interest in Marshall's evolutionary sketch is his introduction of a division of labour within the brain through the development of a reflective level, which has the distinctive ability to conduct thought experiments with newly imagined options. The emergence of this higher-order capability represents an important evolutionary step, for it allows the possibility of co-ordination in time, and therefore of creating mutations which are designed to be favoured by the selection environment into which they are to be introduced, though they remain conjectures; and Marshall (1920: 5) was still emphasising the importance of 'deliberate choice and forethought' in promoting economic development when he came to write his *Principles*. The anticipation of possible consequences does not seem to demand conscious thought, but conscious thought is likely to increase the effectiveness of the procedure, and is therefore likely to be favoured by both biological and social selection.

This new capability opens up the possibility of formalising knowledge by creating conjectures, which may be imposed like Smith's connecting principles rather than emerging from a continuous mixture of reinforcement and amendment. Once connections begin to be imposed, a new class of problems may emerge, such as those considered by Smith in his *History of Astronomy*. The orderings which constitute the physical sciences cannot develop until human beings have learnt how to behave in ways which allow the species to survive; and that cannot wait on ratiocination which is based on codified knowledge. Indeed, it cannot wait on the emergence of language; these capabilities must develop as tacit knowledge. In Smith's account of the growth of science the imagination, which resides in the equivalent of Marshall's higher level of the brain, is roused to action only when phenomena cannot be assimilated to established patterns; but in addition to the desire for coherence between sensory orderings and effective action, there is now a desire for coherence among the ideas of the imagination, especially, as Smith noted, among those who make 'philosophy' into a distinct trade.

As these two categories of coherence become more distinct, there is less and less need for the evolution of science, as 'one of those arts which address themselves to the imagination' (Smith 1980: 46), to be closely linked to the evolution of any individual's sensory order, which addresses itself to effective performance, and no general need for 'knowledge that', and the skills which produce it, to be linked to 'knowledge how'. Indeed, 'the learned [may] give up the evidence of their senses in order to preserve the coherence of the ideas of the imagination' (ibid.: 77). Even science and technology may be differently ordered, and governed by different selection criteria, as we have seen: science increasingly operates within Popper's World 3, the world of ideas, and this extension of the division of intellectual labour presents new, and sometimes difficult, problems of integration – among them the problem which Hayek attempted to resolve by writing *The Sensory Order*. We should not therefore be surprised that 'an enquiry into economic theory and the process of decision making' (Loasby 1976) should find substantial divergences between the two.

The organisation of knowledge

We increase our knowledge, as we make decisions, by making connections. The number of possible connections, single and multiple, that might be

138

made from any single perception or single item of information is beyond imagination. To learn is implicitly to choose, and to choose is to reject, consciously or unconsciously, a host of possibilities. '[T]here are always some alternative constructions available to choose among in dealing with the world' (Kelly 1963: 15), although very few of these alternatives are likely to be visible to any individual at any time. The choice of connections shapes the interpretation that is given to events, and therefore the actions that are taken and the consequences which are offered for further interpretation. Choices differ between people, and these differences continually tend to generate variety; but there are strong pressures to limit this variety within any cohesive group – indeed, cohesiveness might be measured by the limits on variety. Such limits facilitate communication within the group, notably within a clearly focused business or a well-structured discipline, and thereby promote the development of certain kinds of knowledge. Paradigms and research programmes are effective because they impose shared constraints; this proposition is first cousin to Schumpeter's (1943: 88–90) argument that monopolistic restrictions, by providing stability, make innovation easier. The form of these constraints helps to shape the kinds of knowledge or innovation that are produced within the group, and even more clearly helps to determine what kinds are not produced. Therefore some diversity, over time even if not over space, among the institutions of knowledge is desirable in order to preserve the capacity for generating variety.

The construction of economic models gives absolute priority to logical connections, both in the modelling process and in the conception of economic agents as rational actors. But logical operations determine only a small proportion of human actions; even deliberate action often results, not from the application of logic to a well-defined choice set, but from the construction of an action scheme which appears to connect satisfactorily a cluster of objectives with a cluster of constraints – and not only when such action schemes emerge from a group process, as described by Lane *et al.* (1996). When logical operations are used, they depend on the knowledge base from which the premises are drawn, only a small proportion of which is logically ordered. Because our theories of evolutionary economics are appraised by the criteria of logical rigour, as that is interpreted within the economics profession, there is a danger of exaggerating the role in economic progress of logical structures of conscious rationality at the expense of evolved capabilities, even in science-based industries. It is the growth of knowledge about how to get things done that has been the central phenomenon of economic evolution, as Menger (1976 [1871]: 51–5) recognised in defining goods as things, and also relationships, which people know how to use for the direct or indirect satisfaction of human needs. Such knowledge should not be analysed as if it were identical with 'knowledge that'; technology is much more than the application of science, and even now often provides a stimulus and guide to scientific investigation, as

Rosenberg (1982: 141–59) has emphasised. Even within the intellectual world of ideas (Popper's World 3), we should not exaggerate the virtues of logical structures. Otto Frisch (1979: 95) writes approvingly of Niels Bohr 'He never trusted a purely formal or mathematical argument. "No, no" he would say "You are not thinking; you are just being logical".'

The firm

Smith's three categories of improvements still provide a convenient base from which to start an analysis of the ways in which the growth of knowledge is organised. The category of improvements which are originated by specialised workmen needs to be extended, not only to include specialised workers who are not on the production line, but also managers and even business proprietors, especially in small businesses. For all these people, their daily detailed experience requires them to construe events; and variations in the pattern of these events may evoke changes in behaviour, or even referral to the reflective level, within the individual or the organisation, for a more conscious review of the way that things are currently being done. Say's (1964) entrepreneur both manages a business and introduces improvements; and the importance of this connection is spelt out by Marshall:

> [the] manufacturer who makes goods...for the general market must...have a thorough knowledge of *things* in his own trade. He must have the power...of seeing where there is an opportunity of supplying a new commodity that will meet a real want or improving the plan of producing an old commodity.
>
> (1920: 297)

It is his knowledge of 'things' – of materials, machinery, methods of organisation, distribution networks, and patterns of purchases – that generates this power of envisaging improvements, as in Smith's account of 'the prudent man'. Knight (1921: 259) also notes the inseparability of enterprise and management.

Marshall identified the individual business as one of the forms of organisation which aid knowledge; and Raffaelli (1995) argues that Marshall's early model of the two-level brain is reflected in his view of industrial organisation: the operating level is represented by the workmen, who, it should be noted, are thereby assumed, as in Smith's original account, to be the sources of many improvements, and the reflective level is represented by the managing owner, especially if he is at the head of a larger organisation, and therefore 'can keep his mind fresh and clear for thinking out the most difficult and vital problems of his business'. No-one familiar with his manner of writing would be surprised to find that after explaining this advantage of the larger firm Marshall (1920: 284) immediately goes on to observe that a small-scale employer, being more closely engaged in the daily activities of his business, may be more quickly aware of unresolved problems or emerging opportunities at the operating level. In larger firms the employer must strive 'to bring out whatever enterprise and power of origination' his assistants may possess (ibid.: 297).

The experience base is essential; and this experience base differs between firms. 'Each man's actions are influenced by his special opportunities and resources, as well as by his temperament and his associations' (ibid.: 355); each person encounters a different set of events and construes them differently. Differently organised networks, within each organisation and within each individual's brain, generate different operating procedures and refer differently defined problems for explicit consideration; each person's and each firm's reflective level will have its own way of working and so may reach a distinctive conclusion even if problems are similarly defined. Marshall's principle of substitution, which is a principle of search (Loasby 1990: 121), may be applied in many ways, even within a single industry. Of especial value is the presence of those who have been exposed to outside influences (Marshall 1920: 197–8) and whose knowledge is therefore organised into unfamiliar patterns. This is not a model of perfect competition, nor of what might now be called a growth equilibrium; but it does require both competition in Smith's sense of a rivalrous process and, again like Smith, an appropriate set of stable institutions, which might be called an equilibrium of theory and policy (Loasby 1991).

The outstanding modern version of evolution within a single business which is a member of an industrial population has been presented by Penrose (1959, 1995). Firms have different experiences, and interpret them differently: thus the firms in a single industry are likely to develop different, if overlapping, sets of capabilities and to perceive different, if overlapping, sets of opportunities; and both capabilities and opportunities are changed by the very process of seeking to exploit them. Especially Marshallian, though not consciously so, is Penrose's (ibid.: 149) recognition of the importance of organisation: the administrative framework prescribes how labour, and therefore knowledge, is to be divided, and therefore what will be perceived as an opportunity and what capabilities may, and what may not, be developed as the firm follows, and thereby creates, its own growth path.

Movement along this growth path is explained by a process equivalent to that in Marshall's two-level brain: each new venture requires conscious co-ordination, but as events are more effectively construed into patterns a steadily increasing proportion of activities can be handed over to operating routines, thus releasing thinking time for the imagination and exploitation of new productive opportunities. The managerial limit to growth recedes because less and less conscious thought is required for the running of the business. What Penrose does not observe, because her attention is deliberately restricted to firms that succeed in growing, is that smoothly running businesses may therefore be ill-protected against novel threats.

It is an obvious inference from Penrose's analysis that variety within an industry increases the chances of developing valuable new capabilities and of perceiving new opportunities. The value of this differentiation may be enhanced if these firms become linked in a network, which helps to make the experience of each business available to others. The relationships between firms in the same trade, especially but not only if they are located close together, provides opportunities of observing, and indeed discussing, alternative ways of conducting similar businesses, and thus permits not only the transfer of ideas but also the creation of new ideas through the juxtaposition of different interpretations. This is one important way in which the evolution of human systems, being subject to purposeful action, differs from that of biological systems, which rely on purposeless mutation and natural selection.

However, the current enthusiasm of some writers for the virtues of 'industrial districts', to which Marshall devoted a chapter of his *Principles*, should be tempered by a recognition of the collapse of those British industrial districts in which Marshall gathered his evidence. Although such a district typically permits greater variety than is possible within a single firm, effective interchange between its firms requires a broad basis of agreement, often tacit, and so radical ideas are rarely welcome. Moreover, the very effectiveness of such interchange in fostering the prosperity of the group discourages its members from looking outside; they may be so busy learning from each other that they have neither the time nor the incentive to learn from outsiders. Thus a successful district may be no less vulnerable to competence-destroying innovations than a single firm; indeed, it may be even more vulnerable to innovations which require major changes to be closely co-ordinated.

Interfirm relations

It is time to turn to Smith's second category of improvements, those initiated as a consequence of creating a new distinct trade. This category should also be enlarged to include the separation of all kinds of complementary activities. Why this form of the division of labour may generate distinctive kinds of improvements is simply explained by Richardson's (1972) observation that what is complementary need not be similar; it is the grouping of similar activities, and the exclusion of what is not similar, that facilitates the enrichment and extension of particular capabilities. The separation of complementary activities inevitably generates new problems of integration, which may be serious, and sometimes even fatal; but without the distinctive focus which this separation makes possible, the scope for improvement would be greatly reduced. Even when activities are so closely complementary that they appear to be natural candidates for single ownership in order to reduce transaction costs, they often retain their distinct organisational identities, as Richardson pointed out, and as we may currently observe in many alliances and joint ventures.

These co-ordination problems must be resolved by the participants, but Williamson's (1985: 32) organisational imperative, to '[o]rganise transactions so as to economize on bounded rationality while simultaneously safeguarding them against the hazards of opportunism' is not always an adequate guide. Vertical integration may appear to offer safeguards against opportunism, but the increased complexity that is necessarily imported with knowledge which is differently ordered, and which, if not tacit, is coded in ways that may be no more commensurable than Kuhnian paradigms, can impose severe strains on bounded rationality; and even control of opportunism may be illusory if one does not understand what one is trying to control. Some increase in transaction costs may be unavoidable if closely complementary capabilities are to be developed, and it is no accident that transaction costs, as well as distinctive transaction capabilities, are more prominent in highly productive economies. Such considerations do not diminish the importance of the effective management of transaction costs; but they do indicate the need to manage transaction and production costs together, especially when seeking to increase productivity through the Marshallian combination of differentiation and integration.

Marshall's firms do not rely on impersonal contracting in atomistic markets to achieve co-ordination. They seek to reduce the costs of particular contracts, for their partners as well themselves, by investments in market-making, as we have seen in the preceding chapter, and to develop external connections into their internal networks which will guide the development of their capabilities, help them to perceive opportunities, and generate productive work for the organisational equivalent of the higher-level brain. The co-ordination of the growth of knowledge, and the co-ordination of the specialised activities which result from the division of knowledge, both require the development of what Marshall (1920: 458) called a firm's 'external organisation', a source of transaction costs which are deliberately incurred in order to obtain productivity benefits. That prices have not been discussed in this book as an instrument of co-ordination should not be interpreted as a denial of their importance; our focus has been elsewhere. But it is appropriate to observe that the significance of any price, and even more the significance of any price change, can be judged only against the 'knowledge that' and the 'knowledge how' which is embedded in or accessible to the firm's internal and external networks. The information conveyed by any price, and especially by any change in price, depends on the knowledge by which it is interpreted.

This cumulative process of differentiation and integration, in which knowledge is generated and absorbed within and between firms, and each new division of labour enlarges some market within the economy and thereby creates the scope for fresh specialisation, was summarised by Allyn Young.

> New products are appearing, firms are assuming new tasks, and new industries are coming into being. In short, change…is qualitative as well as quantitative. No analysis of the forces making for economic equilibrium…will serve to illumine this field, for movements away from equilibrium, departures from previous trends, are characteristic of it.
>
> (Young 1928: 528)

Increasing return, which is achieved, as in Marshall's definition, through changes in organisation, is pervasive, and improvements in one part of the economy are continually changing the environments of firms in other parts, invalidating hitherto successful plans (Lachmann 1986: 5) and creating new opportunities for those who are capable of both perceiving and exploiting them. 'Every important advance in the organisation of production…alters the conditions of industrial activity and initiates responses elsewhere in the industrial structure which in turn have a further unsettling effect' (Young 1928: 533); Lachmann (1986: 9–11) also draws attention to the importance of intermarket processes. Thus the selection processes that winnow variety simultaneously provide both the incentive and the material for the imagination of new variety.

The consequent variations in performance, between firms, between industries, and over time, may be expected to produce the diversity in rates of productivity growth displayed by Harberger (1998), as well as other kinds of diversity. Harberger (ibid.: 20) argues that economists interested in explaining growth should pay far more attention to the detailed effects of specific externalities and to the specific experiences of individual firms. He does not cite Penrose, Richardson, or Nelson and Winter to indicate a theoretical basis for such investigations, but invokes Schumpeter's vision of creative destruction to suggest that a decline in productivity, to which he draws particular attention, may sometimes be attributable to the failure of attempts to innovate (ibid.: 17). He does not take explicit account of evolutionary processes, in which decline may result from failed conjectures in a broad sense which includes both new ideas which do not succeed and the continued application of once-successful ideas and capabilities in an environment that has changed.

Entrepreneurship

An evolving economy provides a very suitable environment for both Kirznerian and Schumpeterian entrepreneurs. Errors in the assumptions on which people have come to rely are continually being exposed, and those who are particularly sensitive to particular errors may profit by their alertness and improve the effectiveness with which capabilities are deployed. Kirzner's (1985: 78) argument that people are likely to take notice of what they are interested in is a corollary of Smith's theory of economic development; since anyone requires some prior knowledge in order to identify any opportunity, it is reasonable to conclude that alertness, like knowledge, will be highly differentiated, and the finer the differentiation, the more sensitive an individual is likely to be to potentially significant detail which would escape the notice of almost everyone else. It may then seem reasonable to suggest that ten-dollar bills are found lying in the entrepreneur's hand (Kirzner 1973: 48), not on the ground, which Chicago economists tell us is impossible.

However, in Smith's scheme, as buttressed by cognitive psychology, it is not clear that there is much of a role for pure co-ordination; his world seems to work by Cratylus's rules. Rather than alertness to an unquestionable opportunity, it is better to talk of conjecture: the ten-dollar bill might turn out to be a forgery. Conjectures are likely to be more soundly based if they are derived, as in Marshall's and Penrose's expositions, from accumulated expertise; but then the entrepreneurial function becomes linked with management, as Marshall and Penrose have explicitly linked it. Moreover, as Casson (1982) showed in his development from a Kirznerian basis, when entrepreneurship is more than arbitrage, it is likely to require more than successful conjectures. It is not unknown for people to gain little or no advantage from their alertness or invention, even when they are right. That typically requires some skills in running a business, and even in developing a market; here too, one quickly finds oneself in territory well colonised by Smith, Marshall, and Penrose. That Menger has also been another important colonist may encourage further convergence between Austrian and evolutionary economists, as Witt (1992) has been advocating.

Where knowledge is not only dispersed and incomplete but also changing, there is scope for those who are capable of combining together the power of the most distant and dissimilar objects, and thus generating Smith's third category of improvements. Making new combinations is the characteristic role of Schumpeter's entrepreneurs. Unlike Marshall and Casson, Schumpeter (1934) makes a sharp distinction between entrepreneurship and management, but later appears to reverse his position and claims that 'innovation itself is being reduced to routine' (Schumpeter 1943: 132). Langlois (1987) has pointed out that the routinisation of entrepreneurship is foreshadowed in Schumpeter's earlier work, as a direct consequence of the increase in human knowledge: '[t]he more accurately, however, we learn to know the natural and social world, the more perfect our control of facts becomes; and the greater the extent…within which things can be simply calculated…the more the significance of this entrepreneurial function decreases' (Schumpeter 1934: 85). Having been located within an empiricist theory of knowledge, the entrepreneur is progressively squeezed out of an increasingly rational theory. This version of Schumpeter's theory brings him close to Simon, as Langlois points out; it also comfortably accommodates the views of those who believe that all knowledge is potentially codifiable – and therefore, it appears, potentially completable. That was not the view of Adam Smith.

There is another possible interpretation. Schumpeter almost completely ignores the problem of realising the entrepreneur's vision, except for the acquisition of resources and the defeat of the opposition; and surmounting these obstacles seems to depend on personality rather than specific capabilities. That the entrepreneur has the capacity to see things in a way that afterwards proves to be true greatly simplifies Schumpeter's theory, as the equivalent assumption simplifies Kirzner's; but it also limits its value, because it ignores the possibility of failure and, what is more important for a comprehensive account of the contribution of organisation to economic evolution, the possibility of shaping innovations to avoid failure and to augment success. If, however, we interpret entrepreneurial visions as conjectures, and especially if we interpret them as new combinations of complementary conjectures about, for example, sources of materials, skilled labour and finance, and about technology, organisation, and marketing strategy, as Harper (1995) has done, we then have to consider how these conjectures are to be tested, preferably before a commitment to full-scale development and the possibility of very expensive rejection.

Now the entrepreneurial art of 'picking winners' cannot be reduced to routine – nor even the art of picking entrepreneurs who can be relied on to pick winners, as the record of product champions has shown; but the skill of picking losers sometimes can be, at least in part. The testing of conjectures is an activity in which there is considerable scope for logic, for codification, and for quasi-routine behaviour, and this scope has undoubtedly increased greatly in many sectors of the economy. Moreover, testing often reveals flaws in the original vision, which may be remediable by the application of detailed knowledge, particularly 'knowledge how'. That is why development is such an important part of research and development, which is an interactive process of variety generation and selection, and why Japanese companies were able to build world-class businesses by the development of other people's ideas, as Du Pont had done in the 1920s (Hounshell and Smith 1988).

It was no doubt the apparent ability of research and development de-partments in large companies to 'turn out what is required and make it work in predictable ways' which persuaded Schumpeter (1943: 132) that innovations could be produced to order. He may not have been aware that the development process leads to far more rejections than commercial successes (though timely rejection is also a success), or that what is turned out is often rather different from what was first imagined. Development, though not its results, may be reduced, if not to routine, at least to a manageable sequence; but how can one produce to order a new combination from the ever-expanding range of possibilities?

Let us consider an example from mathematics. Fermat's last theorem has apparently now been proved; and a mathematical proof is a strictly logical operation. Yet the assembly of an appropriate combination of pieces of mathematical logic took years of full-time application by an academic entrepreneur, and his effort relied much less on systematic enquiry than on exposure to serendipity. The pieces were collected from diverse parts of the mathematical canon, often of no apparent relevance to the central problem; and mathematics is a far more homogeneous field than is potentially relevant to a business entrepreneur. Once the pieces had been collected, determining whether the new combination was appropriate to the task required a well-defined procedure, though at a rare level of expertise; but no-one could have devised an equivalent procedure for the search. To make the logical operations which constitute the formal proof effective required non-logical operations characteristic of Smith's 'philosophers' (see Aczel 1997; Singh 1997).

The process of conceiving, shaping, introducing, and exploiting a successful innovation typically requires a combination of all three kinds of improvement which were distinguished by Adam Smith. Schumpeterian visions require the prior emergence of new dispersed knowledge, and the realisation of a vision requires a multitude of detailed improvements. Because of the advantages of the division of knowledge, each kind of improvement will normally be undertaken by different people and in different organisations. There may be exceptions, such as George Stephenson, who as a colliery enginewright was asked to construct a locomotive engine – a technology with a very doubtful future, even in coal-mining districts – and eventually became a leading advocate of common standards as an aid to developing a new network of communications, though still concerning himself with detailed improvements; but such exceptions are most likely to be found before the division of labour within the emergent industry has proceeded very far. As it does proceed, variations within each category, and within each specialism in each category, increase the potential for improvement, and attempts by governments or leading firms to control development may frustrate the growth of knowledge, or may fail. The complexity of major innovations often requires the capabilities and financial resources of large organisations; but many large organisations have found that they cannot continue to match the best that can be achieved by specialist businesses which focus their attention on one part of the total production process or product market. One should never forget the contribution of the variation within each specialism, as well as the division of labour between specialisms, to the dynamics of economic progress.

147

Information and knowledge

Economics sets great store by rationality. In economic models, rationality, even when bounded, relies on the agent's information set; information may be incomplete but is not considered to be problematic and yields knowledge directly. But any piece of information gains significance from its connections, and, as we have seen, many different patterns of connection are possible. Thus before we can make deductions from information we must impose some order on it; and this we do all the time, usually without thinking about what we are doing, either through the classification system embedded in our neural networks or by the application of connecting principles, which may be derived from formal education, culture, corporate strategy, organisational routines, accepted sources of authority or any other formal or informal institution. But there are many ways of organising and closing our models, and other people who receive the same information may order it in different ways, and so may rationally take different decisions. In his detailed study of the Japanese computer and communications industry, Fransman (1995) documents the diversity of interpretations which have guided the strategies and the organisational arrangements of companies in apparently similar situations, and which have therefore generated differences in knowledge.

Unless 'interpretive ambiguity' (Fransman 1995) can be resolved it may paralyse action; and if there is an unresolved ambiguity about the prospects for a major potential technology or a major new market then the commitments which are necessary for success, but which might in an alternative plausible scenario lead to disaster, will not be made. For a decade, no-one but George Stephenson persevered with the attempt to make steam locomotives viable; and Keynes (1936) feared that the absence of any reliable basis for long-term expectations would deter the investment needed to support a high level of employment. Fransman (1995: 2) stresses 'the importance of the *beliefs* that are constructed in the firm under conditions of "interpretive ambiguity", and which guide the firm's decisions'. These beliefs, it is worth noting, include beliefs about the relative effectiveness of different governance structures, which have led firms studied by Fransman to make opposite choices about vertical integration in apparently similar situations.

One might perhaps reinterpret Schumpeter's entrepreneur as someone who imposes order on phenomena and persuades others to adopt his connecting principles as their framework for interpreting situations. Persuasion may not be difficult if it simplifies the cognitive tasks of organisation members by providing them with coherent decision premises, and the entrepreneurial vision may therefore dominate their attention and pre-empt opportunism (Witt 1998). Such an entrepreneurial vision may indeed prove true, as Schumpeter (1934: 85) claimed, but it may not; or, quite often, as with Ford's vision of mass motoring and IBM's vision of business computing, it may prove true for a time but then fail. False or failed visions can be very costly for the members of an organisation and for those whose capabilities are closely complementary; but all visions are bounded, and from a systems perspective what matters is the availability of alternative visions. The creation of 'national champions' is a high-risk policy; and at the level of detail a belief in 'the one best way' is the equivalent of a belief in national champions.

An experimental economy needs a variety of connecting principles, and that variety must be supplied from within, for no individual or committee can know where the next viable set of principles will come from. Perfect co-ordination can be bad for the economic health of a region or a nation – and for the intellectual health of an academic discipline. As Richardson (1975: 359) observed, the persistence of competition depends on divergent beliefs; the knowledge assumptions underlying models of perfect competition exclude the possibility of competing. But as Richardson (ibid.: 358) also observed, the continual change inherent in the process of development through increasing returns, which includes the improvement of capabilities and the emergence of new ways of combining knowledge and closing models, continually creates fresh possibilities of divergent beliefs.

Variation between networks, and some differentiation of connecting principles within the division of knowledge, makes alternatives possible, and loosens the constraints of path-dependency at all levels from Schumpeterian visions to the amendment of routines. The potential for continuing variation is assured by the very limitations of human knowledge – of 'knowing how' as well as 'knowing that'. Any set of connecting principles and any neural network omits many connections and simplifies those that it includes; there are always other ways of interpreting events. A universal potential for variation implies a universal potential for entrepreneurship, as Mises (1949) argued, either by extending familiar interpretations to a novel class of phenomena or by interpreting familiar phenomena in a novel way. The creation of new knowledge is not predetermined. It may, however, be in part imagined; and imagination is essential to the formation of new conjectures. As Shackle delighted to remind us, the incompleteness and dispersion of knowledge are a constant source of opportunities for creating new knowledge; as some ambiguities are resolved, more are revealed, and people are inspired to imagine new ways of closing their cognitive systems. There is no discernible end to this process of conjecture and refutation, of the generation and the winnowing of variety – and thus fortunately no discernible end to the continuing evolution of economic systems, and economic theories.

BIBLIOGRAPHY

Aczel, A. D. (1997) *Fermat's Last Theorem*, London: Penguin.

Aiello, L. C. (1996) 'Terrestriality, bipedalism and the origin of language', in W. G. Runciman, J. Maynard Smith and R. I. M. Dunbar (eds), *Evolution of Social Behaviour Patterns in Primates and Man*, Oxford: Oxford University Press, 269–89.

Aiginger, K. (1987) *Production and Decision Theory under Uncertainty*, Oxford: Basil Blackwell.

Alchian, A. A. (1950) 'Uncertainty, evolution and economic theory', *Journal of Political Economy*, 58, 211–21.

Alchian, A. A. and Demsetz, H. (1972) 'Production, information and economic organization', *American Economic Review*, 62, 777–95.

Andrews, P. W. S. (1950) 'Some aspects of competition in retail trade', *Oxford Economic Papers*, 2, 137–75.

Ansoff, H. I. (1965) *Corporate Strategy*, New York: McGraw-Hill.

Argyris, C. (1994) 'Good communication that blocks learning', *Harvard Business Review*, Jul–Aug, 77–85.

Argyris, C. and Schön, D. (1978) *Organizational Learning*, Reading, MA: Addison-Wesley.

Arrow, K. J. (1974) *The Limits of Organization*, New York: W. W. Norton.

Arrow, K. J. and Hahn, F. H. (1971) *General Competitive Analysis*, San Francisco: Holden-Day.

Barnard, C. I. (1938) *The Functions of the Executive*, Cambridge, MA: Harvard University Press.

Becker, G. S. (1962) 'Irrational behavior and economic theory', *Journal of Political Economy*, 70, 1–13.

—— (1976) *The Economic Approach to Human Behavior*, Chicago: University of Chicago Press.

Bianchi, M. (ed.) (1998) *The Active Consumer*, London: Routledge.

Boehm, S. (1994) 'Hayek and knowledge: some question marks', in M. Colonna, H. Hagemann, and O. F. Hamouda (eds) *Capitalism, Socialism and Knowledge: The Economics of F. A. Hayek, Volume II*, Aldershot: Edward Elgar.

Boettinger, H. M. (1974) 'Mental architecture and approaches to decision', presented at Oxford Centre for Management Studies (May).

Caldwell, B. (1997) 'Hayek and socialism', *Journal of Economic Literature*, 35, 1856–90.

Caldwell, B. and Boehm, S. (eds) (1992) *Austrian Economics: Tensions and New Directions*, Boston: Kluwer.

Camerer, C. F. (1997) 'Progress in behavioral game theory', *Journal of Economic Perspectives*, 11, 4, 167–88.

Carroll, G. R. (1997) 'Long-term evolutionary change in organizational populations: theory, models and empirical findings in industrial demography', *Industrial and Corporate Change*, 6, 119–43.

Casson, M. (1982) *The Entrepreneur: An Economic Theory*, Oxford: Martin Robertson.

—— (1990) *Enterprise and Competitiveness: A Systems View of International Business*, Oxford: Clarendon Press.

—— (1991) *The Economics of Business Culture*, Oxford: Clarendon Press.

—— (1997) *Information and Organization*, Oxford: Clarendon Press.

Chamberlin, E. H. (1933) *The Theory of Monopolistic Competition*, Cambridge, MA: Harvard University Press.

Chandler, A. D. (1977) *The Visible Hand*, Cambridge, MA: Belknap Press.

—— (1990) *Scale and Scope*, Cambridge, MA: Belknap Press.

—— (1992) 'Organizational capabilities and the economic history of the industrial enterprise', *Journal of Economic Perspectives*, 6, 79–100.

Choi, Y. B. (1993) *Paradigms and Conventions: Uncertainty, Decision Making, and Entrepreneurship*, Ann Arbor: University of Michigan Press.

Clower, R. W. (1969) 'Introduction', in R. W. Clower (ed.) *Monetary Theory*, Harmondsworth: Penguin.

Coase, R. H. (1937) 'The nature of the firm', *Economica*, N. S. 4, 386–405; reprinted in Coase (1988) *The Firm, the Market, and the Law*, 33–55. Page references are to this reprint.

—— (1960) 'The problem of social cost', *Journal of Law and Economics*, 3, 1–46; reprinted in Coase (1988) *The Firm, the Market, and the Law*, 95–156.

—— (1972) 'Industrial organization: a proposal for research', in V. R. Fuchs (ed.) *Policy Issues and Research Opportunities in Industrial Organization*, New York: National Bureau of Economic Research, 59–73; reprinted in Coase (1988) *The Firm, the Market, and the Law*, 57–74. Page references are to this reprint.

—— (1988) *The Firm, the Market, and the Law*, Chicago: University of Chicago Press.

—— (1991a) 'The nature of the firm: origin', in O. E. Williamson and S. G. Winter (1991) *The Nature of the Firm: Origins, Evolution and Development*, Oxford: Oxford University Press, 34–47.

—— (1991b) 'The nature of the firm: meaning', in Williamson and Winter (1991), 48–60.

—— (1991c) 'The nature of the firm: influence', in Williamson and Winter (1991), 61–74.

—— (1991d) 'The institutional structure of production', in Williamson and Winter (1991), 227–35.

Coddington, A. (1975) 'Creaking semaphore and beyond', *British Journal for the Philosophy of Science*, 26, 151–63.

Cohen, M. D., March, J. G., and Olsen, J. P. (1972) 'A garbage can model of organizational choice', *Administrative Science Quarterly*, 17, 1–25.

Cohen, M. D., Burkhart, R., Dosi, G., Egidi, M., Marengo, L., Warglien, M., and Winter, S. (1996) 'Routines and other recurring action patterns of organizations: contemporary research issues', *Industrial and Corporate Change*, 5, 653–98.

Cohen, W. M. and Levinthal, D. A. (1989) 'Innovation and learning: the two faces of R & D', *Economic Journal*, 99, 569–96.

Colonna, M., Hagemann, H. and Hamouda, O. F. (eds) (1994) *Capitalism, Socialism and Knowledge: The Economics of F. A. Hayek, Volume II*, Aldershot: Edward Elgar.

Conlisk, J. (1996) 'Why bounded rationality?', *Journal of Economic Literature*, 34, 669–700.

Cosmides, L. and Tooby, J. (1994a) 'Beyond intuition and instinct blindness: towards an evolutionarily rigorous cognitive science', *Cognition*, 50, 41–77.

—— (1994b) 'Better than rational: evolutionary psychology and the invisible hand', *American Economic Review*, 84, 327–32.

Dahlman, C. (1979) 'The problem of externality', *Journal of Law and Economics*, 22, 141–62.

De Alessi, L. (1996) Review of H. N. Butler and L. E. Ribstein, *The Corporation and the Constitution, Managerial and Decision Economics*, 17, 345–7.

Debreu, G. (1991) 'The mathematization of economic theory', *American Economic Review*, 81, 1–7.

Demsetz, H. (1988) *Ownership, Control, and the Firm*, Oxford: Basil Blackwell.

Dibben, M. (1997) 'Exploring interpersonal trust in the small business', unpublished PhD thesis, University of Stirling.

Dow, S. C. and Hillard, J. (eds) (1995) *Keynes, Knowledge and Uncertainty*, Aldershot: Edward Elgar.

Drucker, P. F. (1955) *The Practice of Management*, London: Heinemann.

—— (1964) *Managing for Results*, London: Heinemann.

Dubuisson, S. (1998) 'Codification et ajustement: deux moyens pour l'élaboration d'une mémoire de l'organisation: le cas d'une activité de service', *Revue Internationale de Systémique*, 12, 1, 83–98.

Egidi, M. (1992) 'Organizational learning and the division of labour', in H. A. Simon, M. Egidi, R. Marris, and R. Viale, *Economics, Bounded Rationality and the Cognitive Revolution*, Aldershot: Edward Elgar.

Eliasson, G. (1987) *Technological Competition and Trade in the Experimentally Organised Economy*, IUI Research Paper Report No. 32, Stockholm: IUI.

—— (1996) 'Competence blocks of firms', *Journal of Evolutionary Economics*, 6, 125–40.

Foss, N. J. and Loasby, B. J. (eds) (1998) *Economic Organization, Capabilities and Coordination: Essays in Honour of G. B. Richardson*, London: Routledge.

Fransman, M. (1995) *Japan's Computer and Communications Industry*, Cambridge: Cambridge University Press.

Friedman, M. (1953) 'The methodology of positive economics', *Essays in Positive Economics*, Chicago: University of Chicago Press.

Frisch, O. (1979) *What Little I Remember*, Cambridge: Cambridge University Press.

Garud, R., Nayyar, P. R. and Shapira, Z. B. (eds) (1997) *Technological Innovation: Oversights and Foresights*, Cambridge: Cambridge University Press.

Graham, M. B. W. (1986) *The Business of Research: RCA and the Videodisc*, Cambridge: Cambridge University Press.

Groenewegen, P. (1995) *A Soaring Eagle*, Aldershot: Edward Elgar.

Hahn, F. H. (1973) *On the Notion of Equilibrium in Economics*, Cambridge: Cambridge University Press; reprinted in Hahn (1984) *Equilibrium and Macroeconomics*, 43–71. Page references are to this reprint.

—— (1984) *Equilibrium and Macroeconomics*, Oxford: Basil Blackwell.

—— (1993) 'Incomplete market economies', *Proceedings of the British Academy, 80: 1991 Lectures and Memoirs*, Oxford: Oxford University Press, 201–19.

Hahn, F. H. and Solow, R. M. (1995) *A Critical Essay on Modern Macroeconomic Theory*, Cambridge, MA and London: MIT Press.

Harberger, A. C. (1998) 'A vision of the growth process', *American Economic Review*, 88, 1–32.

Harper, D. (1995) *Entrepreneurship and the Market Process*, London: Routledge.

Harrod, R. F. (1939) 'Price and cost in entrepreneur's policy', *Oxford Economic Papers*, 2, 1–11.

Hart, O. (1995) 'An economist's perspective on the theory of the firm', in O. E. Williamson (ed.) *Organization Theory: From Chester Barnard to the Present and Beyond*, expanded edition, New York and Oxford: Oxford University Press, 154–71.

Hayek, F. A. (1937) 'Economics and knowledge', *Economica*, N. S. 4, 33–54.

—— (1945) 'The use of knowledge in society', *American Economic Review*, 35, 519–30.

—— (1948) 'The meaning of competition', in *Individualism and Economic Order*, Chicago: University of Chicago Press, 92–106.

—— (1952) *The Sensory Order*, Chicago: University of Chicago Press.

—— (1978) *New Studies in Philosophy, Politics, Economics and the History of Ideas*, London: Routledge and Kegan Paul.

Heiner, R. A. (1983) 'The origin of predictable behavior', *American Economic Review*, 73, 560–95.

Helmstädter, E. and Perlman, M. (eds) (1996) *Behavioural Norms, Technological Progress and Economic Dynamics: Studies in Schumpeterian Economics*, Ann Arbor: University of Michigan Press.

Hodgson, G. M. (1998) 'The approach of institutional economics', *Journal of Economic Literature*, 36, 166–92.

Horwitz, S. (1995) 'Monetary exchange as an extra-linguistic communication process', in D. L. Prychitko (ed.) *Individuals, Institutions, Interpretations*, Aldershot: Avebury, 154–75.

Hounshell, D. A. and Smith, J. K., Jr (1988) *Science and Corporate Strategy*, Cambridge: Cambridge University Press.

Hutchison, T. W. (1937) 'Expectation and rational conduct', *Zeitschrift für Nationalökonomie*, 8, 636–53.

Johnson, S. (1755) 'Preface' in *A Dictionary of the English Language*, London: W. Strahan for J. and P. Knapton.

Kay, J. A. (1993) *Foundations of Corporate Success*, Oxford: Oxford University Press.

Kay, N. M. (1997) *Pattern in Corporate Evolution*, Oxford: Oxford University Press.

—— (1998) 'Clusters of collaboration: the firm, joint ventures, alliances and clubs', in N. J. Foss and B. J. Loasby (eds) *Economic Organization, Capabilities, and Coordination: Essays in Honour of G. B. Richardson*, London: Routledge, 222–42.

Kelly, G. A. (1963) *A Theory of Personality*, New York: W. W. Norton.

Keynes, J. M. (1936) *The General Theory of Employment, Interest and Money*, London: Macmillan.

—— (1937) 'The general theory of employment', *Quarterly Journal of Economics*, 51, 209–23.

Kirzner, I. M. (1962) 'Rational action and economic theory', *Journal of Political Economy*, 70, 380–5.

—— (1973) *Competition and Entrepreneurship*, Chicago: University of Chicago Press.

—— (1985) *Discovery and the Capitalist Process*, Chicago: University of Chicago Press.

Knight, F. H. (1921) *Risk, Uncertainty and Profit*, Boston: Houghton Mifflin. Reprinted Chicago: University of Chicago Press, 1971.

—— (1933) 'Preface to the re-issue', *Risk, Uncertainty and Profit*, Reprints of Scarce Tracts in Economics and Political Science No. 16, London: London School of Economics, xi–xxxvi.

Kuenne, R. E. (ed.) (1967) *Monopolistic Competition Theory: Studies in Impact*, New York: Wiley.

Kuhn, T. S. (1962, 1970a) *The Structure of Scientific Revolutions*, 1st and 2nd edns, Chicago: University of Chicago Press.

—— (1970b) 'Reflections on my critics', in I. M. Lakatos and A. Musgrave (eds) *Criticism and the Growth of Knowledge*, Cambridge: Cambridge University Press.

Lachmann, L. M. (1986) *The Market as an Economic Process*, Oxford: Basil Blackwell.

Laidler, D. A. (1990) *Taking Money Seriously*, New York and London: Philip Allan.

Lakatos, I. M. and Musgrave, A. (eds) (1970) *Criticism and the Growth of Knowledge*, Cambridge: Cambridge University Press.

Lancaster, K. J. (1966) 'A new approach to consumer theory', *Journal of Political Economy*, 4, 132–57.

Lane, D., Malerba, F., Maxfield, R. and Orsenigo, L. (1996) 'Choice and action', *Journal of Evolutionary Economics*, 6, 1, 43–76.

Langlois, R. N. (1987) 'Schumpeter and the obsolescence of the entrepreneur', paper presented to the History of Economics Society Annual Meeting, Boston. (Working Paper 91–1503, Department of Economics, University of Connecticut).

—— (1992a) 'Transaction-cost economics in real time', *Industrial and Corporate Change*, 1, 99–127.

—— (1992b) 'External economies and economic progress: the case of the microcomputer industry', *Business History Review*, 66, 1–50.

—— (1997) 'Cognition and capabilities: opportunities seized and missed in the history of the computer industry', in R. Garud, P. R. Nayyar and Z. B. Shapira (eds) *Technological Innovation: Oversights and Foresights*, Cambridge: Cambridge University Press, 71–94.

—— (ed.) (1986) *Economics as a Process: Essays in the New Industrial Economics*, Cambridge: Cambridge University Press.

Langlois, R. N. and Robertson, P. L. (1989) 'Explaining vertical integration: lessons from the American automobile industry', *Journal of Economic History*, 49, 361–75.

—— (1995) *Firms, Markets and Economic Change*, London: Routledge.

Lazaric, N. and Monnier, J. M. (eds) (1995) *Co-ordination Economique et Apprentissage des Firmes*, Paris: Economica.

Lazonick, W. (1992) *Business Organization and the Myth of the Market Economy*, Cambridge: Cambridge University Press.

Leibenstein, H. (1976) *Beyond Economic Man: A New Foundation for Microeconomics*, Cambridge, MA: Harvard University Press.

Leijonhufvud, A. (1981) 'Costs and consequences of inflation', in *Information and Co-ordination*, New York and Oxford: Oxford University Press, 227–69.

—— (1986) 'The factory system', in R. N. Langlois (ed.) *Economics as a Process: Essays in the New Industrial Economics*, Cambridge: Cambridge University Press, 203–23.

—— (1998) 'Mr Keynes and the Moderns', *European Journal of the History of Economic Thought*, 5, 169–88.

Lesourne, J. (1992) *The Economics of Order and Disorder*, Oxford: Clarendon Press.

Lester, R. A. (1946) 'Shortcomings of marginal theory for wage-employment problems', *American Economic Review*, 36, 63–82.

Levinthal, D. A. (1996) 'Organizations and capabilities: the role of decompositions and units of selection', presented to Workshop at the University of Trento, 17–19 June.

—— (1997) 'Three faces of organizational learning: wisdom, inertia and discovery', in R. Garud, P. R. Nayyar and Z. B. Shapira (eds) *Technological Innovation: Oversights and Foresights*, Cambridge: Cambridge University Press, 167–80.

Levitt, B. and March, J. G. (1995) 'Chester I. Barnard and the intelligence of learning', in O. E. Williamson (ed.) *Organization Theory: From Chester Barnard to the Present and Beyond*, expanded edition, New York and Oxford: Oxford University Press, 11–37.

Levitt, T. (1980) 'Marketing success through differentiation – of anything', *Harvard Business Review*, 58, Jan–Feb, 83–91.

Loasby, B. J. (1968) 'The decision maker in the organisation', *Journal of Management Studies*, 5, 352–64.

—— (1973) *The Swindon Project*, London: Pitman.

—— (1976) *Choice, Complexity and Ignorance*, Cambridge: Cambridge University Press.

—— (1990) 'Firms, markets, and the principle of continuity', in J. K. Whitaker (ed.) *Centenary Essays on Alfred Marshall*, Cambridge: Cambridge University Press, 108–26.

—— (1991) *Equilibrium and Evolution*, Manchester: Manchester University Press.

—— (1994) 'George Lennox Sharman Shackle 1903–1992', *Proceedings of the British Academy 84: 1993 Lectures and Memoirs*, Oxford: Oxford University Press, 505–27.

—— (1995) 'Acceptable explanations', in S. C. Dow and J. Hillard (eds) *Keynes, Knowledge and Uncertainty*, Aldershot: Edward Elgar.

—— (1996) 'The imagined, deemed possible', in E. Helmstädter and M. Perlman (eds) *Behavioral Norms, Technological Progress and Economic Dynamics: Studies in Schumpeterian Economics*, Ann Arbor: University of Michigan Press, 17–31.

Lucas, R. E., Jr (1981) *Studies in Business Cycle Theory*, Cambridge, MA: MIT Press.

Lundvall, B. A. and Johnson, B. (1994) 'The learning economy', *Journal of Industry Studies*, 1, 23–42.

Machlup, F. (1946) 'Marginal analysis and empirical research', *American Economic Review*, 36, 519–54.

Marshall, A. (1919) *Industry and Trade*, London: Macmillan.

—— (1920) *Principles of Economics*, 8th edn, London: Macmillan.

—— (1994) 'Ye machine', *Research in the History of Economic Thought and Methodology, Archival Supplement 4*, Greenwich, Conn.: JAI Press, 116–32.

Maslow, A. (1954) *Motivation and Personality*, 2nd edn, New York and London: Harper and Row.

Meade, J. E. (1936) *An Introduction to Economic Analysis and Policy*, Oxford: Oxford University Press.

Medawar, P. (1984) *Pluto's Republic*, Oxford: Oxford University Press.

Ménard, C. (1994) 'Organizations as co-ordinating devices', *Metroeconomica*, 45, 224–47.

—— (1995) 'Markets as institutions versus organizations as markets? Disentangling some fundamental concepts', *Journal of Economic Behavior and Organization*, 28, 161–82.

Menger, C. (1963 [1883]) *Problems of Economics and Sociology*, ed. L Schneider, and translated by F. I. Knock, Urbana, IL: University of Illinois Press.

—— (1976 [1871]) *Principles of Economics*, translated by J. Dingwall and B. F. Hoselitz, New York: New York University Press.

Merton, R. K. (ed.) (1972) *The Collected Scientific Papers of Paul A. Samuelson*, Volume 3, Cambridge, MA and London: MIT Press.

Minkler, A. P. (1993) 'The problem with dispersed knowledge: firms in theory and practice', *Kyklos*, 46, 562–87.

Mises, L. (1949) *Human Action*, London: Hodge.

Nelson, R. R. and Winter, S. G. (1982) *An Evolutionary Theory of Economic Change*. Cambridge, MA: Belknap Press.

Nooteboom, B. (1992) 'Towards a dynamic theory of transactions', *Journal of Evolutionary Economics*, 2, 281–99.

Norburn, D. and Schoenberg, R. (1994) 'European cross-border acquisition: how was it for you?', *Long Range Planning*, 27, 4, 25–34.

O'Brien, D. P. (1984) 'The evolution of the theory of the firm', in F. H. Stephen (ed.) *Firms, Organization and Labour*, London: Macmillan.

Olson, M. (1982) *The Rise and Decline of Nations*, New Haven and London: Yale University Press.

Penrose, E. T. (1952) 'Biological analogies in the theory of the firm', *American Economic Review*, 42, 804–19.

—— (1959, 1995) *The Theory of the Growth of the Firm*, 1st and 3rd edns, Oxford: Basil Blackwell (1959), Oxford University Press (1995).

Popper, K. R. (1959) *The Logic of Scientific Discovery*, London: Hutchinson.

—— (1963) *Conjectures and Refutations*, London: Routledge and Kegan Paul.

—— (1996) *The Myth of the Framework: In Defence of Science and Rationality*, ed. M. A. Notturno, London and New York: Routledge.

Prychitko, D. L. (ed.) (1995) *Individuals, Institutions, Interpretations*, Aldershot: Avebury.

Raffaelli, T. (1995) 'The principles of organisation: a forgotten chapter of Marshallian economics', paper presented to the European Conference on the History of Economics, Rotterdam.

Reynaud, B. (1996a) 'Types of rules, interpretation and collective dynamics: reflections on the introduction of a salary rule in a maintenance workshop', *Industrial and Corporate Change*, 5, 699–721.

—— (1996b) 'Collective co-ordination in a workshop: distributed knowledge, rules and routines', presented to Workshop at the University of Trento, June 17–19.

Richardson, G. B. (1960, 1990) *Information and Investment*, Oxford: Clarendon Press. 2nd edition 1990, with new material including Richardson (1972).

—— (1972) 'The organisation of industry', *Economic Journal*, 82, 883–96; reprinted in Richardson (1990) *Information and Investment*, 224–42.

—— (1975) 'Adam Smith on competition and increasing returns', in A. S. Skinner and T. Wilson (eds) *Essays on Adam Smith*, Oxford: Oxford University Press, 350–60.

Robbins, L. (1932) *The Nature and Significance of Economic Science*, London: Macmillan.

Robertson, D. H. (1976) *Economic Commentaries*, London: Staples Press, 147–54.

Robinson, J. V. (1933, 1969) *The Economics of Imperfect Competition*, 1st and 2nd edns, London: Macmillan.

Robinson, R. (1970) *Edward H. Chamberlin*, New York: Columbia University Press.

Rogers, E. M. (1983) *The Diffusion of Innovations*, 3rd edn, New York: Free Press.

Rosenberg, N. (1965) 'Adam Smith on the division of labour: two views or one?', *Economica*, N. S., 23, 127–39.

—— (1982) *Inside the Black Box: Technology and Economics*, Cambridge: Cambridge University Press.

—— (1994) *Exploring the Black Box: Technology, Economics, and History*, Cambridge: Cambridge University Press.

Rühl, C. and Laidler, D. (1998) 'Perspectives on modern macroeconomic theory and its history: an interview with David Laidler', *Review of Political Economy*, 10, 27–56.

Runciman, W. G., Maynard Smith, J. and Dunbar, R. I. M. (eds) (1996) *Evolution of Social Behaviour Patterns in Primates and Man*, Oxford: Oxford University Press.

Ryle, G. (1949) *The Concept of Mind*, London: Hutchinson.

Samuelson, P. A. (1972 [1967]) 'The monopolistic competition revolution', in R. E. Kuenne (ed.) *Monopolistic Competition Theory: Studies in Impact*, New York: Wiley, 105–38; reprinted in R. K. Merton (ed.) *The Collected Scientific Papers of Paul A. Samuelson*, Volume 3, Cambridge, MA and London: MIT Press, 18–51. Page references in text refer to this reprint.

Say, J.-B. (1964) *A Treatise on Political Economy*, 4th edn, New York: Augustus M. Kelley; 1st edn published in 1803.

Schotter, A. (1994) *Microeconomics: A Modern Approach*, New York: HarperCollins.

Schumpeter, J. A. (1934) *The Theory of Economic Development*, Cambridge, MA: Harvard University Press.

—— (1943) *Capitalism, Socialism and Democracy*, London: Allen and Unwin.

—— (1954) *History of Economic Analysis*, London: Allen and Unwin.

Shackle, G. L. S. (1967) *The Years of High Theory*, Cambridge: Cambridge University Press.

—— (1972) *Epistemics and Economics*, Cambridge: Cambridge University Press.

—— (1979) *Imagination and the Nature of Choice*, Edinburgh: Edinburgh University Press.

Simon, H. A. (1957) *Administrative Behavior*, 2nd edn, New York: Free Press.

—— (1978) 'Rationality as product and as process of thought', *American Economic Review*, 68, 2, 1–16.

—— (1982) *Models of Bounded Rationality*, 2 volumes, Cambridge, MA and London: MIT Press.

—— (1992) 'Introductory comment', in H. A. Simon, M. Egidi, R. Marris and R. Viale, *Economics, Bounded Rationality and the Cognitive Revolution*, Aldershot: Edward Elgar.

Simon, H. A., Egidi, M., Marris, R. and Viale, R. (1992) *Economics, Bounded Rationality and the Cognitive Revolution*, Aldershot: Edward Elgar.

Singh, S. (1997) *Fermat's Last Theorem*, London: Fourth Estate.

Smith, A. (1976a) *The Theory of Moral Sentiments*, ed. D. D. Raphael and A. L. Macfie, Oxford: Oxford University Press.

—— (1976b) *An Inquiry into the Nature and Causes of the Wealth of Nations*, ed. R. H. Campbell, A. S. Skinner and W. B. Todd, 2 volumes, Oxford: Oxford University Press.

—— (1978) *Lectures on Jurisprudence*, ed. R. L. Meek, D. D. Raphael and P. G. Stein, Oxford: Oxford University Press.

—— (1980) 'The principles which lead and direct philosophical enquiries: illustrated by the history of astronomy', in *Essays on Philosophical Subjects*, ed. W. P. D. Wightman, Oxford: Oxford University Press, 33–105.

—— (1983) *Lectures on Rhetoric and Belles Lettres*, ed. J. C. Bryce, Oxford: Oxford University Press.

Stephen, F. H. (ed.) (1984) *Firms, Organization and Labour*, London: Macmillan.

Streissler, E. W. (1990) 'The influence of German economics on the work of Menger and Marshall', *Annual Supplement to History of Political Economy*, 22, 31–68.

Swann, G. M. P. (forthcoming) 'Marshall's consumer as an innovator', in S. C. Dow and P. E. Earl (eds) *Economic Knowledge and Economic Co-ordination*, Aldershot: Edward Elgar.

Tooby, J. and Cosmides, L. (1996) 'Friendship and the banker's paradox: other pathways to the evolution of adaptations for altruism', in W. G. Runciman, J. Maynard Smith and R. I. M. Dunbar (eds) *Evolution of Social Behaviour Patterns in Primates and Man*, Oxford: Oxford University Press, 119–43.

Van de Ven, A. H. and Grazman, D. N. (1997) 'Technological innovation, learning and leadership' in R. Garud, P. R. Nayyar and Z. B. Shapira (eds) *Technological Innovation: Oversights and Foresights*, Cambridge: Cambridge University Press, 279–305.

Vincenti, W. G. (1990) *What Engineers Know and How They Know It*, Baltimore and London: Johns Hopkins University Press.

Vromen, J. J. (1995) *Economic Evolution*, London and New York: Routledge.

Weitzman, M. L. (1996) 'Hybridizing growth theory', *American Economic Review*, 82, 2 (Papers and Proceedings), 207–12.

Whitaker, J. K. (ed.) (1975) *The Early Economic Writings of Alfred Marshall, 1857–1890*, 2 volumes, London: Macmillan.

—— (ed.) (1990) *Centenary Essays on Alfred Marshall*, Cambridge: Cambridge University Press.

Whitehead, A. N. (1948) *An Introduction to Mathematics*, Oxford: Oxford University Press; 1st edn published in 1911.

—— (1951) 'Immortality', in P. A. Schilpp (ed.) *The Philosophy of Alfred North Whitehead*, 2nd edn, New York: Tudor Publishing Company, 682–700.

Whitley, R. (1984) *The Intellectual and Social Organization of the Sciences*, Oxford: Oxford University Press.

Williamson, O. E. (1964) *Economics of Discretionary Behavior: Managerial Objectives in a Theory of the Firm*, Englewood Cliffs, NJ: Prentice-Hall.

—— (1967) 'Hierarchical control and optimum firm size', *Journal of Political Economy*, 75, 123–38.

—— (1975) *Markets and Hierarchies*, New York: Free Press.

—— (1981) 'The modern corporation: origins, evolution, attributes', *Journal of Economic Literature*, 19, 1537–68.

—— (1985) *The Economic Institutions of Capitalism: Firms, Markets, Relational Contracting*, New York: Free Press.

—— (1986) *Economic Organization: Firms, Markets, and Policy Control*, Brighton: Wheatsheaf.

—— (1996) *The Mechanisms of Governance*, New York and Oxford: Oxford University Press.

—— (1997) Review of H. Demsetz, *The Economics of the Business Firm: Seven Critical Commentaries*, New York: Cambridge University Press, *Journal of Economic Literature*, 35, 129–30.

—— (ed.) (1995) *Organization Theory: From Chester Barnard to the Present and Beyond*, expanded edition, New York and Oxford: Oxford University Press.

Williamson, O. E. and Winter, S. G. (1991) *The Nature of the Firm: Origins, Evolution and Development*, Oxford: Oxford University Press.

Winter, S. G. (1991) 'On Coase, competence, and the corporation', in O. E. Williamson and S. G. Winter (1991) *The Nature of the Firm: Origins, Evolution and Development*, Oxford: Oxford University Press, 179–95.

Witt, U. (1992) 'Turning Austrian economics into evolutionary theory', in B. J. Caldwell and S. Boehm (eds) *Austrian Economics: Tensions and New Directions*, Boston: Kluwer.

—— (1998) 'Imagination and leadership – the neglected dimension of an (evolutionary) theory of the firm', *Journal of Economic Behavior and Organization*, 35, 161–77.

Wittgenstein, L. (1922) *Tractatus Logico-Philosophicus*, London: Kegan Paul.

Woo, H. K. H. (1992) *Cognition, Value and Price*, Ann Arbor: University of Michigan Press.

Young, A. (1928) 'Increasing returns and economic progress', *Economic Journal*, 38, 527–42.

Zajac, E. J. and Olsen, C. P. (1993) 'From transaction cost to transaction value analysis: implications for the study of interorganizational strategies', *Journal of Management Studies*, 30, 131–45.

Ziman, J. M. (1978) *Reliable Knowledge*, Cambridge: Cambridge University Press.

NAME INDEX

SUBJECT INDEX

absorptive capacity 96
abstraction 14
access 57, 96, 97, 117, 118, 128
activities 49, 57, 61, 87–8, 94–5, 135;
  and transactions 84–5
adaptation 28, 81
adaptations, evolutionary 33, 34, 36, 92
administrative framework 41, 90, 94,
  141
agency theory 16, 27, 28, 65, 81–3, 91;
  economics as 84
allocation, efficiency of 3, 22, 27, 33,
  56, 70, 72–4, 76, 78, 80, 84, 103,
  125
ambiguity: of capabilities 60, 67; causal
  99; interpretative 10, 148–9; of
  product definition 111
archaeology 53
architecture, mental 58
Austrian economics 41, 112, 123, 145
Austrian capital theory 34, 92
authority 47–8, 83, 100–3, 105–6, 133,
  148; in academic disciplines 102–3
axiomatic reasoning 14–15

biological evolution 33, 36, 40
biological models, relevance of 22,
  24–5, 26, 28, 29, 135, 142
boundaries, viable 11
bounded rationality 4, 5, 7, 12, 65, 79,
  80, 143
brain, human 32–3, 37, 39, 59, 67, 87,
  130, 132, 137; evolution of 33–4,
  38
British Telecom 121

budget constraints 21–2
business behaviour 19–21
business strategy 91, 99, 100, 117
businessmen 19, 133, 140–1

Cambridge 110, 111, 120, 128
capabilities: and activities 49; cognitive
  foundations of 57–9; concept of
  49–51; developed by education 53–5;
  and division of labour 132–3, 137–8;
  indirect 56–7, 97–8, 104; as
  'knowledge how' 51–7; and markets
  114, 118, 125; and networks 97–8;
  organisation of 87–9, 123; orientation
  of 49, 60, 92; and plans 127–8; and
  routines 64–5; scope and quality
  59–60; similar and complementary
  93–6; and strategy 99–100; and trust
  104–5; using 59–62; see also firms
capital markets 22
causal explanations 15
change, problems of 5–6, 14, 30, 65,
  76, 81, 108, 149
characteristics of goods 42
chemical engineering 56
choice 24–5, 29, 62–3, 65, 139; see also
  decision premises; rational choice
classification 12, 35, 43, 46, 88, 93,
  148
closure 4, 12–14, 27–8, 43, 55, 63, 64,
  65–6, 88, 91, 109, 112, 116, 128,
  130, 134, 148
Coase Theorem 74
Coase's problem 69–71
codification 66–7, 96, 146

163